AF352706

The Land Is Sung

Thomas M. Pooley

THE LAND IS SUNG

Zulu Performances
and the Politics of Place

Wesleyan University Press   Middletown, Connecticut

Wesleyan University Press
Middletown CT 06459
www.wesleyan.edu/wespress
© 2023 Thomas M. Pooley
All rights reserved
Manufactured in the United States of America
Designed by Mindy Basinger Hill
Typeset in Minion Pro

The Publisher gratefully acknowledges support from the AMS 75 PAYS
Fund of the American Musicological Society, supported in part
by the National Endowment for the Humanities and the
Andrew W. Mellon Foundation.

Library of Congress Cataloging-in-Publication Data

Names: Pooley, Thomas M., 1983– author.

Title: The land is sung : Zulu performances and the politics of place / Thomas M. Pooley.

Other titles: Music/culture.

Description: Middletown : Wesleyan University Press, 2023. | Series: Music/culture |
Includes bibliographical references and index. | Summary: "An ethnography of Zulu
performances in post-apartheid South Africa, drawing on a decade of fieldwork showing
how performances of song, dance, and praise poetry are political acts in communities
still defined by their relationship to traditional leadership, land, and custom."
— Provided by publisher.

Identifiers: LCCN 2023018053 (print) | LCCN 2023018054 (ebook) | ISBN 9780819500571
(cloth) | ISBN 9780819500588 (trade paperback) | ISBN 9780819500595 (ebook)

Subjects: LCSH: Zulu (African people)—Music—Political aspects. | Zulu (African people)—
Rites and ceremonies. | Zulu (African people)—South Africa. | Music—Political aspects—
South Africa. | Dance—Political aspects—South Africa. | Laudatory poetry—Political
aspects—South Africa. | Land tenure—South Africa. | BISAC: MUSIC / Ethnomusicology |
SOCIAL SCIENCE / Ethnic Studies / African Studies

Classification: LCC ML3917.S62 P65 2023 (print) | LCC ML3917.S62 (ebook) |
DDC 780.8996/3986—dc23/eng/20230518

LC record available at https://lccn.loc.gov/2023018053

LC ebook record available at https://lccn.loc.gov/2023018054

5 4 3 2 1

We shall not cease from exploration

And the end of all our exploring

Will be to arrive where we started

And know the place for the first time.

T. S. ELIOT "Little Gidding"

CONTENTS

LIST OF MAPS

All maps created by S3 Technologies.

ACKNOWLEDGMENTS

This book is dedicated to the memory of my father, Tony Pooley (1938–2004), and to my mother, Elsa Pooley. Growing up in Natal and Zululand, and journeying in what later became KwaZulu-Natal, enabled me to develop an understanding for this beautiful land and its extraordinary people. I was lucky to have parents who appreciated the diversity of South African cultures and who took a keen interest in music, sound, and the natural world, instilling in me a sense of commitment and conscience in advancing a just cause.

Research on this book was made possible by many friends, colleagues, and institutions. Thank you to everyone who helped me along the way. I am grateful for fellowships from the Booth Ferris Foundation and the University of Pennsylvania, which enabled me to complete the initial fieldwork, and for research funding from the University of South Africa. I am also grateful for a publication subvention from the AMS 75 PAYS Fund of the American Musicological Society, supported in part by the National Endowment for the Humanities and the Andrew W. Mellon Foundation. My colleagues in the Department of Art and Music have offered valuable advice and support over the past decade. Tilman Dedering, Marc Duby, and Nombe Mpako offered guidance and encouragement, and Jabulani Nene assisted with many of the translations from isiZulu..

At Penn, I was fortunate to work with inspiring teachers. Gary Tomlinson set me on an exciting path of graduate study in biocultural musicology and supervised my dissertation, challenging me to think differently about sound and music. Carol Muller received me in Philadelphia with kindness as a fellow South African. Teaching African music with her was an unexpected joy. Gene Narmour mentored me into the field of cognitive music theory. He and Kathy were kind hosts during my visits to Media. Jairo Moreno introduced me to some of the key texts on the anthropology of the senses with enthusiasm. I am grateful to all the extraordinary teachers I had at Penn, including Carolyn Abbate, Emily Dolan, Emma Dillon, Jeff Kallberg, Guy Ramsey, Tim Rommen, and Michael Weisberg. My thanks also to Audrey Mbeje and her Fulbright-Hays students for engaging conversations about Zulu music and culture over the years. My fellow graduate students and friends at Penn shaped my thinking and offered tremendous support when I was far from home. Thanks to Karin Meyer, Myron Gray, Glenn Holtzman, and Peter and Dayna Mondelli for their friendship and generosity. Thank you to James and Christine Bond, who made Georgetown a home away from home for me.

This research has been presented at seminars and conferences in many places, and I would like to thank some individuals who contributed to my thinking, including Naomi André, Yolanda Covington-Ward, Jendele Hungbo, Lee Watkins, Annabel Cohen, Liz Gunner, Angela Impey, Brenda Mhlambi, Clorinda Panebianco, Gavin Steingo, Kathryn Olsen, Barbara Titus, and Simon Pooley. Thank you to Diane Thram, Lee Watkins, and Elijah Madiba at the International Library of African Music.

Thank you to Suzanna Tamminen at Wesleyan University Press, who commissioned this book and saw it through each stage of the process with grace and kindness. I am also extremely grateful to my copyeditor, Natalie Jones, who read the manuscript with thoughtful precision, and to Hannah Krasikov, who managed the work through production. Thank you also to Nigel Berjak at S3 Technologies, who created the maps, and to Kate Mertes for the index.

Fieldwork is an art of collaboration. At Ndumo, I learned a great deal through my adventures with Thulani Gumede. Thank you for being an expert guide, translator, and musical investigator, and for your friendship. I am grateful to the entire Gumede family with whom I grew up, including Busisiwe, Dumisani, Phumzile, Phumelelo, and Nthuthuko. At Mdukatshani, Mlamuli Magasela, Zamani Madonsela, Gugu Mbatha, Ndididi Dladla, and Mthethowakhe Dladla were skilled and patient. Thanks also to Elliot Banda, Caiphus Mthabela, and Zama Nzuza for their help in the mountains.

The Alcocks were kind and thoughtful hosts at Mdukatshani. Creina has been an incisive but generous reader, research collaborator, adviser, and archivist. She is a formidable source of authoritative information on the history and culture of uMsinga whose companionship during the ups and downs of fieldwork was invaluable to me. Rauri quietly arranged introductions and guides. His advice on protocol and pragmatic reciprocity were important to the success of my fieldwork. GG kindly checked and commented on translations and other ethnographic details in several chapters, making useful corrections and observations, and helping me out in Johannesburg. My sincere thanks to each of you.

Research on the *umemulo* ceremonies at uMsinga and Weenen was facilitated by two powerful women: Isainah Masoka and Nokulunga Mchunu who were the conduit for all information on events among the Thembu and Mchunu tribes respectively. Thank you to Inkosi Mvelase of the Thembu and to Inkosi Mchunu and Inkosi Miya for their hospitality and guidance. Many others contributed to my fieldwork on music and dance, including Eric Biyela, Rose Hlophe, Mvezi Khumalo, Mafutha Enkukhu, the Mbhele family, Vincent Mbatha, Jabulani Mthembu, J. J. Mthethwa, Nkosi Ngcobo, Musa Ngoza, Menzi Ngubane, Sula Ngwenya, Nomusa Nhlapho, Gana Nyawose, Brother Clement Sithole, Pessa Weinberg, Gill Whittington Banda, and Sithembile Xulu.

I traveled a lot to conduct this research, and the cost of accommodation would have been prohibitive had it not been for the generosity and kindness of friends and family. A warm thank you to Eddie and Lauren Germiquet, William and Winifred Bond, and Anne Rennie. Everyone at the Cavern treated me like family. To Megan, Hilton, Leslie, Murray, Peter, and Rhona: thank you for your friendship, hospitality, and expert advice in the Drakensberg. Siwakhe Wiseman Mbatha and I have collaborated on many projects now, and I am grateful for his gracious hospitality at Mazizini and for inviting me to his family's events and concerts. I am also grateful to Ezemvelo KZN Wildlife for research accommodation at Ndumo Game Reserve, and to Sonto Tembe, Bongani Mkhize, Chris Ngubane, Joseph Gumede, and Catherine Hanekom who assisted me in the reserve.

My brothers, Simon and Justin, were fellow travelers on this journey and served as confidants and advisers from start to finish. The love of family has enabled so much of what I have accomplished. Mom, you encouraged and supported me, and more than anything, you understood what this journey meant to me. You and Dad inspired me to do this work, and your convictions continue to guide my own decisions. To my dear wife, Nicole, thank you for reading, editing, and checking many drafts of this book with a smile, and for accompanying me on trips across KwaZulu-Natal. Your unflagging enthusiasm, insight, and rigor have made a real difference to the preparation of this manuscript. More than anything, your boundless love made it possible for me to see this project through.

NOTE ON LANGUAGE

This book makes extensive use of isiZulu terminology, place names, and lyrics. Anglicized spellings for isiZulu terms are avoided. The original terminology is retained throughout the text with a parenthetical gloss at the first mention of each term including both singular and plural forms. A glossary is included for terms that recur frequently in the book.

The decision to make isiZulu words an integral part of this text serves several purposes. I recognize that African languages need to be understood and appreciated on their own terms, and that certain concepts do not have a direct translation into English. For accuracy it is important to use the correct isiZulu words and to explain their usage. Consider two examples: the general term for "dance song" is *ingoma*, whereas specific styles of dance song include *umzansi*, *isishameni*, *izingilili*, *indlamu*, and *isigekle*. A second example is the distinction between the isiZulu words *utshwala* and *umqombothi*. Both may be translated as "beer" in English, but only the latter is brewed specifically for rituals involving *amadlozi* (ancestral spirits).

The decolonial turn, with its emphasis on knowledge production emanating from the Global South, aims at the recognition and revitalization of African languages and knowledge systems. By including song texts and terms in isiZulu, I have sought to open a space for dialogue on their meanings and interpretations. This avoids an "authoritative" reading of cultural practices where several are in fact plausible. It seems valuable to make such texts (and sounds) available to readers, including those involved in the research, rather than to make these texts the preserve of the ethnographer.

Specific features of isiZulu and its orthography should be noted. First is that isiZulu, unlike English, is an agglutinative language in which words are compounds of prefixes, roots, and suffixes that change the meaning and grammatical function depending on the context of the word in a sentence. By convention, isiZulu prefixes are not capitalized in titles and at the beginning of sentences—for example, in the case of places: eMpangeni, eThekwini; institutions: umKhosi woMhlanga; and genres of music: isiCathamiya, uMaskandi. The singular and plural forms of words share the same root, but differ in prefix (e.g., isigodi/izigodi; tribal ward/s). The glossary is organized to show this relation of singular to plural terms.

The word "Zulu" is used when discussing aspects of culture and history in a general context. Whenever I refer to the language, however, I use the term "isiZulu." Less frequent is "amaZulu," which refers to the nation or to a large group of Zulu people, and "umZulu," which refers to a deep sense of culture. isiZulu is a language that employs a system of contrastive linguistic tones. The nature of this system is discussed in detail in chapter 5. Those interested should consult the comments on orthography and tone systems included in the standard *English-isiZulu, isiZulu–English Dictionary* published by Wits University Press in 2014.

The Land Is Sung

INTRODUCTION

Sounding a Way

FEBRUARY 2012

I went down to the Phongolo with Thulani, Ben Gumede's son. I wanted to speak to the musicians our fathers had listened to all those years before, and I was curious to know whether their songs were still sung. I had traveled up from Umkomaas, my hometown, crossing the broad expanse of the turbulent Thukela River into KwaZulu. I passed by the place of my birth, eMpangeni, then on to Mkhuze where my father, Tony, began his journey.[1] I crossed the steep pass over the Lebombo mountains and into Maputaland taking the road from Jozini to Kosi Bay. At Shemula, there is a fence and cattle barrier to prevent foot-and-mouth disease from spreading south. The steel grates vibrate a familiar rhythm through tires and teeth, a visceral reminder that I'm close. The Gumede homestead is located only a few hundred yards from the T-junction. That's where I meet Thulani. Ben worked with my father for decades, and our families have remained close since the 1960s. Thulani is the only one of his five siblings still residing here because work is so scarce. We pause for a cheerful greeting before starting our journey. Our route takes us along a rough gravel road skirting the Phongolo floodplain to the east and the escarpment to the west. A dusty heat makes a blur of the summer day. An expanse of wilderness stretches before us into Mozambique. Irrigated fields fringe the floodplain, but otherwise the terrain is arid, scattered with homesteads, schools, and thornbush. The road angles away to the west where olive green groves of fever trees tilt awkwardly over the watercourse, discarding leaves and salted branches. The heat is ameliorated in the cool shadows of giant sycamore figs near the low-level causeway over the

Ngwavuma River. The road banks steeply upward before we get to the town, police stations, and army barracks. Up we climb to Ndumo, place of thunder, and to the paths our fathers trod.

The humidity hangs thick in the air. Driving slowly along the crest of Ndumo Hill, we reach a sandy strait fringed by thickets, *ehlatini*. As the road dips I accelerate gently into the soft orange grit. Thulani interjects, "Bra Tom, let's go in here. My ma is visiting." Taken by surprise, I turn sharply up the embankment. Carefully, we follow dual tracks into densely wooded bush. Through the greenery I can just about make out the features of a homestead, a few stools dotted amid the sun-dappled clearing between dwellings. I park the car beneath the shade of the mottled canopy. Thulani raises his voice to announce our arrival, and motions for me to sit down. Busisiwe emerges, smiling, laughing, clapping her hands together in joy. "Hawu, kunjani umNyonyovu?" she says, greeting me by my Zulu name.[2] I am put at ease by the tone and tune of her voice, engrained as it is in my sense of place. This is her sister's *umuzi* (homestead), she explains.

I am introduced to a tall, elderly man, who exclaims: "Ah, yes, you are Mashesha's son! I recognized his straight hair." Last he saw Mashesha was in May 1964, nearly fifty years ago, when my father recorded his *isizembe* (a single-string, ratcheted musical mouth bow played by friction with a short stick) at the back gate to Ndumo Game Reserve.[3] Madolwane is holding an isizembe identical to the instrument I know from our family home. Madolwane lives near Lake Sibayi, about sixty miles away, where he makes and plays these bows, he tells me. The string of the wooden bow is made from *ilala* palm fronds indigenous to the sandy planes of Maputaland.[4] The palm frond is attached to a small bow that has grooves carved into it. The rapid alternation of a stick across these grooves creates sound by friction with the mouth used as a resonator to alternate harmonics, thereby creating a melody. Mashesha recorded the haunting hum and buzz of this extraordinary instrument on magnetic tape. It is a sound that I have come to know through the crackle and hiss of a record. Everyone knew Mashesha in those days, says Madolwane, recalling a time beyond my ken. There were other instruments played then, but no more, he says. He mentions the *stiloti* (a herder's flute) and the *genqe* (a rattle). There is also a single-stringed plucked bow that you insert into your mouth to amplify the harmonics, the *mqangasi*. Some of my father's recordings were released on an LP, *Sounds of Tongaland*, in 1966. Side A contains wildlife sounds recorded at Ndumo Game Reserve and is conceived as a kind of soundscape, without narration, depicting the passage of day. Side B is a compilation of music: singing, dancing, drums, and bows recorded not in studio conditions but rather with the backdrop of natural sound. Most of the music tracks were recorded live at friends' homes outside the reserve, including here on Ndumo Hill. Madolwane's performance is one of the most striking on record and he has an extraordinary tale to tell. He relates to us how he walked two days from Lake Sibayi to Ndumo to make the recording. My father had a reel-to-reel recording device, a novelty in those days, and Madolwane was curious to hear himself play. When they finished recording, he listened to the playback before returning home on foot. That's the last time he saw Mashesha.

Madolwane is visiting us with a purpose. Word of my purpose has traveled before me thanks to Busisiwe and Thulani. Thulani takes us off to find Msani, better known as Mafutha Enkukhu (Fat Chicken). Msani lives a few miles further down the road, and only a few hundred yards from the Phongolo floodplain where he plows vegetables. We pass an *umaskandi* (colloquial term for a singer-instrumentalist) guitarist on the way, Masombuka Gumede, with whom we talk briefly about musicians in the area; then we venture further down the hill and off into a maze of red sand tracks that disappear into the bush. I can't imagine how farmers succeed in growing mealies and spinach on this arid land. The sand stretches out, and soon there is no cultivation and little sign of human habitation. I spin the little car gently along the faint tracks until we can go no further. We must find Mafutha Enkukhu on foot. Madolwane knows where he is going, and soon ventures off on his own. Thulani and I reach a hedge marking the boundary of a homestead. This surely belongs to Mafutha Enkukhu, so we wait in the shade. I am surprised to discover that his homestead is much larger and older than the others, measuring perhaps two hundred yards in diameter. Having rested for a few minutes, we encounter a woman who knows Msani. He is plowing in the fields down near the Phongolo River, she says, but she'll find him. Looking around, we discover a collection of plows that is matched in size and number only by a separate collection of drums and bull-roarers. An awning has been built to house the instruments, some of which are elevated on timber poles, others hanging from the rafters. Through the green-hedged foliage, the outlines of forest are visible in the distance.

Mafutha Enkukhu is a wiry, bearded man whose upright bearing exudes authority. He is elderly now, perhaps seventy years old, but has a tough vitality. His right arm was blown off by a landmine many years ago, during the civil war in Mozambique. I explain to Msani that I am here with Thulani to conduct research on music and dance. He seems to know this already and is getting straight to business. He has a dance group, he says, that performs *ingoma* (a generic term for "song," "dance"). This much we had deduced from the impressive collection of cowhide drums. The group performs often, he says, and won a big dance competition at Shemula Lodge in 1997 at the opening of the water supply to the area.[5] Mafutha Enkukhu is proud of his group and says we must make an appointment to discuss my project with his team. I explain that my research involves the study of different genres of Zulu music and dance from across the KwaZulu-Natal province, investigating the relationship of music to language, and taking an interest in its diversity. Recording is important to my study of music and dance styles, and I offer to provide an edited audio or video recording for each group. I hand him an informed consent document to review. It is printed in isiZulu and English. Thulani explains what it means and helps me answer Mafutha Enkukhu's questions.

When Mafutha Enkukhu learns that Mashesha is my father, he is excited and suggests other musicians for me to contact. This calls to mind the chance meeting we had with the guitarist, Masombuka. He was playing gospel, not umaskandi, says Thulani. But Msani knows a true umaskandi in the area, Jonathan Mathenjwa, and Masombuka will know how to contact him. As our discussions conclude, Mafutha Enkukhu directs us to ePhosheni where we will find *umakhweyana* bow players at the home of Sula Ngwenya. This large single-stringed bow has a gourd resonator and is said to have originated with the Thonga people before it was borrowed by the Zulu. In this border region there is a complex admixture of cultures.

It is noon by the time we drive back to meet Busisiwe, dropping off Madolwane. By now it is hot, the air drenched in humidity. There is at least some respite from merciless mosquitoes on the drive back. We drop Busisiwe and her sister at Ndumo Spar, a large grocery store. At the crossroads we turn in a northwestern direction, traveling parallel to the game reserve. There we are to find Sula Ngwenya at the "second right turn." It's about five miles, and sure enough a rough entrance leads us straight into his homestead. We are welcomed by an elderly woman, who tells us to wait for Sula. She talks about two women living close by who play the umakhweyana. This is exciting news because the instrument is extraordinarily rare. Eventually Sula arrives. He has good memories of my father even though he was only a boy back then. "Mashesha, he who talks with birds!" exclaims Sula, looking at us with kind eyes. We are introduced to Zenzile Khumalo, who plays music with the group of women at ePhosheni. Sula says the group played for Maputaland Community Radio based in Jozini—but that was a long time ago, and there are no such opportunities now. Work is scarce, but some members of the group are employed by Ndumo Game Reserve to remove invasive non-native plants as part of the Working for Water initiative.[6] Later on, as we leave, I notice a faded sign with the official Ezemvelo KZN Wildlife logo on it denoting the provincial department tasked with managing the park. On future visits to the game reserve, I discover this sign in the most unexpected places: in the bushveld adjacent Nyamithi pan, deep in the thickets of the Mahemane, and in the Madiphini fig forest where truckloads of workers unclog the waterways and clean up the bush. And so my journey begins with the memory of birds and bows, and plants, and music, in a community of people who remember my family and our shared past.

———

From highways to regional routes, single-lane carriageways to dusty dirt tracks: new roads have been forged to the very ends of KwaZulu-Natal. A generation ago, many rural communities in this province of South Africa were isolated from the conventions of urban life. The postapartheid state's developmental agenda has changed all that. Networks of communication and information have cascaded to places long isolated. Following the deprivations meted out by the apartheid regime, the democratic dispensation inaugurated by President Nelson Mandela in 1994 has seen to the provision of basic services, and to just principles, which are now protected in a Bill of Rights.[7] Connections to electricity, water, sanitation, education, and health care have gradually spread, and the disparities between urban and rural lifeways have narrowed with the widening of roads. When I began my research, many of these roads were unpaved, some impassable. Now, a decade later, tarmac licks its way to remote corners of the country. Trucks trek merchandise to new rural hubs. Cellular technologies and digital satellite television excite expectations for a newly connected world. Concrete strip malls dispense commodities mixing trusty brands like Boxer, Pep, and Ellerines with designer labels, furniture, and building supply stores. Boom boxes draw customers with umaskandi beats. Sidewalks are overrun by vendors, shoppers, and minibus taxis. This economy of retailers, wholesalers, and street vendors is sustained by a small population of wage earners, by income from migrant workers, and by the millions of child support, disability, and pension grants from national government. With crippling unemployment levels, nearly a third of South Africa's population depend on these grants as their primary mode of income. In juxtaposition, the creeping tendrils of corporate development etch their way into the once barren hillsides. Homesteads sprawl in myriad formations, each with its own road. Concomitant to these developments are changes in lifestyle, culture, and performance that have molded the sensibilities of musicians, dancers, and orators in the age of social media.

This book is an ethnography of Zulu performances in which I show how song, dance, and praise poetry articulate a politics of place in postapartheid South Africa. It is based on multisited fieldwork conducted from 2011 to 2021 in the provinces of KwaZulu-Natal and Gauteng. I chart the changing lifeways of rural and migrant Zulu communities focusing on how the everyday experiences of those struggling for a living wage are expressed in performance. My writing is rooted in ethnomusicology, anthropology, and sound studies. It is complemented by audio and audiovisual recordings, which are included on this book's companion website and tied to specific passages flagged in the text using the symbols ◀⟩ and 🔊. These recordings are integral to the analysis of sound and music and to the phenomenology of performance that I develop in this book. This phenomenology explores how ways of being-in-the-world are structured by the overlapping cultures and regimes of traditional governance in the rural polity of KwaZulu-Natal and how these are in dynamic relation with the strategic objectives of the democratic state.[8] Studies of traditional and neotraditional genres of music advance new methods for musical transcription and analysis. Spiritual and political ties to land are explored in studies of ritual, ancestral belief, and the environment. Voice and movement are chronicled in transcription and thick description, in dialogue and critical reflection. The emphasis on *performances* rather than *performance* in the book's title makes the point that Zulu identities are multiple, irreducible, and adaptable.

The journeys I traveled in order to record performances have immersed me in a society undergoing radical transformation. The politics of land, identity, and belonging in South Africa are suspended across deep fault lines. Migrancy continues to hollow out the adult population in rural areas, and the neglect and corruption of municipalities leaves many communities vulnerable. Institutions of justice and democracy are under threat, and the role of traditional leaders in this mix is vexed. These leaders are formally recognized by the state as custodians of the land who administer justice in accordance with law and custom. But what role do traditional leaders play in the lives of their communities, and how are the dynamics of power performed? How do performers play with the politics of custom to address their needs, desires, and expectations in a fast-changing world?

This introductory chapter provides a context for the interpretation of contemporary performance focusing on the politics of identity and governance in the postapartheid state, as well as recent work in ethnography and sound studies that weighs the ambiguities of democracy and traditional governance in South Africa.[9] Singing is ubiquitous and distinctive of performances in nearly every genre discussed in this book, and it is through singing that land, genealogy, and ancestral belief are connected in Zulu cosmology. How do musicians, dancers, and orators perform their ways of being-in-the-world? I will show how performance is a mode of political action: singers sing of justice; dancers dance their freedom. The nexus of belief that structures the worlds of musicians, dancers, and orators is embedded in epistemologies of land, genealogy, and spirituality. By approaching performance through the lens of phenomenology and sound studies, this book aims to render the experience of performance vividly. The remainder of this chapter describes the ethnographic methods deployed to study performances before turning to a discussion of Zulu identities and genres of performance.

ON METHOD

The interpretive and reflexive ethnographic strategies employed in this book are influenced in different ways by anthropologists Clifford Geertz, James Clifford, and George Marcus,[10] as well as by recent ethnographic writing in ethnomusicology and sound studies. Thick description is a stylistic strategy that I use to envision the sensory world.[11] I draw on work by Maurice Merleau-Ponty in phenomenology, as well as Paul Stoller, Deborah Kapchan, Steven Feld, Veit Erlmann, Louise Meintjes, and others in the anthropology of the senses and sound studies.[12]

The advent of sound studies has set in motion a new wave of ethnographic writing that first emerged after the writing culture moment in the 1980s.[13] Writing culture fashioned a literary response to the crisis of representation in anthropology. At the time, Clifford argued that the "literary or rhetorical dimensions of ethnography can no longer be so easily compartmentalized," pointing to the ways in which "academic and literary genres interpenetrate."[14] Familiar codes and modes of representation suddenly became contested ground while the poetic and political were now inseparable. For Clifford, ethnography entails "the invention, not the representation of cultures."[15] But this invention is no less valid as a mode of interpretation. Ethnographers began to place themselves squarely within the narratives they told as interested observers who were constrained, but also empowered, by their own unique perspectives. "Transparent modes of authority" that positioned the ethnographer as the arbiter of objective fact were now open to criticism.[16] This reflexive positioning of the ethnographer as central to the construction of the text informs my writing. Transcription and thick description are used to foreground other voices while evoking a sense of space, place, and somatic immersion.[17]

The lessons of reflexive ethnography resound in new musicological perspectives that emerged in the 1990s and after.[18] The contexts for this shift in method were a postmodern turn in the humanities and social sciences, the rise of the postcolony and postcolonial theory, feminism, as well as a resistance to authoritarian and patriarchal modes of authority and representation that undermined the rights of minorities. These factors were registered in ethnomusicology through an emphasis on research in situ through participation, observation, interviews, and the analysis of texts and performances gathered through ethnography.[19] The ensuing decades have seen numerous new paths into and out of ethnography. Ethnographies of African musics, such as those of Michelle Kisliuk and Steven Friedson, offer different ways of exploring reflexivity and phenomenology as research strategies.[20] Here I turn to recent literature in anthropology of the senses and sound studies to discuss how these fields have refashioned the poetics of ethnography.

An ethnography of somatic emplacement is poetic in its evocation of sound. Deborah Kapchan captures this when she observes that "the body begins with sound, in sound. The sound of the body is the sound of the other, but it is also the sound of the same. From the beginning, subjectivity emerges from intersubjectivity, the one is born from the many. We resound together."[21] We "resound together" in an environment. The sounds of the natural and humanmade worlds; of the birds, insects, animals, wind, leaves, trees, and grasses; of water, fire, and rain; of machines and technologies; all these elements situate us and shape our acoustic ecology.

Steven Feld's *Sound and Sentiment* pioneered a way to give voice to these elements in ethnography, both in observing the poetic dimensions to a culture situated in its natural habitat, but also in evoking that ethnoscape through a poetics of ethnographic writing.[22] This approach has gained new momentum in studies of "the Global South."[23] In *Remapping Sound Studies*, Gavin Steingo and Jim Sykes explain a new commitment to "situating sound in and from the South not as a unified, alternative notion of what sound is but as diverse sonic ontologies, processes, and actions that cumulatively make up core components of the history of sound in global modernity."[24] Sound studies and sound writing, then, are critical to the approach to history and culture developed in this book. The conceptual imaginary that informs these fields needs further elaboration and refinement before it is employed in the chapters that follow.

SOUND WRITING

A soundscape encompasses the totality of sounds experienced in an environment and depends for its identity on elements both synchronic and diachronic. Thinking of the soundscape through semiosis enables a careful sense-making of sound. R. Murray Schafer explains how a soundscape "consists of events *heard* not objects *seen*."[25] The "keynotes" to a soundscape are its "fundamental tones" carved out "by its geography and climate: water, wind, forests, plains, birds, insects and animals. Many of these sounds may possess archetypal significance; that is, they may have imprinted themselves so deeply on the people hearing them that life without them would be sensed as a distinct impoverishment. They may even affect the behavior or lifestyle of a society."[26] For Schafer, the sonic identity of an environment is culturally embedded over time. This approach to soundscape is not adopted as a method, but his insights about the rootedness of a society in its environmental sounds are crucial to the perspectives on place, space, and identity that I articulate in later chapters.

In a reorientation of the "ethnographic ear," Veit Erlmann explains how anthropologists are "overcoming the hegemony of textual analogies" as part of a broader interdisciplinary effort to rethink the place of auditory perception in the study of the senses. Erlmann introduces the idea of "hearing cultures" to encourage ethnographers to "conceptualize new ways of knowing a culture and of gaining a deepened understanding of how the members of a society know each other."[27] The move away from textual signifiers to sounds enables us to gain insight into the ways people relate and understand their place in the world differently.[28] The recognition that ways of knowing are sounded in a sense of hearing articulates a politics important to this project, particularly in the chapters of this book that explore questions of justice and ethics. Deborah Kapchan writes of the practice of listening as compassionate scholarship, adopting an experimental approach to sound writing that is political.

Writing *about* sound and writing *sound* are two different processes. The first maintains the positivist position of subject (writer) and object (sound). The second breaks out of duality to inhabit a multidimensional position as translator between worlds—the writer listening to and translating sound through embodied experience, the body translating the encounter between word and sound, sound translating and transforming both word and author. This is sound writing. When she flies, how extraordinary![29]

It is the intersection of ethics and politics in poetics that makes sound writing a powerful new approach for ethnographers. How does writing *sound* a world? Poetic writing facilitates a record of listening, and sensory responses to it, whose meanings cannot be reduced to a familiar order of things. Recorded sound enables a way of listening to the voices that figure this book and is used as a method for tracing my auditory footprints in the sonic spaces of which I am now part.

Sound studies offers a perspective that is posthuman in its emphasis on worlds beyond our own, or rather, that encompass natural worlds too often alienated by our anthropocentrism. Steven Feld's "acoustemology" speaks in important ways to the potential for sound studies to advance this agenda. Feld explains, "The anthropology of sound idea advocated for an expanded terrain when engaging global musical diversity. That expansion acknowledged the critical importance of language poetics, and voice; of species beyond the human; of acoustic environments; and of technological mediation and circulation."[30] Shedding anthropology meant embracing a new terminology that is likewise defined against others. "Unlike acoustic ecology," for instance, "acoustemology is about the experience and agency of listening histories, understood as relational and contingent, situated and reflexive."[31] Feld's acoustemology responds to soundscape without privileging sound. Like Tim Ingold, he is careful to relinquish the conceptual apparatus of landscape that is embedded with visual terminologies and ocularcentrism.[32] Listening is conceived as a relational practice that embraces feedback. Listening to the land makes sound studies an important domain of scholarship in which to present concerns regarding environmental justice and the loss of biodiversity threatening our planet. Sound writing figures the disciplinary orientation of a book that is vested in notions of relationality, reciprocity, and dialectic that are germane to recent ethnomusicology.

ETHNOGRAPHY IN ETHNOMUSICOLOGY

This book is about performances as political acts.[33] To understand the nature and meaning of these acts in everyday life, I advance interpretations that are the product of dialogue and feedback from my participants. The perspectives on the political acts recorded here are nevertheless partial, idiosyncratic, and incomplete. It was often the case that my understanding of a concept began with a misunderstanding and subsequent clarification from one of my interlocutors. This book is conceived in the spirit of this continuous and evolving dialogue as a technology of connection. This recognition of my own doing and making in the process of ethnography is explained by Gregory Barz and Timothy Cooley, who write: "By creating a reflexive image of ourselves as ethnographers and the nature of our 'being-in-the-world', we believe we stand to achieve better intercultural understanding as we begin to recognize our own shadows among those we strive to understand."[34] How we engage with others determines what we learn and come to know about their worlds in addition to our own. Reflexive ethnography rejects the confident essentialism of colonial-era representations of the Other, as well as the idea of cultural practices as "wholly objectively observable," and aims instead to position the ethnographer in relation to, and in conversation with, persons in the cultures studied.[35] Personal attachments and interactions are not hidden away in footnotes and acknowledgments. Instead, these idiosyncrasies of scholarship are recognized for what they are: motivation and rationale for scholarship that is humanistic. How we feel about our experiences shapes how we write about them.

The ethnographic texts that figure the narratives in this book alternate voices and registers, sometimes marking closely the descriptive and transcriptive while at other times analytical and reflexive modes of writing foreground my voice as well as those of my participants. I approach fieldwork as an ethical project founded on reciprocity. The nature of this reciprocity had to be negotiated at every stage of research. For the vulnerable, where day-to-day realities present critical challenges to subsistence, I found it essential to engage with the needs of communities before asking them to commit time, effort, and resources to activities for which they did not accrue a tangible benefit. The positivistic documentation of cultural practices should not be the measure of "access" or the basis for reciprocity. The appeal to posterity, which I find to be insufficient as a rationale for research, has for too long been the refrain of some anthropologists and historians. In South Africa, the weight of an exploitative history enjoins us to resist the ideology of research as an autonomous pursuit of intrinsic value. Decades of research on *Volkekunde* (folk studies) at South African universities were conducted in service of the apartheid state with the distinct purpose of advancing its policies of separate development and the repression and exploitation of Black South Africans while supposedly adopting a scientific methodology.[36] The contemporary ethnographer must tread with trepidation when encountering ethnic and racial difference. Throughout the research process, I have negotiated a complex postapartheid racial dynamic, which meant that trusting relationships were usually established over extended time periods. It is by returning year after year that committed reciprocal relationships have been made possible. The complexities involved in relating to and explaining the experiences of others motivates my approach to a dialogical mode of scholarship. It is also why I envisage this book as a route marker in an unfolding program of research rather than its summation.

Ethnographers make sense of the cultural contexts out of which, and into which, performances are fashioned. This book explores how culture plays a decisive role in how we conceive, construct, and interact with the world around us, and how embodied knowledge is crucial to how we express ourselves in it.[37] I have adopted a holistic approach to the study of performance because music, dance, and praise poetry are performed as integral arts in Zulu societies. I use the term "performance" to describe the modes of expression through which persons explore their immediate and imagined worlds as amalgamations of sound, movement, and gesture. The emphasis on consciousness as an overarching frame of reference for ways of being-in-the-world also points to the patterns of thought and action that link performers from across a wide range of genres in shared conventions of practice. This powerful social connectionism is acquired and activated instinctively.[38] In the sections that follow, I focus on how Zulu performances emerge from Zulu identities and how genres of Zulu performance interrelate.

ZULU IDENTITIES

What does it mean to belong? In 1994, at the dawn of South Africa's democracy, belonging was open to all. The question has become fraught over the past decade with identity politics now a zero-sum game. Archbishop Desmond Tutu's vision for a "rainbow nation" has withered in the shadow of corruption and social acrimony. Claims to authenticity now appear to threaten principles of diversity and inclusion. Desperate acts of exclusion are common and characterized by acts of hostility toward "foreigners." The power of ethnic mobilization in South African politics remains strong in KwaZulu-Natal and has been used by politicians and monarchs to threaten disorder. In these contexts, Zulu identity is a crucial site of contestation for the polity.

Speakers of the isiZulu language constitute the largest language community in southern Africa. Most live in the provinces of KwaZulu-Natal, Gauteng, Mpumalanga, and the Free State. isiZulu is the lingua franca for urban residents of many metropolitan areas.[39] The dialects of present-day isiZulu are the product of long and complex genesis over the past two centuries.[40] Clement Doke described two dialects: *ukuthefula* (meaning "to be oily, slippery") and *ukuthekeza* (meaning "to quiver, to speak in a quavering voice"). The former is spoken on the east coast of the province, whereas the latter is spoken to the south and from the Thukela River northward to eSwatini (Swaziland).[41] Southern tribes in the (eastern) Cape province speak the related *ukuthetha* (meaning "to speak sharply, to scold") languages of the amaMpondo, amaXhosa, amaMpondomisi, amaThembu, and amaGcaleka. To the west of the Drakensberg and into Lesotho and the Free State are the *kubuwa* influences of the Sotho languages. To the north, in Mpumalanga and southern Mozambique, are siSwati, xiRonga, and xiTsonga speakers.[42] The region of Maputaland is populated by persons speaking Thonga, also a Nguni language. This is the root of the name Tongaland, which was originally given to the area encompassing the Jozini and uMhlabuyalingana districts in which I conducted work for this book (chapters 5 to 7). However, this border region between South Africa, Mozambique, and eSwatini is populated by speakers of Thonga, siSwati, xiTsonga, and isiZulu. The predominance of isiZulu is partly the result of the annexation of Tongaland into Zululand and Natal (chapter 1). The politics of language play out in schools where children are taught isiZulu rather than Thonga and are encouraged to compete in performances of *indlamu, ingoma, isicathamiya,* and *amahubo* that normalize cultural and linguistic features specific to Zulu cultures (chapter 6). The introduction of literacy in the twentieth century as well as the widespread availability of radio, television, and social media have changed the ways people communicate and express themselves.[43] Features of dialect are important to the analysis and interpretation of all forms of orature, including song, speech, and praise poetry, and especially in districts on the edges of nations where languages are in transition and performers switch or mix codes.

Zulu identities demonstrate important similarities and differences across KwaZulu-Natal. The idea of an undifferentiated Zulu identity has been rigorously contested in recent literature in anthropology, archaeology, and history.[44] Since the 1970s, regional differences within KwaZulu-Natal have to some degree been ameliorated by province-wide efforts to reassert a pan-Zulu identity through Inkatha, and through nationalistic performances of various kinds, such as the cultural activities programs promoted by the Department of Arts and Culture in KwaZulu-Natal schools, and the mass events hosted at the Zulu royal residences.[45] The focus here is on performance practices at places within *izigodi* (tribal wards), and their relationship to groups, some of which have as yet received only limited attention from social scientists surveying the scope of this region's culture and history. Patrilineal groups are sometimes defined as "tribes" who fled Zululand during the reign of Shaka kaSezangakhona (c. 1787–1828), the monarch recognized as the founder of the modern Zulu nation and its enduring symbol of power. Recent scholarship recognizes these complexities through careful reconsideration of the archive.[46] The relationships between cultures in and across this region have been fluid for many centuries—before and after European colonists arrived in the eighteenth and nineteenth centuries.

Zuluness and Zulu national identity are not coterminous. In uMsinga, for instance, the Mchunu and Thembu tribes have historically maintained independence from monarchical supremacy. The idea of granting uniformity on ethnic groupings at first served colonial agendas where territories were divided by treaty and fiat, and where international borders were established at the whim of administrators with no understanding of or care for their local impact. Successive Union and apartheid governments sought control over the lives and livelihoods of Black South Africans, as well as their land.[47] Thus, questions of ownership and belonging are tied to identities to which persons may or may not subscribe. Or rather, the construction of ethnic identities is itself a fluid and contested space characterized by its heterogeneity rather than its homogeneity. Commonalities are recognized rather than assumed. The question of territorial homogeneity and difference is discussed in the next chapter, where questions of tribe, nation, and culture are weighed in relation to the vexed issue of land and identity in postapartheid South Africa.

In scholarly research on representations of Zuluness in the media and popular culture, anachronistic and stereotypical representations of Zulu "warrior culture" have been thoroughly debunked. The image of a mythic Shaka is still associated with war, conquest, and annihilation in the popular imagination. Historians and anthropologists have sought to rethink these and other stereotypes about Zulu culture and identity that have been used to advance political agendas in the past.[48] In this context, the militancy of some contemporary Zulu cultures of performance, as well as the ubiquity of martial symbols and gestures, require nuanced interpretation. To reduce these symbols to a global exoticism is to mistake the stereotypes of the past for the complex representations of the present, including those of contemporary Zulu political movements like Inkatha.[49] Louise Meintjes has written vividly of the exploitation of Zulu bodies by apartheid ideologues and colonialists, and of their dehumanization through the circulation of ferocious images in global markets.[50] There is no closed inventory of Zulu signs signaling distinctness, difference, or coherence. There is no ur-Zulu conferring an organic unity on the plethora of individual units. This book tells specific stories about Zulu cultures of performance, describing thickly the conventions of genre and style in dance, music, and praise poetry that give meaning to the everyday. The specificities of context and culture foreground the political dimensions of performance, and these need to be understood in their proper historical contexts.

The "insidiously resilient stereotypes" that sustain fallacious representations of Zuluness today are widely condemned as essentialist and denigrating.[51] These images are contested by Zulus themselves who refuse to be associated with the cultures of violence to which they have sometimes been tied. The constructs of "tribe" and "tradition" persist in the postapartheid political imaginary, and not simply as the product of global narratives of desire. Tribe and tradition are woven into the workings of society and tied to systems of governance and representation with origins in the nineteenth century. These terms are still widely used in school textbooks, in tourist brochures, in government policies, and in the media.[52] "Tribe" refers to large patrilineal political formations under the leadership of a single patriarch or matriarch. In South Africa, tribes fall under the authority and administration of South Africa's Department of Cooperative Governance and Traditional Affairs (CoGTA). "Tradition" is used to refer to indigenous knowledge systems, practices, and modes of performance considered specific to South Africa and consistent with its African pasts. Tradition invokes a sense of authenticity even in forms that are distinctly hybrid. Constructions of Zulu tribe and tradition are in flux and so are treated here as historically contingent.[53] In this play of postcolonial signs, the rich canvas of Zulu performances needs to be interpreted reflexively, allowing for textured arts of parody, caricature, and appropriation. The intensely personal performances recorded in women's and men's bodies articulate an aesthetics that is embedded in circumstance and convention, and which is conceived for an audience of fellow dancers, kith, and kin.

In her book *Dust of the Zulu*, Louise Meintjes is careful to identify and distance her readings from a global Zuluness by deconstructing the essentialist ideology of fixed, timeless, and unchanging Zulu identity through close analysis of the warrior hero-villain. She chronicles the lives and exploits of ingoma dancers from rural esiPongweni in South Africa, tracking their voices, bodies, and careers, and situating their performances in the context of South Africa's violent transition to democracy. Meintjes shows how the brutal legacies of colonialism and apartheid still shape contemporary ingoma practice and its commodification. Her chronicle of *umzansi*—one of several distinct styles of ingoma danced in the province of KwaZulu-Natal—raises urgent questions about South Africa's impoverished rural communities and the status of migrant labor in its urban ghettoes.

Reading Zulu signs through a global lens risks missing their local intent, reducing their relevance to discursive regimes aimed at a northern readership. In advancing scholarship on the Global South, this book focuses on everyday representations in Zulu performances by taking account of both historical and contemporary factors in structuring worlds of experience. The singing, dancing, and praising of musicians from across the region demonstrates important commonalities indicative of shared frames of reference and a sense of shared consciousness. "Consciousness" refers here to ways of being-in-the-world, principles of thought and action made normative through practice. These principles are evident in language usage and cognition, in music, dance, and orality, and in genres of performance whose genealogies reach back several decades. This coalescence of consciousness is a product of history.

Zulu societies are continuously evolving to take account of a changing social dynamic shaped by factors of economy, health, morality, and media. In rural country districts, social distinction and status are still shaped by factors of gender and generation. The expression of these relationships is embedded in language, performance, and bearing, and is made concrete in the practice of *inhlonipho* (behavior that exhibits respect, reverence, and honor in accordance with specific social norms).[54] Marriage and associated rituals are institutions tied to Zulu cosmologies that acknowledge the centrality of modes of being-in-the-world associated with "tradition." But the fluidity of tradition is thematic to the concerns of this book. Lifeways are changing, and have been changing, since the early nineteenth century. Decades ago, in traditional law it was common for men to marry multiple wives and occupy homesteads organized hierarchically. But these practices are less common today with the institution of marriage understood quite differently, and with a high proportion of adults living in relationships that are not formally recognized as marriages. The material conditions of present-day society make different demands, and the idea of the nuclear family is increasingly undermined by other ways of imagining community. The consequences of these changes are felt across the structure of Zulu societies. The architecture of the umuzi itself used to be shaped by principles of Zulu cosmology with its emphasis on veneration for ancestors and patrilineal descent. In some places, these factors remain strong; in many others, they are gone.

Labor migrancy is a way of life for those who rely on subsistence farming to supplement their incomes. A large proportion of adults live and work most of the year in cities and towns far from their rural homes. This disrupts the rhythms of rural life, which are beset by the challenges of poverty, unemployment, and disease. Often it is those who cannot work because of disability who remain at home in the rural districts. Factors of gender and status to some extent determine the sorts of musical performances women, men, and children engage in and can access. Even those genres that are not tied to specific communal rites—such as popular forms of isicathamiya and umaskandi—tend to be performed by all-male or all-female groups. At uMsinga, for instance, married women usually only perform in private, whereas unmarried women perform at rituals and ceremonies attended by whole communities. There are both cultural and historical reasons for these divisions, as we shall see in the chapters that follow. For instance, adolescents are socialized in peer groups whose lifelong bonds are established through rites of passage. Other codes of interaction are based on marriage practices and taboos. These relations inscribe themselves in music and dance and are evident in the public performance of gender.[55]

GENRES OF ZULU PERFORMANCE

Zulu genres of performance are marked by commonalities in sound and movement. Music is seldom independent of dance and gesture. Genres classified into ceremonial and dance songs are termed *izingoma* (singular, *ingoma*). Genres of izingoma are further delineated by gender and regional differences and are sometimes classed using the pan-Bantu term *ngoma*.[56] The Zulu societies discussed in this book are predominantly patrilineal. A clear separation of male and female roles and responsibilities is made such that performances by and for men, women, boys, and girls are largely autonomous. The demarcation of sonic spaces reinforces the relative autonomy of these groups (see chapter 3). Two popular genres of women's dance songs that I focus on in this book are wedding and *umemulo* (a coming-of-age ritual for girls and women indicating their readiness for marriage) songs. These dance songs are associated with ceremonies and rituals but are sometimes performed outside of these contexts. The umemulo is attended by the entire community who feast and dance together to celebrate the transition, and communicate this to their *amadlozi*, or ancestral spirits (chapter

3). At these events the focal point is the young women celebrated by their parents. The dancing is accompanied by singing, clapping, and stamping, and sometimes by the beating of large bass drums.

Communal song is characterized by at least two voice parts in antiphonal call-and-response, solo and chorus, singing different texts nonsimultaneously (chapter 5). Songs tend to be cyclical with the same melodies returning repeatedly, and with no fixed cadence or end point. These dance songs are designed for communal activities and encourage participation, including ululation, gesticulation, praising, and singing. Men's dance songs employ similar techniques and include subgenres that are regionally distinct and marked by specific choreographies, rhythms, and, in some cases, by instrumental accompaniment.[57] Performances at weddings, funerals and umemulo ceremonies are often accompanied by *izaga* (battle cries), which "usually comprise rhythmical or ('choral recitation') without fixed musical pitches. There is a common rise and fall of pitch, determined by the speech tones of the words, but no uniformity of absolute pitch, among the participants."[58] Adult men also sing *amahubo* (serious anthems).[59] "Each clan has its own *ihubo*, sung only on special occasions, with great reverence, and without dancing . . . The term *ihubo* is also used for war song, *ihubo lempi*, however, for regimental song, *ihubo lamabutho*."[60] In the past, amahubo were sung only when traditional beer was brewed, and served as a means of communication with ancestors. In this book, amahubo are discussed in relation to wedding ceremonies and performances at the umemulo. In both cases, communion with ancestors is a basic function, but so, too, is group identification and genealogy. Musa Xulu has shown how amahubo have been incorporated into nearly all the major genres of Zulu music, thus demonstrating the fluidity of cultural practices and the ways in which popular forms have become synthesized indigenous forms.

Many of the musical instruments and sounds associated with rural life disappeared in the twentieth century. Bow music used to be popular but these instruments have been replaced by the guitar, harmonica, and concertina.[61] Two neotraditional genres of Zulu popular music are umaskandi, a guitar-drum-and-bass style that is also performed with concertinas and violins, and isicathamiya, an a cappella vocal genre with close-knit harmonies and a distinctive call-and-response heterophonic structure that is choreographed to light stepping movements and gestures.[62] These genres are performed widely on radio and television, and I have recorded umaskandi artists all across KwaZulu-Natal. There are many other genres that we might include in this short survey of Zulu genres of performance, such *amakhwaya*, jazz, gospel, house, and *kwaito*;[63] but the focus of this book is on the traditional and neotraditional genres, including umaskandi, as well as the songs, dances, and praises that accompany rituals and public celebrations in contemporary life.

OUTLINE OF THE BOOK

In this chapter I have focused on the disciplinary contexts for studying cultures of performance in situ in sound studies, anthropology, and ethnomusicology. A reflexive ethnography invested in the politics and poetics of writing culture, and the interpretive strategy of sound studies, informs the narrative strategy of this book. Zulu identity politics in the postapartheid period will be explored further in the chapters that follow, focusing on popular and traditional genres of performance.

This is a book about the politics of place, and so land tenure, governance, and representation are important themes (see chapter 1). Land is administered in rural KwaZulu-Natal by two contrastive but complementary institutions of the postapartheid state. Democratically elected councillors administer wards while traditional leaders oversee separately designated izigodi (tribal wards). Land tenure in the izigodi is administered by traditional authorities under the control of *amakhosi* (kings, or what were formerly known as "chiefs" in the apartheid era). The Zulu monarch is the custodian of the Ingonyama Trust, which is responsible for all tribal land in KwaZulu-Natal. The land question is central to the politics of South Africa because of the history of colonial dispossession and apartheid, the nature of communal land tenure, the violence associated with contestations over land, the failure of many land reform programs, and heightened political rhetoric demanding expropriation without compensation. I explain how certain aspects of land tenure and governance work, focusing on the history of these practices at key sites of fieldwork in KwaZulu-Natal. The dynamics of land tenure figure in the performances I record. Songs, dances, and orature articulate the spiritual and spatial politics of lifeworlds conceived as an extension of land. Land is thus a determining context for understanding the political economy of the rural polity, and for making sense of Zulu culture and consciousness in the postapartheid era.

Chapter 2 takes its title from the word *umsindo* (meaning "noise," "din," "uproar," or "quarrel"). It is also the colloquial term for weddings and other large communal celebrations featuring performances of music, dance, and praise poetry. The word encapsulates the polyphonic textures of Zulu acoustemology in which voices are immersed in the simultaneity of dancing, singing, ululating, praising, chanting, and gesticulating in heightened states. This aesthetic of "simultaneous doing" is a key characteristic of Zulu performances at weddings and umemulo ceremonies (see chapters 2–4).[64] Chapter 2 is built around a thickly sounded description of a single wedding at Ncunjane in central KwaZulu-Natal and explores the aesthetics of immersion embodied in performance. In this chapter and in the two that follow, I theorize the concept of sonic space, focusing on the ordering of Zulu homesteads and communities. The competitive social dynamics displayed in performances by Mchunu and Thembu groups at this wedding illustrate how sonic spaces are constructed on the basis of reciprocity.

Chapter 3 describes features common to umemulo events drawing on multi-sited ethnographic fieldwork from across KwaZulu-Natal but focusing on events in the izigodi of Dakeni, Mazizini, Mashunka, Ncunjane, Nkaseni, and Shemula. These umemulo rituals had in common the goal of celebrating and recognizing the conduct and chastity of a daughter by her parents. The umemulo serves as the public announcement of a young woman's readiness for marriage, and of the parents' elevated status within the community. I argue that umemulo songs and dances temporarily suspend the taboos governing everyday social discourse and propriety, thus enabling and normalizing a mode of intergenerational communication otherwise forbidden. The role of sacrifice and seclusion as a mode of communication with ancestral spirits is central to this analysis.

iNgoma dance is performed at celebrations, competitions, and festivals, and after weddings and rituals. Chapter 4 explores the phenomenology of ingoma in hostel life, focusing on the genre of *isishameni* (a style of unaccompanied dance characterized by its high kick) performed by teams of Thembu men at Jeppe, the Wolhuter men's hostel in Jeppestown, Johannesburg, and back home at uMsinga. This chapter reflects on the experiences of dancers who performed at the uMsinga wedding and umemulo ceremonies recorded in chapters 2 and 3. These men are migrants accommodated in the inner-city hostels who perform ingoma on weekends and after hours. Their lifeworlds in the city have come under increasing social and economic pressures in the postapartheid era from rising unemployment, poverty, violence, and competition from other migrants. I argue that dance articulates belonging, territorializes space in the inner city, and articulates a bodily response to the challenges of worlds under threat. In this chapter I draw on the work of Maurice Merleau-Ponty and Jonathan Clegg to unpack the spatial dynamics of the hostel and the relation of these communities to their surroundings.

Chapter 5 focuses on how popular praises in umaskandi guitar music are used to record history, genealogy, and identity, and how they are used as a political tool for social critique. These praises are characterized by rapid, tonally nuanced phrases of incisive social commentary set to the rhythms of instrumental and electronic music. Praises articulate the experiences and heritage of their orators and are replete with idioms and lyrical encodings intelligible only to those familiar with the contexts, symbols, and sounds specific to their perspectives. I offer interpretations of the shared conventions and martial imagery used by musicians and orators from the izigodi of Mkhomazi, Mashunka, Nongoma, Ndumo, and Nkaseni who use praises to evince sharp social critique. The genealogy in this chapter links umaskandi to other popular praises, to genres of dance and bow music, and to *izibongo zamakhosi* (the praises of kings). The politics of popular praises are tied to land, identity, and tradition in a changing world. New musico-analytical approaches are introduced to show how the prosodic dimensions to these praises reinforce their political messaging.

Themes of poverty, inequality, and performance are elaborated in chapter 6. With many parents in rural KwaZulu-Natal working far away as migrants, I found that some of the most vital performances take place in schools. The hugely popular cultural competitions facilitated by the Department of Arts and Culture are an important site for performances of indigenous music, dance, and praise poetry. But what purpose do such competitions serve in a system of education that privileges notation over performance? I argue that an inclusive vision for music literacy in South Africa would help revitalize a curriculum predicated on Western norms.

Chapter 7 is a study of sound and environmental justice at Ndumo Game Reserve, a place where communities and conservationists are in conflict over land. My father's writings on Ndumo, and his recordings on *Sounds of Tongaland*, imagined the coexistence of humans and wildlife while recognizing a history of dispossession and exploitation. When I returned some fifty years after he made the Tongaland record, I discovered a community in crisis with conservation authorities seemingly unable to maintain the integrity of the reserve's boundaries. I argue that the loss of biodiversity and the threat of extinction at Ndumo make urgent the need for interventions to support communities and conservation bodies alike in finding solutions of mutual benefit. Chapter 8 is an essay on reciprocity and the ethics of ethnography that reflects on my own recording practice in this book, developing ideas from earlier chapters. The conclusion offers an analytical summation and final thoughts on themes of land and belonging that recur throughout this book.

Zulu performances embody ways of being-in-the-world that respond dynamically to the politics of place in postapartheid South Africa. The violent contestations over land and belonging that are voiced in these performances are symptomatic of a nation in turmoil. By adopting a multisited and multigenre perspective on Zulu performances, I have sought to illuminate some of the common historical, cultural, and spiritual factors that are at play in these contestations. Land is a powerful spiritual and emotive force that binds persons and communities. The land question remains unresolved and is a bitter site of political contestation in postapartheid South Africa. The sense of dislocation that many Zulu communities feel as a result of segregation and apartheid has yet to be resolved by state interventions. To understand the importance of land in postapartheid South Africa, and its thematic role in Zulu performances, the next chapter engages with the history and politics of land tenure and governance in the province of KwaZulu-Natal.

ONE

The Politics of Belonging
Land, Culture, and Representation
in KwaZulu-Natal

The land is sung. For people of the sky, ancestral lands are the spiritual nexus to their worlds.[1] The singing of Zulu cultures in the land of their forebears is a powerful rendering of spiritual commitment across generations. To sing the land is to mark the contiguities of past and present. To be in and of a place is to draw strength from it. Singing realizes the territories of spiritual life, transcending the barriers of the terrestrial world. Singing releases other worlds in a commingling of life histories and experiences, of past and present. In Zulu cultures, singing is a cognitive extension of the lifeworld. It is a means of becoming, of knowing, and of reaching beyond limits. Singing enables the spiritual connectedness that resides in the bonds of land and kin performed in dance, orature, and music. Performances demonstrate the importance of land as a signifier of identity and spiritual connectedness among kith and kin.

This chapter explores the history and politics of land in KwaZulu-Natal, focusing on the governance of the *isigodi* (tribal ward) and *isizwe* (nation) as contexts for interpreting Zulu cultures of performance.[2] Images of land, nation, and identity recur in Zulu performances and are tied to genealogy, ancestry, and spirituality. The lyrics of songs and praise poetry show how the isigodi is an important symbol of identity and belonging. Land figures in praises and songs that extol virtues, deride vices, and identify orators in addition to their genealogies. Praise poetry is replete with geographic references rendered in imaginative detail: rivers, mountains, and valleys signify places of origin and of belonging. Singers call on their ancestors, connecting place with spirit. The amahubo performed at weddings and public ceremonies affirm kinship and belonging through these tropes. Cultures of song define this land.

In this chapter I offer a brief history of Zulu societies since the nineteenth century, focusing on the rural country districts and the tribal authorities once administered as Bantustans under the apartheid government, but now under the leadership of izinkhosi appointed by the postapartheid state. The overlapping tribal and municipal boundaries complicate peoples' relationships with the land. In the former Bantustan regions of KwaZulu-Natal, a dualistic system of governance has democratically elected councillors and traditional leaders working alongside one another. Through the institution of *ubukhosi* (kingship), Zulu traditional leaders have considerable authority in matters of customary law and land tenure and are often present at community events and performances to keep the peace. amaKhosi administer tribal land on behalf of the Ingonyama Trust, which falls under the authority of the Zulu paramount. This means that most persons living on ancestral lands do not own title deeds and have limited means to extract benefit from the land they occupy. This is partly a consequence of the colonial and apartheid policies that kept land within the ambit of "native reserves." Resolving this problem is one component to the land question in South African politics. The second has to do with the return of ancestral lands to the communities dispossessed during the colonial and apartheid eras. The present contestations over land are a product of the failure of land reform programs postapartheid and heightened political rhetoric demanding expropriation of land without compensation to fast-track the process. This chapter also provides an introduction to the history and politics of place at the main sites at which I conducted fieldwork in KwaZulu-Natal.

A HISTORY OF KWAZULU-NATAL

Bantu-speaking peoples have occupied the coastal plain of southern Africa since at least the fifth century CE.[3] Their interactions with the hunter-gatherer societies who sang this land in the centuries prior gave distinctive shape to the patterning of speech and song. Through intermarriage and cultural assimilation, some of the Bantu clans adopted features of San music, language, and dance. Those groups that borrowed the click-consonants from the San languages were eventually to form a distinct subset of Bantu that linguists class Nguni.[4] *Nguni* is a linguistic term that refers to speakers of isiNdebele, isiXhosa, isiZulu, siSwati, and other related groups. It has also been used to describe a form of cattle culture practiced across southern Africa.[5] As an ethnic identifier it is contested on the basis that "the historically known African societies of the region did not 'migrate' into it in fixed ethnic units but emerged locally from long-established ancestral communities of diverse origins and heterogeneous cultures and languages."[6] This emergence took place over the past five hundred years or so. As archaeologist Tim Maggs explains, "After about [CE] 1500 the evidence clearly indicates that the Iron Age people of the Natal region were directly ancestral, culturally, linguistically, and physically, to today's Black population. There is nothing to suggest that the cultural traits that distinguish Nguni-speaking groups from others within the Late Iron Age originated or developed outside the historic Nguni-speaking regions."[7] The differentiation that gave rise to isiZulu took place over several centuries, taking root in the late eighteenth and early nineteenth centuries.

The Zulu were at first a minor clan among several more powerful conglomerate states on the southeast coast. The inspirational leadership and military brilliance of Shaka, son of Senzangakhona (reigned 1816–1828), quickly expanded their power base precipitating a major shift in the political economy and social structure of the region. Shaka replaced a system of autonomous chiefdoms with a centralized Zulu kingdom that sought tribute from the *amakhosi* (chiefs) through surpluses, and through conscription. Shaka's successors were his brothers Dingane kaSenzangakhona (r. 1828–1840) and Mpande kaSenzangakhona (r. 1840–1872); they, together with Cetshwayo kaMpande (r. 1872–1884), were less successful militarily than Shaka had been, and their legacies were undermined by infighting.[8] Careful policies of intermarriage and the training of regiments of young men (*amabutho*) with strict discipline and enculturation into Zulu lifeways facilitated a system of statecraft that created shared cultural norms for the tribes of Zululand.[9] Powers of patronage enabled the conquest of large stretches of southeast Africa. It also laid the foundation for a formidable response to the European colonists whose forays into Zulu territory became increasingly assertive in the mid to late nineteenth century.

Europeans first arrived in southeast Africa in the late fifteenth century. Portuguese explorers rounded the Cape of Good Hope in 1488, and theirs are the first written records of the southeast coast of Africa.[10] Musical encounters were recorded from the point of first contact between Europeans and Africans, but these meetings were characterized by misunderstandings and violence.[11] When the Indian Ocean trade began in the sixteenth century, it lent impetus to the establishment of way stations in southern Africa, and thus to the permanent presence and influence of Europeans. These outposts for colonial expansion would in the eighteenth century serve as a base for settlers at the Cape, although Natal, then inhabited by Nguni and San populations, was only settled by Europeans in the nineteenth century. Shipwrecks along the coast resulted in sporadic encounters with Nguni speakers, but for the most part these interactions were limited.[12] It was the gradual northern spread of the Cape frontier that facilitated European exploration of the southern African interior. The destruction to indigenous lifeways incurred during the colonial wars of the eighteenth and nineteenth centuries precipitated a seismic shift in the worlds of Africans. The establishment of the Portuguese trade routes was thus only the beginning of an aggressive period of European colonialism that in South Africa was principally the project of the Dutch and then British.

The British first occupied the Cape in 1795 and annexed it from the Dutch in 1806. A small delegation from the Cape landed at Port Natal in 1824. The initial settlement was small, but the impact would soon be felt across the east coast and inland as far as present-day Zimbabwe. Traders, missionaries, and colonial officials introduced new ways of life for indigenous peoples by imposing their values and beliefs through systems of education, economics, politics, law, and public administration.[13] The colonists were ruthless in acquiring and then protecting lands and livestock, and in the colony of Natal they instituted a series of bloody attacks on San peoples, driving them from the coastal belt and mountains. Initially, Zululand remained relatively unscathed by these forays to the south.[14] But the gaze of the British soon turned to the Zulu nation, and by the mid-nineteenth century hostilities had commenced.

The British annexed the colony of Natal from the Boers in 1843. Natal was at this time defined as the land to the south of the Thukela and Buffalo Rivers, stretching to the Umtamvuna River in the south and with the Drakensberg mountains on its northwestern border. Zululand had the Thukela River as its southern boundary with Natal and stretched northward to the Lebombo mountains and Tongaland in the east, the Swazi kingdom to the north. Many Boer trekkers were driven out of Natal or left to escape the expanding British influence. They helped establish the republics of the Transvaal and Orange Free State, which would form the northwestern borders of Zululand. Some Boer trekkers ultimately remained in Natal, including a small group who established the first towns at Pietermaritzburg, Congella, and Weenen.

With the discovery of diamonds in the Cape colony in 1867, and a gold rush on the Witwatersrand in 1884, the political economy of the entire region shifted dramatically. Industrialization fueled the labor market, and many Zulus were recruited for work on the mines. It was in this context that an independent Zulu kingdom became a hindrance to the colonists' exploitation of southern Africa. The British sought control of the coastal harbors in addition to the industrial and mining centers in the interior. The imperial armies moved into Natal and destroyed the Zulu kingdom in the Anglo-Zulu War of 1879. But it was nearly a decade before Zululand was annexed by the British in 1887. In 1888 Cetshwayo's heir, Dinuzulu, was arrested and found guilty of revolt. He was imprisoned on the island of St. Helena for ten years before returning to Natal in 1898 as "Government Induna."[15] With the Natal Act 37 of 1897, Zululand was annexed to Natal. One main purpose was to extend opportunity for European farmers into Zululand. With the disbandment and exile of the Zulu royal house, there was little coordinated response to the British claims on their land. Even so, resistance grew, and the British had to defeat a fierce rebellion in 1906.[16] By then, reserves had been demarcated for "natives," and most of the best arable land was granted to Europeans.[17] Initially, Zulus were allowed to purchase freehold land, but they were later prohibited from doing so with the passing of the Land Act of 1913. This Act precluded "natives" from purchasing or renting land in areas designated for Whites and prevented "persons other than natives" from purchasing or renting land in areas designated for Blacks.[18] A schedule to the act described the areas allotted for Blacks as "native territories" and "locations" that initially "comprised only 7.3 percent of the total area of the Union of South Africa. With subsequent additions, this was increased to 8.3 percent."[19] The Union government aimed "to establish a hegemonic order in South Africa"[20] that would enable the continued dominance of settler economic and social interests as an extension of imperial rule. Its first prime minister, Louis Botha, allowed the former Zulu monarch, Dinuzulu kaCetshwayo, to live out his days on a farm in the eastern Transvaal. But the segregationist policies of the Union (1910–1961) further eroded the already diminished holdings of Zulus and rendered Solomon Nkayishana Maphumuzana kaDinuzulu (r. 1913–1933) little more than a figurehead. Solomon and his son, Nyangayezizwe Cyprian Bhekuzulu kaSolomon (r. 1933–1968), were not recognized as kings. The Native Administration Act of 1927 (Act No. 38 of 1927) handed powers to the governor general of the Union of South Africa to act as the paramount chief of all Black populations in South Africa. One purpose of this act was to enable the colonial government to appoint amakhosi and izinduna who would support their conquest of the land.[21]

The election of the Afrikaner Nationalist government in 1948 resulted in aggressive changes to land policy to favor Europeans. The state cleared so-called White areas of Black families, and those Blacks with title to land were bought out. In the 1950s the Nationalists segregated the country into distinct ethnic homelands. The removal of "Black spots" (i.e., those Black families with title) was intensified, and the tenure of Blacks living on farms was also suspended. Laborers on Black-owned farms were forced to move into locations. A system of labor tenancy had been in place allowing Blacks to trade their own labor for access or residence on a farm, but in 1969 this system was revoked in some areas. Government agents moved in to relocate Blacks to makeshift shelters in the Bantustans, often with limited or no access to water, grazing, and arable land; their possessions were dumped in the veld. This deeply inhumane treatment inflicted a cruel toll on individuals, the consequences of which were extreme poverty. By the 1970s the distinct ethnic enclaves were reconceived as independent homelands, which served the dual purpose of keeping Blacks out of "democratic" White South Africa while containing resistance movements aimed at broader political representation for Blacks. The state installed leaders in these homelands who were promised a measure of autonomy from the apartheid state while benefiting from its patronage. Deborah Posel points out that this strategy of separate development was aimed at "reinvigorating, refashioning and rewarding 'traditional' African notions of authority and political culture—indeed, reinventing, bureaucratizing and disciplining tradition as part of the wider project of creating political 'order'—at the same time as fragmenting African peoples into discrete ethnic components."[22] The urban-rural dichotomy created by these homelands was entrenched as a form of double-consciousness that became the harsh reality for millions of Black South Africans in the twentieth century: work in the cities and slums, home in the country. Movement between the two areas was restricted according to lines of race, gender, and ethnicity, and the state required all Blacks to carry passes or passports with proof of employment.

The Bantu Administration Act of 1952 and other legislation was designed to further delegitimize the rights of Blacks to live and work outside of a homeland system. Black leaders were convinced or coerced to serve the ends of the state by running sham independent states, partly as a propaganda tool to ameliorate South Africa's reputation as a racist state. This strategy was tried on the Zulu monarchy in the 1950s and 1960s until the KwaZulu Traditional Authority (KTA) was established by the state as a semiautonomous unit under the leadership of the monarchy in 1970. The Zulu paramount, King Goodwill Zwelithini kaBhekuzulu, regained limited powers on December 3, 1971, when he was officially installed by the apartheid government as overlord and king. But it was Mangosuthu Buthelezi who became the chief executive officer when the KwaZulu Legislative Assembly replaced the territorial authority in 1972, and it was he who had ultimate authority over the Bantustan. This was a step toward the ideal of independence that the apartheid government used to advance its policies of segregation.[23] Buthelezi consolidated his power through the institution of Inkatha yaKwazulu, which in 1975 he revived as a cultural organization in service of the Zulu nation. As Anne Mager and Maanda Mulaudzi point out, Inkatha was a "vehicle for mobilizing ethnic nationalism" that Buthelezi used for decades to reinforce his ideology of tradition, thereby "further alienating the king."[24] The apartheid government, by extending colonial policies of segregation, cultural essentialism, and ethnic coherence, was expedient in supporting these forms of ethnic nationalism because it furthered the doctrine of separate development. The political consequences were far-reaching. In the 1980s the province became the site of extreme violence in clashes between supporters of the Inkatha Freedom Party (IFP) and the African National Congress (ANC).[25] Buthelezi codified the protocols of traditional leadership in KwaZulu and published regulations for chiefs and headmen that specified their "duties, powers, authorities and functions."[26]

The 1980s were a decade of turmoil that saw South Africa reach the brink of civil war. Economic sanctions hit hard and ultimately forced political and social reforms and the gradual repeal of apartheid laws. The transition to a democratic South Africa was accelerated in 1990 when F. W. de Klerk unexpectedly decided to release Nelson Mandela and other political prisoners, paving the way for a period of negotiation leading to the first democratic elections in 1994 and the formation of a government of national unity. Mandela and the ANC took power. The transition period had been marred by some of the worst violence in South Africa's history, much of it located in KwaZulu-Natal, but also in the migrant hostels of Johannesburg and Soweto.[27] Infighting between and within Zulu political factions continued through the 1990s and reemerged in the late 2010s and early 2020s. A surge in land occupations and an unprecedented spike in political assassinations have again stretched the fibers of South Africa's democracy. Initially, the "new" South Africa was widely heralded for its embrace of democracy, nonracialism, nonsexism, reconciliation, and inclusion. Nelson Mandela and F. W. de Klerk were awarded the Nobel Peace Prize in 1993 and worked together in the first democratic government. Plans for the country's democracy were optimistic and ambitious. But challenges remained. The promise of idealistic new economic and social policies was not fully real-

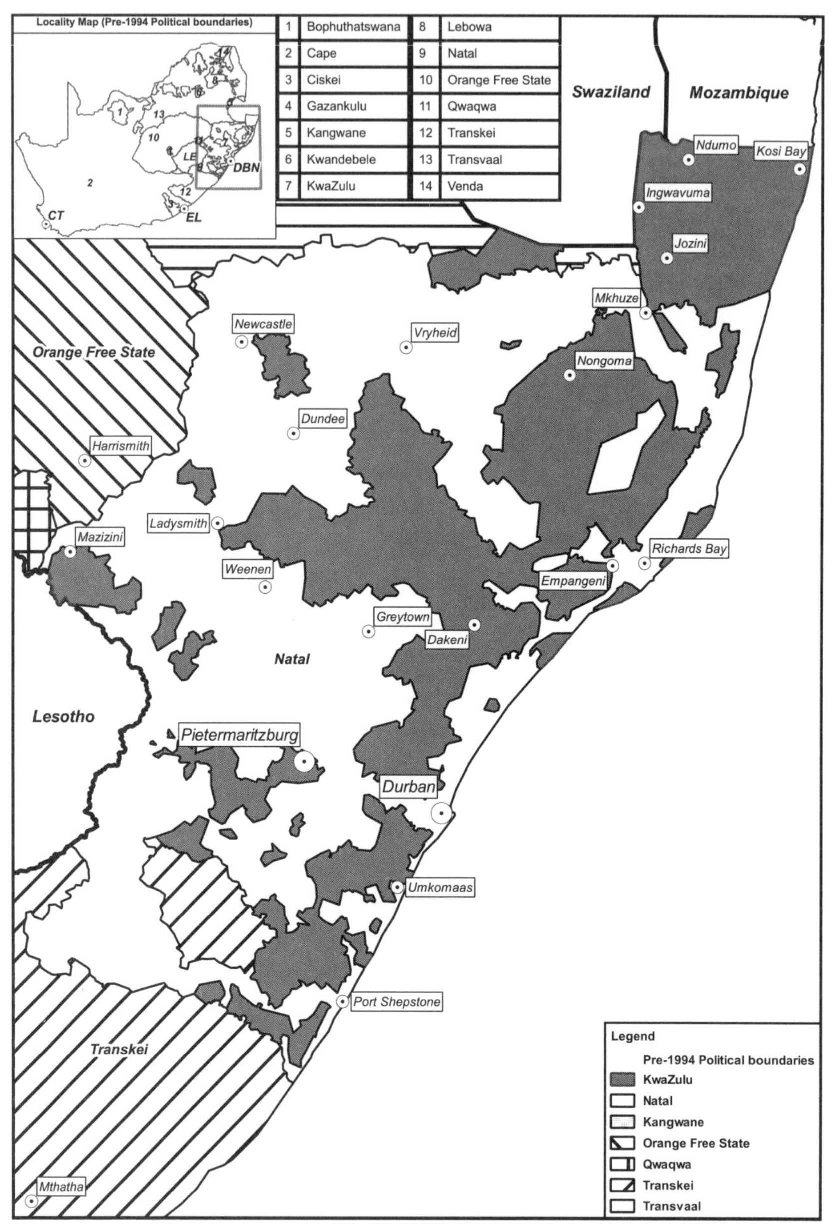

FIGURE 1.1 Map of Natal and KwaZulu, 1990. Created by S3 Technologies.

ized. Still, the immediate impact on everyday South Africans was felt in marked improvements in the general socioeconomic position of the rural poor and a turnaround in the economy. Electricity, running water, sanitation, education, social grants, health, and other forms of support became available to the poor. The economy improved under the Mbeki government in the early 2000s, before dipping under Jacob Zuma's administration. The decline in governance and the rise of corruption and crime in the 2010s undermined growth and frustrated opportunities for youth. The specter of state capture and the hollowing out of institutions of governance and security negated some of the gains made during the first decade of democracy.

Between the years 2010 and 2020, there was a steady decline in South Africa's economic growth. In 2021 unemployment reached an all-time high, compounded by the wide-reaching effects of the coronavirus pandemic, and by the fourth quarter the official figure of unemployed adults in South Africa stood at 35.4 percent for persons who are economically active, and a horrifying 46.2 percent for persons not working but who are looking for work.[28] Statistics South Africa estimates that this last group constitutes approximately 17.4 million persons who are unemployed. The rate of unemployment among individuals between fifteen and thirty-four years old was 43.6 percent in 2021. Structural concerns over the levels of inequality, joblessness, landlessness, and general lack of opportunity indicate a crisis, and this has spilled over into the realm of public violence, looting, and the ugly spectacle of xenophobia.[29] These socioeconomic factors contributed to the outpouring of violence that accompanied the July 2021 insurgency, which has been described by President Cyril Ramaphosa as a coordinated attack on the state and its infrastructure. The riots were triggered by the jailing of Jacob Zuma, the first South African president to be found guilty of contempt for refusing to appear before the inquiry into state capture (the ransacking of state resources for personal gain). Zuma's incarceration and the violence and criminality that followed took place along ethnic lines. Zulu nationalism and identity remain powerful tools for mass political mobilization. To understand the structural means by which the ANC and IFP continue to draw on Zulu nationalism, it is important to recognize the patterns of demography and settlement figured by apartheid and negotiated in the democratic compromise of 1994. The experiences of persons in Zulu communities who are at the margins of South African society continue to be shaped by structures of traditional governance and land tenure that were instituted after apartheid.

UBUKHOSI AND TRADITIONAL LEADERSHIP IN KWAZULU-NATAL

The institution of chieftaincy, ubukhosi, is a hybrid political mechanism used to effect traditional governance in KwaZulu-Natal.[30] It is a composite of indigenous practices and colonial policies that have gradually evolved since the first native policy was implemented in 1849 by the secretary for native affairs in Natal, Theophilus Shepstone. Past and present governments have used policy mechanisms to advance their own political objectives. The authenticity of state-sanctioned ubukhosi is a vexed issue because the authority to appoint and recognize traditional leaders is vested in the minister of cooperative governance and traditional affairs and the president. While ubukhosi depends on paternal succession, there have been cases in which the state appointed pliant leaders in place of resistant or revolutionary chiefs. More than this, the government appointed their own administrators in place of a Zulu overlord of ubukhosi in 1927. The fabrication of traditional leaders by European colonists meant that "traditional authority was no longer traditional."[31] The subsequent marshaling of tradition by the KTA under Buthelezi reclaimed its legitimacy, and many features were retained postapartheid with the codification of the national and provincial houses of traditional leaders.

The geopolitical structure of ubukhosi is constituted by izigodi (literally "valleys"), which are tribal wards within districts. Each isigodi contains *imizi* (homesteads) governed by an *umnumzane* (homestead owner). An *induna* (headman) presides over a single isigodi and forms part of a larger group of elders (*ibandla*) who report to and advise the inkosi (chief) of a tribe. *iziNduna* are assisted in turn by *amaphoyisa* (tribal police officers), *amagoso* (leaders of men),[32] and *amaqhikiza* (unmarried women). During war or unrest, the induna remains prominent even though the *igoso* (leader in dance or music) becomes the primary leader of the isigodi. Within these wards are sub-wards called *imihlathi*, where young men's behavior is regulated by the *amapini* (deputies to the amagoso).[33] The *induna mkhulu* is the chief headman who assists the inkosi in the administration of justice. The induna mkhulu acts as a prosecutor and witness in a tribal court whose jurisdiction follows that of a magistrate's court. The latter is determined by the regional authority, which itself is determined by the provincial legislation. The ibandla come together at events such as weddings and consist of a diverse range of persons of high rank and respect in the community, including *izinduna*. It used to be that the choice of izinduna fell under the authority of the inkosi, but under democratic rule in the postapartheid era this has changed so that persons may now nominate izinduna subject to the approval of the inkosi. Councillors also make representations before the inkosi and on his behalf. The inkosi is not an elected leader with a fixed term in office, and thus cannot be removed from office by ballot, but there are other ways by which elders may persuade their leader.[34] Such practices vary from tribe to tribe in KwaZulu-Natal, but the hierarchy of powers is uniform. The relationship of the head of a household, the umnumzane, to his local induna, the ibandla, and inkosi is enduring. Obligations to kin are complexly woven into the fabric of Zulu societies because genealogy and ancestral belief go hand in hand for Christians and non-Christians in KwaZulu-Natal. In cultures where ancestral spirits intercede in the lives of the living, there are powerful bonds between these persons and their relatives.

Traditional leaders in KwaZulu-Natal are power brokers who must be consulted on all events of ritual significance. Performances at ceremonies and rituals reinforce these relationships through communal displays of social identity. Rituals and public ceremonies are attended by izinduna and amaphoyisa and must be registered with the secretary to the inkosi because they are subject to the payment of tariffs. The inkosi will work through the izinduna who represent him at events or public gatherings and serve as custodians of the peace. They are appointed by the tribal elders on an honorary basis, but their duties are sometimes onerous. I sent letters to amakhosi and visited tribal courts to obtain permissions for my research. It was also essential to be interviewed by the induna for the district, and sometimes by the induna mkhulu, before attending an event like an umemulo or recording musicians from a particular isigodi. The close relationship between traditional leaders and their communities is recognized by the postapartheid government and tied to the rights and privileges of the Zulu royal house. Even so, the status of the Zulu monarchy is not universally accepted and has been the subject of violent confrontation in the postapartheid era.

MONARCHY

All traditional land in KwaZulu-Natal falls under the trusteeship of the Zulu monarch. King Goodwill Zwelithini kaBhekuzulu was installed as head of the ubuKhosi in KwaZulu-Natal in 1994 upon the transition to democracy, and was recognized as paramount king of the amaZulu until his death, on March 12, 2021.[35] This conglomerate of Zulu clans is the largest grouping of traditional leaders in South Africa. The Zulu monarch sits on the KwaZulu-Natal legislature and is the most powerful representative on the Congress of Traditional Leaders of South Africa (CONTRALESA). Traditional leaders gained official recognition in South Africa's Constitution of 1996 and are served through the national ministry CoGTA. In postapartheid South Africa, traditional leaders are responsible for administering justice and managing lands under their control. In KwaZulu-Natal, these lands fall under the administration of the Ingonyama Trust.

The administration of land after apartheid has been the subject of several state commissions. Questions of landownership and land restitution are emotive issues under intense scrutiny from political parties, the media, and civil society. In KwaZulu-Natal, the controversy over communal land tenure centers on the powers of the Ingonyama Trust. A deal was made right before the first democratic election in 1994 between President F. W. De Klerk, ANC leader Nelson Mandela, IFP leader Mangosuthu Buthelezi, and King Zwelithini, to cede all communal lands to the Zulu monarch under the Ingonyama Trust Act. This act was passed by the KwaZulu legislature on April 24, 1994, three days prior to the election. King Zwelithini was made the sole trustee of the Ingonyama Trust and was handed control of roughly one-third of all land in KwaZulu-Natal.[36] Currently the Ingonyama Trust Act governs two hundred fifty traditional councils listed, or a population of approximately 5.2 million (2011 estimate). The total land holding consists of some 2,883 million hectares.[37] Ownership of land on this scale is unprecedented in South Africa. With so little land available to Black South Africans, there is now intense debate over the rights to ownership, and to rightful ownership.[38]

King Zwelithini and the IFP leader and former prime minister of the KwaZulu homeland, Mangosuthu Gatsha Buthelezi, argued that the Ingonyama Trust is essential to the Zulu monarchy, marshaling support from Zulu traditionalists at numerous public celebrations of Zulu culture and history. Buthelezi said that "the ITA was meant to make certain that 'land in traditional areas could continue to be administered according to indigenous and customary law.'"[39] But the consultations documented in the report of the High-Level Panel (HLP) show that residents often do not enjoy the rights to land conferred by the Constitution of 1996, and the question of indigenous and customary law is not settled.[40] Zwelithini had countered the prospect of reform and "threatened to call on his subjects to take up arms to defend the land under the Ingonyama Trust if the need arose,"[41] and asked "loyal" Zulus to contribute funds toward its defense. During his address at the annual *umKhosi woMhlanga* (reed dance ceremony) in September 2019, Zwelithini warned against the appropriation of the Ingonyama Trust land. "The provocation of us as Zulu people has reached a high, they are no longer just provoking me, but it has spilled on to you, my children. In the last two years, the king's enemies have shown themselves very clearly by saying we must be stripped of our blanket, which is the land of our ancestors."[42]

The tense public debate over the role of traditional leaders in KwaZulu-Natal is indicative of a broader set of contestations that democratic norms have brought to the fore.[43] The Traditional Leadership and Governance Framework Act, passed in 2004, serves to underscore the role of chiefs presiding over traditional councils that operate in collaboration with local government authorities. The phrase "cooperative governance" is used to embrace a communal form of leadership exerted through consultation with conventions rooted in custom. Recent legislation and the outcomes of the Nhlapo commission have shifted the equilibrium. The ANC government has effectively guaranteed the authority of traditional leaders with legislation ensuring their permanence in the postapartheid state. Communities have the power to establish traditional councils that are elected in terms of custom, but always under the authority of a designated chief. Land in the former homelands is still not under the control of individuals or homestead owners; instead, it is held in trust under communal tenure that is controlled by traditional councils who are accorded a key role "in the allocation of land, serving to enhance the power of traditional leaders to control property rights."[44] The status quo was reinforced when President Ramaphosa signed the Traditional and Khoi-San Leadership Bill into law on November 20, 2019.[45]

Some leaders in the province petitioned the government for recognition, but the Nhlapo Commission determined that Zwelithini is "king of amaZulu as a whole," having far-reaching consequences.[46] Critics of traditional leadership claim that the "freezing of political dynamics and the pre-colonial competitive, shifting, fluid imbalance of power and influence" has resulted in a hegemonic yet constitutionally sanctioned chieftaincy in South Africa.[47] The powers of the king over land deny his subjects access to capital, and thus to the possibility of developing their land for a better life.[48]

Performances of music, dance, and praise show how citizens and subjects engage these power dynamics in izigodi. The logic of communal land tenure orders lives. But is it just? Popular artists like Phuzekhemisi, and his brother, Khethani, rose to prominence by contesting chiefly authority and giving voice to the protestations of the rural poor (see chapter 5). The power and authority of the amakhosi and king are generally respected, often in pragmatic contexts where communities cannot afford taxes and levies, or where decisions about land are made without consultation. Democratic institutions foster a different culture of governance, justice, and representation, and this leads to tensions in the governance of wards. The parallel modes of governance are the system of democratically elected officials from political parties appointed as salaried councillors, and the semiautonomous system of traditional leaders who appoint izinduna and amakhosi in consultation with their ibandla. Traditional leaders work in collaboration with CoGTA to assist with law and order as well as the maintenance and functioning of traditional courts of justice.[49] With land redistribution under apartheid and the resettlement of large numbers of Zulu speakers in areas far from their ancestral homes, the division of land poses a central political problem for postapartheid South Africa. The injustices of land have created enormous social and spiritual tensions, resulting in faction fighting, land grabs, invasions on state land (including conservancies and parks), and violent attacks on smallholdings and farms in rural areas. The politics of place in specific locations is important, then, to understanding the meanings of performance and how they articulate with questions of land and belonging. I explore these sites in the section that follows.

SITES IN KWAZULU-NATAL AND GAUTENG PROVINCES

The performances of music, dance, and praise poetry I describe in this book were recorded at rural homesteads, schools, community halls, and courthouses in the province of KwaZulu-Natal, and in Johannesburg in the province of Gauteng. I focus here on two places around which most of the fieldwork sites are anchored: Mdukatshani, near the town of Weenen, in the Inkosi Langalibalele Local Municipality, and Ndumo in the Jozini Local Municipality. Other sites are located across six municipalities that include the uMzinyathi, uThukela, uMkhanyakude, King Cetshwayo, Zululand, and Harry Gwala District Municipalities.

Sites in the Inkosi Langalibalele and uMsinga Local Municipalities

The blue skies at Weenen conceal the stains of past injustice. This land has been the site of violent struggle since the early nineteenth century. The Thembu and Mchunu tribes originated in the uMzinyathi region but ventured south in search of independence from Shaka. Both lost their chiefs in Pondoland before migrating back north.[50] The Thembu initially occupied a territory near the confluence of the Thukela and uMtshezi (Bushman's) Rivers but were displaced in 1839 when

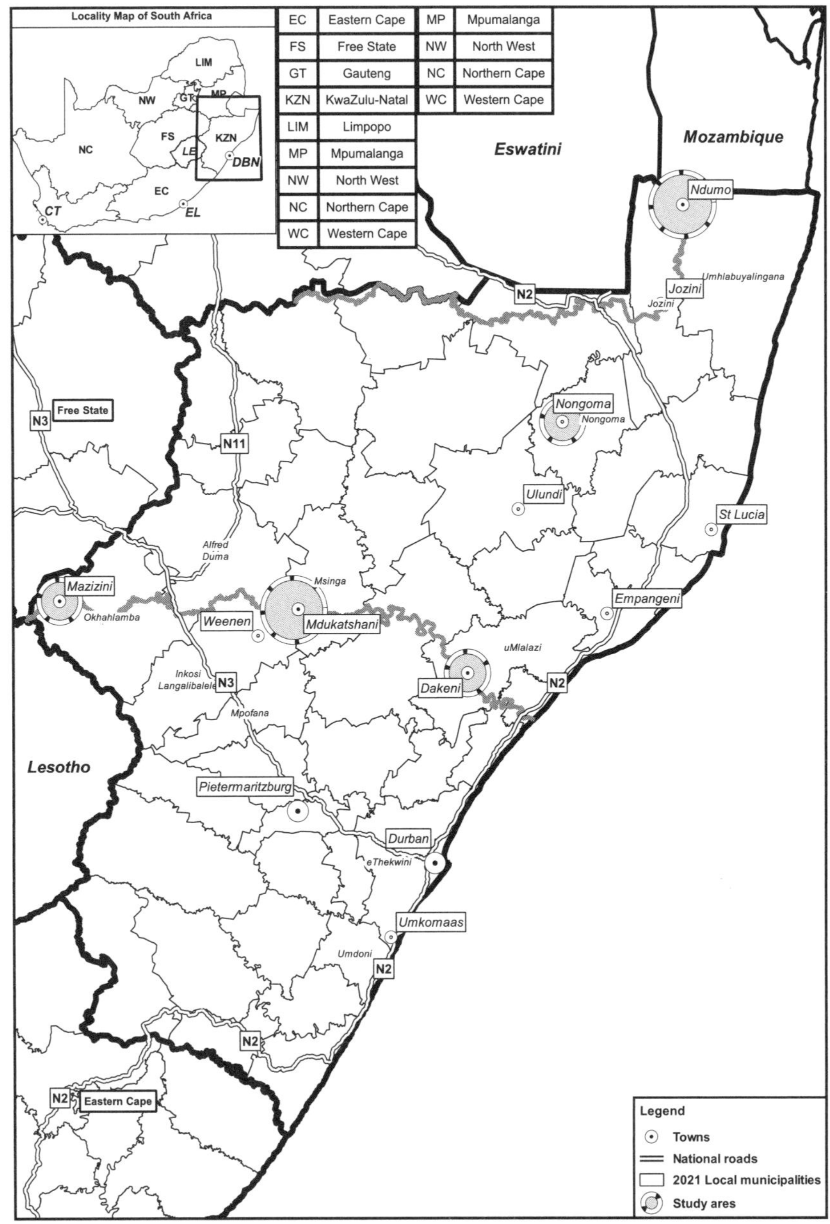

FIGURE 1.2 Site map of KwaZulu-Natal. Created by S3 Technologies.

the Boers forced them onto land near the Mnambithi (Klip) River. The Mchunu settled alongside the Thembu to the south. In the 1840s both of these border tribes were living outside of the authority of the Zulu king, Mpande.

The British colony of Natal was established in 1843. In 1849 the Natal colonial administration proclaimed a series of locations for indigenous peoples. The Thembu were designated residents of the Mzinyathi location while the Mchunu lived on land defined as part of the Mpofana location.[51] Both tribes had a fractious relationship with the Boers who wanted the colonial government to force them to work as cheap labor on their farms. For much of the nineteenth century, the amakhosi of these two tribes relied on the British secretary for native affairs, Theophilus Shepstone, to intercede in times of political instability and conflict.[52] The Mchunu tribe settled much of the Weenen district, including farms owned but not occupied by settlers of European origin. The Thembu initially occupied only a sliver of land south of the Thukela around Mashunka mountain. Most were resident north of the Thukela until their territory was extended further south to Tugela Ferry. The British considered these tribes a useful buffer against the Zulus for the settler populations of Natal.

Land surveyors staked out farms in the Weenen District in the 1850s, and some farmers settled where there was access to water and irrigation. The rocky ravines were of little interest as they were not suitable for livestock. These farms were left unfenced well into the twentieth century; Mchunu and Mthembu families lived on them as tenants. "The Africans had the hills to themselves, vast unfenced hinterlands that were 'practically small locations.' They had a tribal identity, with allegiance to a chief, but none of the obligations usually owed."[53] These were the largest tribes in Natal, but most resided on White-owned farms.[54] During the twentieth century the area was marked by violent conflicts in these districts. A war was fought at Ngongolo on the boundary between the Mchunu and Mthembu lands in 1944. Later, the amakhosi sought peace between the tribes but violence continued thereafter that was both intra- and inter-ethnic.[55]

Land tenure on the farms in the Thukela valley has long been contested because of legislation that forced Blacks off their land or into exploitative relationships with White farmers. The Native Trust and Land Act of 1936 legislated a labor tenant system in which Black laborers were granted permission to reside on White farms as tenants where they could graze their cattle and make use of arable land on condition that they provide unpaid labor to the White landowner for six months each year.[56] The rezoning and repopulating of designated Black and White areas destabilized Weenen, leaving many Blacks homeless. Segregationist policies determined that Blacks should not be resident on White-owned land, leading to labor tenancy being outlawed by the state in 1969. Only Black families who were permanently employed were allowed to remain on White farmland.[57] This precipitated evictions and the hasty establishment of new settlements for Black families who would now be required to live in the neighboring KTA or on lands owned by the South African Development Trust.[58] Chizuko Sato observes that "Africans who refused to work full time were served with eviction notices, and eventually an estimated 10,000 to 20,000 people in the district were forcibly removed."[59] The effects were devastating. There was overcrowding on lands that lacked the necessary resources for subsistence, and competition between individuals led to violence.[60] The demarcation and control of land for these communities later fell under the jurisdiction of the KTA, setting up an unhappy coalition of governance that did nothing to improve the plight of the displaced peoples. Most of the relocated families lost their livestock or were forced to sell off their cattle and goats cheaply to White farmers who took advantage of their desperate plight by paying a pittance. Evicted labor tenants from the Weenen District were resettled at Thukela Estates in what came to be known as Sahlumbe, Nomoya, Susamphi, and Mashunka.[61] The Department of Bantu Administration and Development did not provide even basic facilities for water, sanitation, health care, and schooling.[62]

Access to arable land and grazing is of daily consequence. Conflicts over land among poor communities living in high-density areas are commonplace. The establishment of the African reserves and the forced removals resulted in greater population density with associated tensions and gave rise to generational violence. Jonathan Clegg has described the emergence of an ideology of vengeance in the uMsinga District in the early 1930s, pointing out that violence both within and across districts could be attributed to "the problem of insufficient land."[63] Hostilities over land and related matters are embodied in performances at weddings, and in other rituals and cerebrations that involve inter-district dances that have taken on a martial character. For instance, the practice of *umgangela*, a ritualized form of stick-fighting, sometimes results in dangerously violent escalations where weapons are drawn and persons are killed and injured. In some ways, dance, music, and praising offer the means not only to express aggression but also to contain it. We see this in the music of umaskandi artists who in their *izibongo* (praises) adopt an aggressive and threatening tone (see chapter 5), deriding their leaders. In chapter 4 I show how isishameni dance is used to express a sense of belonging in situations where a community's unique identity is threatened.

Mdukatshani

The town of Weenen was planned on the banks of the Bushman's River in 1840; today, Weenen is a small farming town with a single gas station and a post office. While conducting my research, I stayed at Mdukatshani, some twenty miles from the town, along a scenic route that stretches through cultivated fields, orchards, and bush in the direction of Tugela Ferry. At Nkaseni, the road runs parallel to the Thukela River, hugging the hills before meandering to a second meeting with the Bushman's River shortly before a confluence. The route through the valley parts ways with the Thukela at the approach to Mashunka mountain. Mdukatshani lies at this bend in the river and consists of three farms first surveyed in 1864 that had never been occupied by Whites: Koornspruit, the Spring, and Loraine. These frontier farms had been settled by Thembu and Mchunu families who worked six months of each year by way of rent. One hundred and forty-six families were forcibly removed in 1969 and were settled at locations near and far, including neighboring tribal izigodi. The three farms were purchased by the Church Agricultural Projects (CAP) in 1975 for a program of rural development directed by Neil Alcock and his wife, Creina, my aunt. CAP's new home was named Mdukatshani, meaning "place of lost grasses."[64] In winter, Mdukatshani's arid, rocky landscape is decorated by aloes and tough thornveld. The farms were acquired when the forced removals had already left many Black communities with nowhere to go and no one to turn to for help.[65] CAP had established the farm as a resource for these displaced families. Sustainable agriculture was practiced with the aim of rehabilitating the land to make it productive. The invisible boundaries that divided the properties scored a troubled history. Koornspruit, otherwise known as "top farm," spills out onto Ncunjane isigodi, home to families from the Mchunu tribe in the Inkosi Langalibalele Local Municipality. The CAP offices and the Alcock homestead are located on Loraine, a narrow strip of land adjacent the Thukela River. Loraine sits lower down in the valley and runs onto Mashunka isigodi occupied by the Thembu tribe in the uMsinga Local Municipality.

LAND TENURE ON THE FARMS When the Alcocks arrived at Mdukatshani in 1975, they knew nothing of the complex history of this contested land. Creina records how there were no less than "twenty-one conflicts that turned project areas into war zones which were out of bounds to staff for months at a time. Not one of the conflicts was inter-tribal. Mthembu fought Mthembu, or Mchunu

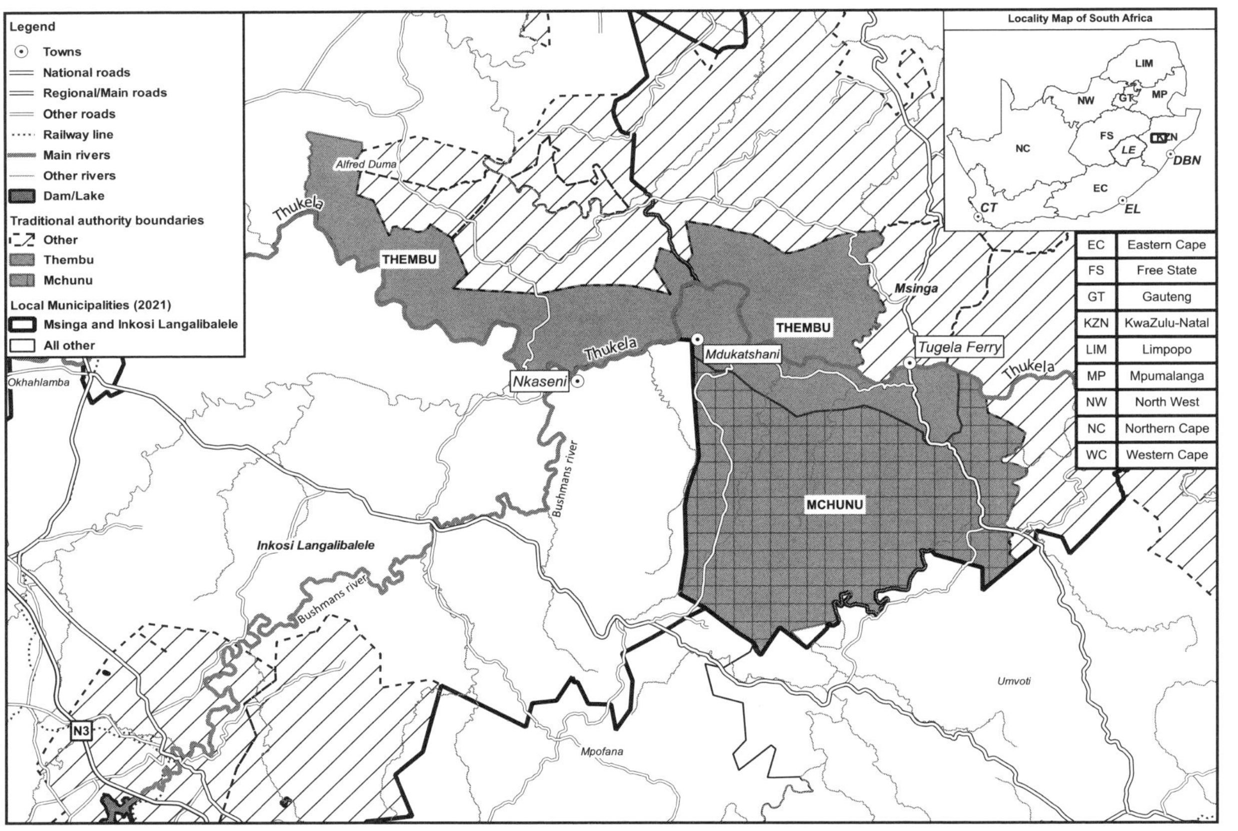

FIGURE 1.3 Site map of the Inkosi Langalibalele and uMsinga Local Municipalities. Created by S3 Technologies.

fought Mchunu."[66] Over the past five decades, the Alcocks have developed a powerful bond with these communities that has been crucial to their own sense of belonging in the district. The process of land restitution that they jointly initiated through CAP began in 1991 when a formal land claim was instituted on behalf of residents in the area. CAP has since ceded Koornspruit and the Spring to land claimants, with Loraine still in process.[67] In 2017 the Koornspruit land was handed over to the Mchunu Tribal Authority, who administer it for the fifty-three families now living there.[68]

I first came to Mdukatshani as a child, and remember the enormity of Neil's *imisebenzi*, a "return of the spirit" ceremony, held in July 1988. In September 1983 Neil had been killed in an ambush on his way home from a peace meeting.[69] Creina chose to remain on the farm to continue CAP's work as an administrative clerk. The management committee and board of directors ensured that the project went on, now under the leadership of the Mchunu chief induna Petrus Majozi, Peter Brown, and Elliot Mngadi. Creina's sons, Mark ("GG") and Rauri ("Khonya"), would eventually take on additional responsibilities in 1990 when Creina turned to the community beading business that she had established with over two hundred local women. Creina's commitment to Mdukatshani and to beadwork has established her deep bond with the community. Khonya later built a cottage adjacent to Creina's and elevated above the banks of the Thukela. He manages the renamed Mdukatshani Rural Development Project with donor funding.[70] The relationships the Alcocks established with communities in and around Mdukatshani were an important enabler of my work there.

uMkhanyakude

The second location of importance to this book is situated in a border region in the far northeast of KwaZulu-Natal near the town of Ndumo. This land also fell under the KTA during apartheid even though it was largely independent of Zulu influence until well into the twentieth century. Alfred T. Bryant places the Tembe king as the progenitor of a lineage that is continuous with the present inkosi, who is recognized by the South African government as a traditional leader in the uMhlabuyalingana Local Municipality, and who is independent of the Zulu royal family. This remote quadrant of KwaZulu-Natal was formerly known as Tongaland in reference to the Tembe-Tonga peoples, but its ethnic and linguistic fabric is complexly woven. When Zululand was first annexed by Natal in 1887,

Tongaland was not included but was instead specified as its northern boundary. "In November 1897, Tongaland was finally annexed and added to Zululand, and in December 1897, Zululand (including Tongaland and the Trans-Pongola Territories) was incorporated in Natal."[71] When the KwaZulu government took over the region, Buthelezi renamed it Maputaland, thereby negating its Thonga identity. But the cultural and, to a lesser degree, linguistic presence of the Tembe Thonga, Tsonga, and Swazi remains, particularly among women who speak these languages. The social dynamics of this multicultural border region have been mapped out in historical accounts by Leslie and Alfred T. Bryant, and by anthropologists Walter Felgate and Angela Impey.[72] Here, two important points about this region require emphasis: first, the growing influence of Zulu cultural and linguistic dominance and its promotion; and second, the integration of this region into the structures of traditional leadership and democratic governance that now apply across KwaZulu-Natal.

The political structure of this northern sector of the uMkhanyakude District Municipality is split into the Jozini and uMhlabuyalingana Local Municipalities by the Phongolo River (figure 1.4). The Jozini Municipality borders Swaziland to the west and north and Mozambique to the northeast.[73] The Mathenjwa Tribal Authority is in the Jozini Local Municipality with an office at Ingwavuma, and the Tembe Tribal Authority is in uMhlabuyalingana with an office at Manguzi.[74] The songs I recorded in this area (chapters 4 to 7) are almost exclusively in isiZulu. Angela Impey's careful elaboration of the complex network of languages and identities that persist in the Ndumo region shows this complexity,[75] and it was significant that when Thulani and I introduced my research project to the Tembe izinduna at Manguzi, they complained about the dominance of isiZulu to the detriment of Thonga culture. This shift toward Zulu cultural hegemony is undeniable and has had a major impact on the cultures of performance at Ndumo. The main sites I studied are in the izigodi of ePhosheni, Makhane, Shemula, and Ndumo. The isigodi of Mbangweni, adjacent Ndumo Game Reserve, is in the uMhlabuyalingana Local Municipality of the Tembe Tribal Authority. The introduction and chapters 6 to 8 focus on fieldwork conducted in this region. What is of marked importance to the politics of place at Ndumo is how Zulu culture and identity are contested rather than normative. This raises important questions about the nature of tradition and its performance in postapartheid South Africa.

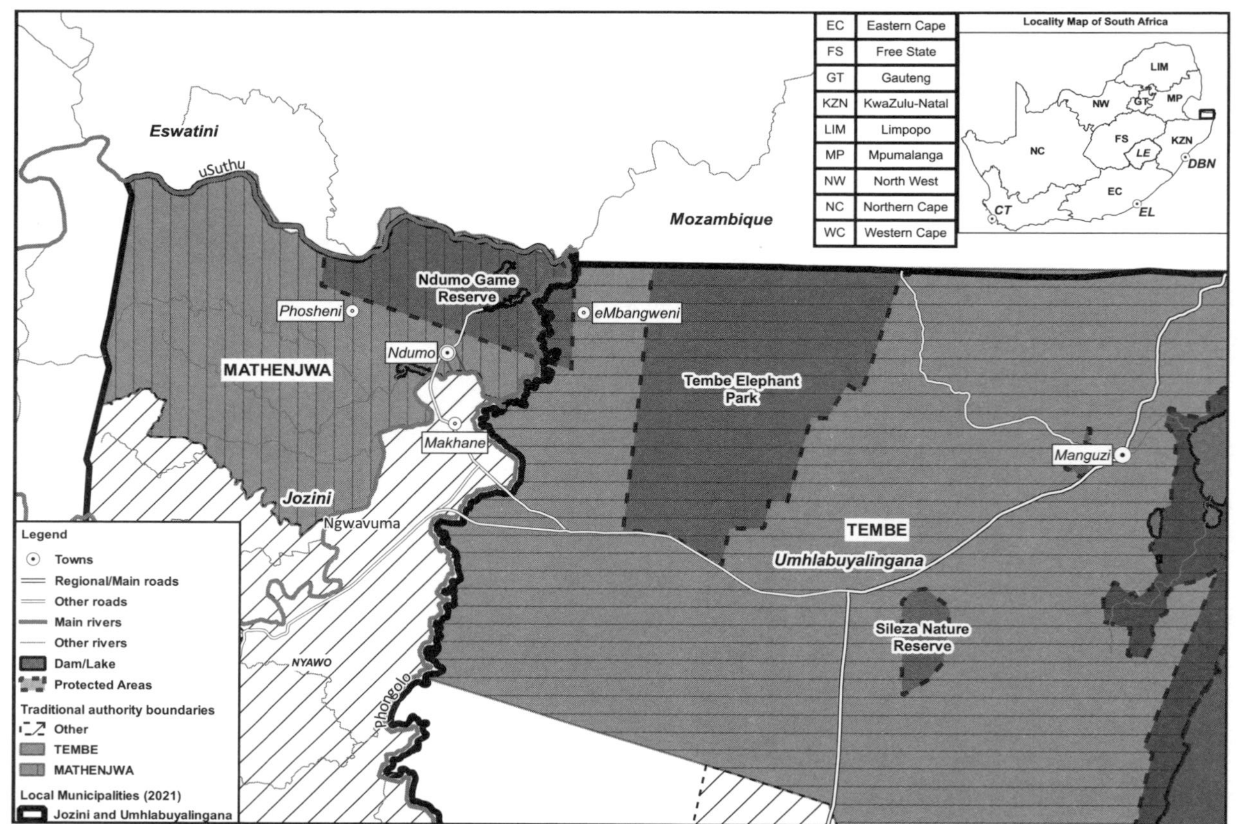

FIGURE 1.4 Map of the uMkhanyakude District showing sites in the Jozini and uMhlabuyalingana Local Municipalities. Created by S3 Technologies.

CULTURE, TRADITION, AND GOVERNANCE

Tradition in all its guises is an important context for interpreting Zulu performances. But whose traditions are at stake? This chapter has reflected on the ways in which tradition was constructed to legitimize very different systems of governance under the Union and apartheid governments, and now, with the institution of ubukhosi, under the authority of the Zulu king.[76] Performances, I argue, are central to the spectacle and embodiment of Zulu traditions that have been invented and reinvented to serve political purposes. Terence Ranger describes the invention of "European traditions of subordination" in Africa,[77] of which ubukhosi is a case in point, forged by colonial administrators for colonial ends and reappropriated by the postcolonial state. The invention of traditional despots in South Africa may have been the product of colonial invention, but the process was undoubtedly reciprocal and adaptive rather than passive. As Ranger puts it, "Europeans believed Africans belonged to tribes; Africans built tribes to belong to."[78] What this book shows is how the politics of tribe and tradition are performed, constructed, and contested in contemporary South Africa.

The idea of traditional Zulu culture in the twenty-first century is overdetermined as much by the legacy of colonial invention as by its reinvention in the postcolonial imagination. The assertion of an unchanging tradition in the face of radical social change is indicative of a strategy that suited apartheid ideologues, and which has been appropriated by postapartheid politicians and the Zulu royal house to exert authority over their subjects. In democratic South Africa, claims to tradition have been used to justify the continued dominance of institutions of traditional authority and to make claims to ownership and stewardship of the lands of rural dwellers. This despite national commissions that have given voice to opposing views, and which have recommended the abolishment of the Ingonyama Trust. In *Citizen and Subject*, Mahmood Mamdani describes this relationship of colonial to traditional leadership. Colonial administrators sought to liken their patronage to monarchical systems of control in Africa, imposing a new regimen on societies in flux. The failure of this imposition is well-documented. Colonial governments were drawn to similarities. "Their own respect for 'tradition' disposed them to look with favor upon what they took to be traditional in Africa. They set about to codify and promulgate these traditions, thereby transforming flexible custom into hard prescription."[79] These traditions have remained. According to Mamdani, "the invented traditions of African societies—whether invented by the Europeans or by Africans themselves in response—distorted the past but became in themselves realities through which a good deal of colonial encounter was expressed."[80] The annual umKhosi woMhlanga is one example of these inventions at which performances of Zulu culture are seen to reinforce the supremacy of the king through acts of supplication.

This book is about the performance of cultures at a time when the stereotypical images of identity have waned, when the notion of tradition has been historicized, when the representation of others has been thoroughly interrogated. And yet what we find in the performance cultures of KwaZulu-Natal is a complex mix of indigenous and contemporary, of tradition and modernity. The rituals most closely guarded by communities—such as the wedding and coming-of-age ceremonies documented in the following two chapters—are no less syncretic than genres of popular music like umaskandi and isicathamiya. The chapters that follow draw close attention to the sounds and symbols of these rituals to reflect on the politics of tribe and tradition and how these constructs are applied to twenty-first-century cultures in flux.

TWO

umSindo!
The Politics of Sonic Space
at a Zulu Wedding

The sounds of an *umsindo* can be heard for miles around. The Zulu word means "noise," "din," "uproar," or "quarrel."[1] It is also the colloquial term for a wedding (formally an *umgcagco* or *umshado*) or for other events that bring the community together in song, dance, and ritual. The din at weddings is created by groups of women, men, and children singing, dancing, clapping, ululating, shouting, and gesticulating together. It would be easy to mistake this noise for discord because the sheer volume of sound is often overwhelming. But what is the social function of this noise, and how is it used to advance the interests of groups in a community? This chapter on the dynamic intensity of an umsindo describes a wedding that took place at Ncunjane, KwaZulu-Natal. I introduce the concept of sonic space to show how sound is used to identify persons and groups, and to establish power relations between them.

Two approaches to sound and space are commingled in this chapter: the anthropology of social space, which focuses on social relations across territories and how these are structured;[2] and an analysis of sonic space that shows how space is figured in sound, and how sound is used as a physical and symbolic means of shaping and representing social space.[3] The dimensions of social space—that is, its concrete features and their arrangement—may or may not be explicable in terms of their social construction. This approach to sonic space as a zone of interpenetrating sounds differs from other theories of social space. For instance, Claude Lévi-Strauss adopts a linguistic explanation: "any manifestation of social phenomena—a mode of marriage, the arrangement of a village—constitutes a language in the sense that it can be reduced to a set of abstract rules and expressed in different models." In this method, "social space is analyzed as part of the total system which can be expressed at different levels and through different models of organization."[4] Maurice Merleau-Ponty argues that the experience and expression of space is not Euclidean. He observes that "we can no longer draw an absolute distinction between space and the things which occupy it, nor indeed between the pure idea of space and the concrete spectacle it presents to our senses."[5] Space is not experienced as the objective parameters to which our lives are fitted. It is not reducible to a set of points mapped in abstract dimensions. Instead, the person is conceived as a "mobile spatial field—a spatiotemporal unit."[6]

Sound is a mode of occupation. Sounding is a way of making claims over the properties, boundaries, and distinctions that space affords. A sonic space is defined by its spatiotemporal dimensions and how these are perceived. Visual co-ordination to space is complementary to sonic orientation. Sonic space is unique in one important dimension: it is porous, unbounded. The aural dimension to space is seldom remarked upon, and yet sound is used for determining location as much as sight. My concern is not so much with a universal concept of spatial dimensions and social construction, nor with territoriality and its expression, but rather with declarations of the territorial in sound and their implications for social and political institutions. How is sonic space inhabited, imagined, and manipulated to advance persons' interests?[7] The spatial dimensions to sound are too often faded out of this conception of reality. Sound has location, and it locates us relationally to others, to things, to the world. A place is a point in space whereas space itself is the experience of being in place. Moving between places, and across spaces, is a social phenomenon. How we move, and who we move with, matters.

DECEMBER 29, 2011

Zamani Madonsela is the driver for the Mdukatshani Rural Development Trust. He is responsible for driving me around the farms. Without him, I wouldn't know how to find anyone at Ncunjane, Nkaseni, or Mashunka. The visits are a departure from his everyday work delivering beads, transporting women from the bead project, ferrying patients to and from the mobile clinic, and the occasional drive to Tugela Ferry for provisions or a hospital visit. A drive to Weenen is usually punctuated by a dozen stops for hitchhikers who jump on and off the trailer. Zamani drives the project's powder-blue 1978 Toyota Hilux single-cab *bakkie* (van). The windows are cracked, having endured the tectonic challenge of Mdukatshani's roads. Only he knows how to turn on the ignition without starting a fire. Zamani lives within earshot of the offices on the cliffs above Mdukatshani. He's quick to help, and when my car got stuck on the access road, it was he and Mla Magasela who helped me dig it out.

Today we are en route to an umemulo ceremony at Ncunjane. This section of Mdukatshani is commonly referred to as "top farm" because it sits atop a plateau several hundred feet above the river. Our ascent to Ncunjane is slow. Creina and I crouch on the back of the truck with two elderly men seated in the cab, one in poor health. We drop them off within sight of the umemulo. A young man approaches us with an elder from the community. He asks whether I will return tomorrow to film a wedding. The day will mark the acceptance of the *umakoti* (bride, married woman)[8] into the family homestead. Creina says I will think about it and let them know. I am pleased with the invitation and decide to accept right away but say nothing. Reticence is a mark of respect, after all, and this is Creina's domain. The young man is Ngamulakhe Ndlovu, the *umkhwenyana* (bridegroom) who invited us to his umshado (wedding) asking that I "shoota" (film) the proceedings. The event is to take place at the umuzi of his father, Mbuzeni Ndlovu, in the Ncunjane isigodi of the Mchunu Tribal Area. Ngamulakhe's umakoti, Bhekile Masoka, is from the Nkaseni isigodi in the Thembu Tribal Area, about eight miles from Ncunjane.

The next day, Zamani drives us up the steep hill to Ncunjane and we park just inside the fence to the *isango* (main gate) of the Ndlovu umuzi. A smart double-cab Toyota Hilux pickup truck is parked outside the homestead, and I wonder whether this belongs to the bridegroom. Ndlovu is wearing the green and gold springbok rugby jersey he had on yesterday. It is early afternoon, and we are greeted warmly with a spread of cakes and drinks. Men and women busy themselves in distinct spaces across the umuzi. There is no sign of the *umthimba* (bridal party). It is only a while later that I discover them settled in a glade of trees a short distance from the entrance. Two groups of men have clustered in the umuzi. One is seated under a large red-and-black tent with the name *Mkhize* emblazoned on it. The second group of Nkaseni men, the bride's party, sit thirty yards away toward the back of the umuzi under a tree adjacent a rondavel. All are drinking beer. Young men roast meat over an open fire and serve it to Ncunjane elders in the tent. Raw strips are sutured to the barbed wire fence in preparation.

Behind the *izindlu* (homestead buildings), women stew meat in black cast iron pots over an open fire in the outdoor kitchen. The sacrifices took place yesterday. The slaughter of cattle in the *isibaya* (cattle byre) has ritual significance,[9] and I see evidence of this in the middle of the isibaya where a large hide has been laid out to dry, layered thick with blood and pegged down at the edges.[10] The significance of the isibaya as the seat of the amadlozi, or amathongo (ancestral spirits), makes it the focal point for ritual.[11] The isibaya is also home to the cattle, who are the wealth and pride of the family. Adjacent to the isibaya is the family's main granary. Above it is a burial place for deceased family members, although in this case Ndlovu's father's grave is inside the isibaya.[12] "Ancestral shades" brood over their family members from the isibaya itself, and so this is where sacrifices are made. It is enclosed by a ring fence of twisted branches and barbed wires, the ground a deep-brown mound rough strewn with generations of rocks, roots, and bovine excretions: nourishment for two hardy trees that cling to its upper slope. The spirits of the umuzi rest here with its cattle. Set on a gentle slope, the isibaya has one isango immediately below the leveled platform of the *indlu enkhulu* (large house) and another at its lower extremity. The dwellings set about the umuzi consist of a rectangular house, the indlu enkhulu, and four rounded izindlu positioned above and to the right of the isibaya. The *umsamo* is a sacred space, a room in which a wedding or umemulo ceremony will generally start with the sacrifice of a goat. The umsamo is marked by horns placed above its entrance. It is here that the spirits will be told about the marriage ceremony that is about to take place.[13] A broad path curves its way from the main gate along a rooted maze through the homestead. Trees greened in summer rains smatter shade over the growing crowd.

Mchunu migrants have returned home from the cities and industrial complexes to the thin, quiet air of Ncunjane. For most, this is a period of annual leave and a time for rest and recreation. Workers knock off on December 15 and return early in the new year. The heaviness of the year's load is dissolved in laughter, music, and dance. Today's excitement carries a heightened sense of anticipation. Slowly trickling into the umuzi are small parties of kith and kin. As the sun waxes, the afternoon swells into an umsindo and the final rites of the *ilobolo* (bride wealth) ritual that has been negotiated between the two families prior to the wedding.

The midsummer sun commands a deep sweep of blue sky, its crisp breeze collecting dust. Jubilant troupes arrive in pockets of three or four at a time. Two distinct groups are congregating in the umuzi. *Amasoja* (soldiers) dressed in

FIGURE 2.1 iKhetho men from Ncunjane congregating and singing *amahubo* (anthems) in preparation for the umsindo. All photographs by Thomas Pooley.

military garb—acquired through duty or purchased at the local trading store—pace the meandering footpaths singing amahubo (anthems). Each *ihubo* (anthem) signifies place, identity, genealogy; each song is a symbol of the *ibutho* (regiment) or isizwe (nation) from which they hail.[14] To the rear of the umuzi is a small clearing beneath an acacia tree. This is the destination for a group of *izinsizwa* (young men) who have walked from the Nkaseni isigodi, some eight miles away, down into the steep Thukela valley and up the jagged ascent to Ncunjane. The plateau commands no view of the river. It is dry, sandy, stony; a concaved stomach threaded by the wizened vein of an abandoned riverbed running dry through its belly. The men are quiet now, their dialogue quenched en route. A much larger congregation of Ncunjane residents are seated inside the red marquee some fifty yards away. Strips of charred meat are still being meted out to sustain them.

A teenage boy blows a borrowed bugle. The shrill screech resonates a twinge through my neck. He's struggling to pitch the contorted tube to a tune. The result is a mashup of piercing squeaks, low breathy sucks, and wheezy belches. The piercing din soon gains the attention of a soldier from the tent nearby who takes the bugle from him. Under supreme effort the instrument succumbs to its master, and the soldier's percussive interjections ring across the landscape. The repetitious chorus of spluttering valves echoes over the plain, summonsing the community and sounding the occasion. From time to time, the distant salvos of other buglers answer as they approach on foot.[15]

The sun has passed its midpoint by the time the elders join the izinsizwa. They file out through the lower gate of the isibaya, singing. The path takes them through the long grasses, stony earth, and thorn trees, to where, three hundred yards away, a group of women sits at the *esihlahleni* (place of preparation). This is the umthimba, which includes the umakoti and her attendants, all family. uMakoti is wearing her *isicholo*, a broad, circular, red headpiece balanced atop rings of leopard skin and braids of white cotton. She wears one red and one green *isiqhaza* (earring) attached not to her ears, hidden as they are beneath the expanse of the isicholo, but to the braided white cotton. The isicholo identifies her unmistakably as a married woman. Tied to her neck like a mane down her back is a blond *ishoba* (bull's tail). She is distinct from the others wearing a white vest matched to a soot-black *isidwaba* (leather skirt). A red hoop of cotton is strung over her right shoulder crisscrossing at the navel with a matching green hoop hung from her left shoulder. Across her breast is a string of *umcimelo* (folded bank notes), a donation from her family. She carries two items with her: an *ummese*, a large knife that she clasps throughout the umshado and uses to signal to her umkhwenyana;[16] and a small cowhide *ihawu* (shield). Brown leather bangles clasp her forearms. White sandals match her top. *amaFahlawana*[17] are emptied metal cool-drink cans, folded in half and filled with small stones. These are tied to her ankles and used for percussive effect as rattles. A white metal whistle is pursed between her lips. She blows it in short sharp bursts while dancing. Two items are clipped to her isicholo with safety pins: a condom filled with water, and a fifty rand note.

The umakoti's attendants are *amatshitshi* (young girls), *amaqhikiza* (unmarried women), *izinkehli* (elders), and *omakoti* (married women). The amatshitshi are bare-breasted, beaded, and dressed in hide skirts. The amaqhikiza wear *umqele umthini* (hide headdresses), black braziers, beads, and *izidwaba* (plural: isidwaba). Their legs are tightly coiled with *amagadasi* (copper bangles), and their

ankles adorned with the same amafahlawana rattles worn by the umakoti. The elder women are fully clothed with long capes, T-shirts, and closed sneakers; the married women are distinguished by their magnificent *izicholo* (plural: isicholo).

A second ibandla arrives from the umuzi to collect the umthimba. They, too, are singing and chanting amahubo in call-and-response, calling out *izaga* (battle cries) and shouting repetitious salutations, *izibongo* (praise names) and *izithakazelo* (clan names). A bugler punctuates their singing with shrill, percussive blasts. The ibandla collect the bridal party for procession to the umuzi. A man from the ibandla takes command. He is wearing an impressive zebra hide and carries an ihawu and *induku* (fighting stick), his neck draped with a mane-like ishoba, and he is wearing an *isinene* (loincloth made from soft tassels of leather), *ibheshu* (buttock-covering skin), and *izimbadada* (dancing sandals made from tire tread). The men are ready to fight, ready to dance.

Movement among the umthimba is slow. Every effort is subjected to the gravity of the moment. A quiet suspense has enraptured the party. The young umakoti is departing her family for a new life. The transition to new *imithetho* (laws) and new roles as wife and daughter is upon her. When she crosses into the space of the isibaya, her state of belonging will change. This forging of familial alliances will alter the force of commitment and responsibility formerly owed to her parents. The change is symbolized by the large *umbogisi* (chest) carried on the head of one of her *amaqhikiza*. The matching pedestal is balanced on an *inkehli* (elder). Contained within the oversized chest are belongings gifted from her family that will be useful in her new life as a wife and mother.[18] The umbogisi is painted red with black stripes on the front. Two rectangular mirrors are inset to the left and right of a central panel depicting Joseph with a shepherd's staff overlooking a haloed Jesus in his crib. The umthimba get up one by one and circle into the formation in which they will file up the hill to the isibaya. The bugling is now muted and the singing an undertone as the solemn march to her new umuzi begins. A python trail takes shape as the women march into the umuzi with the men singing behind them.

iBandla: Ayojabula amanqa	Vultures will be happy
ayodla thina.	to eat us.
umThimba: Mhlawumbe	Maybe they'll chase us away
azosxosha thina.	(refrain to men's singing).

This is the ihubo sung by the umthimba as they enter the isibaya. Bugle blasts and ululating punctuate the air intermittently. The lower entrance to the isibaya is chained and so the umbogisi cannot be carried upright into the kraal. One by one the party enter with men congregating on the lower fence line where they will be positioned for most of the afternoon. The women divide; by custom they are not permitted to enter the isibaya for this space is the domain of men and cattle. But these spatial and spiritual taboos are suspended for today, and those carrying the umbogisi move to the very center of the isibaya where they carefully place the pedestal and chest, one atop the other. The men continue singing, standing in a line behind the second group of women. The youngsters are singing *umcushulo* (a genre of dance song).

iBandla: Undaba haka kwanguye.	This issue of our ancestors.
umThimba: La kwela phezu	Pholoba's words rose over us.
kwethu ilizwi loPholoba.	

Now that the umthimba have established themselves in the isibaya, it is the turn of the *ikhetho* (bridegroom's party). They file out of the red marquee in the umuzi and march down past the isibaya and out of the umuzi even as the umthimba continue their singing and dancing. The umthimba are singing *umgezo wezintombi* (a genre of cleansing song). Goats were slaughtered for the umakoti's attendants. This song washes them clean as the young women dance in front of the umthimba. The mood is somber, reserved, and respectful, and the lyrics offer a laconic commentary on the unfolding drama.

umThimba: Sadlala amadoda awadikadika umntanami.	We were played by the men who are weighing down my child.

Lined up, the umthimba sing and dance, the young women taking the lead.

umThimba: Nangu ubaba ethangenze ngibe igongobala naku nyizoshiya bakwethu. Yibekin' gongobala.	Here is my father, I say let me be unmoved as I'm going to leave my kin behind. We see you are unmoved.[19]

The sound of the ikhetho's singing can once again be heard approaching the umuzi from below. The umthimba men start to *giya*, making mock attacks at invisible assailants and chanting. The women respond to each giya with rhythmic gestures of their ankle rattles (see figure 2.4). Giya is a form of dancing in which men imagine their roles within a potential conflict, advertising their willingness to join the battle and establishing their credibility before the assembled company. During the giya their peers call out praise names, heightening their sense of purpose. The dancer's actions will often imitate the movements and sounds of a bull. Charging across the isibaya from left to right, dragging their feet to lift clouds of dust into the air, the men use their arms and dancing sticks to rampage like a bullock's horns. The clattering of sticks and shields, fearsome facial expressions, and baring of teeth exhibit a righteous anger (*ulaka*).[20] This must be quelled by the umthimba women, who boldly stamp the ground back into place during and after each giya. This is designed to have a calming effect, closing off the momentary turbulence. It also completes the intrinsic cycle of call-and-response.[21]

The ikhetho is outside the umuzi. It may be out of sight, but it is audible from inside the isibaya. Now they are singing and chanting amahubo anthems together, thereby reinforcing their bonds of community and family, and heightening their resolve. At last, they enter the main path into the umuzi singing in medium voice, traversing the isibaya, and entering by the lower isango. Their tone recognizes the presence of others in their isigodi, in this umuzi, in this isibaya.

iKhetho: Uyezwa, sivul'indlela.   Listen, we are opening the way.

Simultaneous to this intrusion by the ikhetho, the alternation between the giya of the men and the uqashiya of the women in the isibaya continues. But the sounds from these two large groups are now closer than before, and the element of competition comes into play. Standing opposite their adversaries, the ikhetho begin chanting their amahubo over the singing and chanting of the umthimba. The ihubo they sing offers up a challenge, asserting their dominance.

iKhetho: We hlab' indlovu.   The elephant stabs.

The ikhetho men crouch on their haunches, their izinduku to hand, aggressively chanting izaga.

iKhetho: Izwa, izwa seskhona.   Listen, listen we are here.
Silindele ukufa kuyeza.   We are waiting to die, it's coming.
Mabamanga kwanumzane   The headman has given us a
    was'thela ngeqala.   sentence to begin.

An ihubo follows:

iKhetho: Wayishiyaphi   Where did you leave the
    indlovu?   elephant?
Indlovu enomboko.   The elephant with a trunk.

The women in the umthimba continue dancing and singing:

Ngihlulekile wu-ithathe   I have been beaten, take her,
    ithathe ithathe.   take her, take her.

So continues the to-and-fro between the umthimba and the ikhetho. A male soloist enters the fray wearing a camouflage-printed brown shirt. He chants:

Soloist: Hup, hup, kwamnandi
    Nkaseni!
iKhetho men: Kwamnandi
    Nkaseni!

Hey, hey, it's wonderful
    at Nkaseni!

He strikes his shield, beating out a rhythm to the giya. The men respond with their shields setting a cross-rhythm to the girls' singing and dancing, which continues unabated.

Soloist: Kophela imithombo,
    kophela imali,
    soyeka ibiya!
umKhongi: Umfazi uyadula,
    indoda ayiduli!
Girls: Ubani ubengalobolo
    ngeZamalek?[22]
Ngoba inkomo kaziko

The malt will be finished, the
    money will be finished, we will
    stop having beer!
A wife is expensive,
    a man is not!
Who can court marriage [*lobola*]
    with a Carling Black Label beer?
Because we have no cattle
    [to lobola with]!

These taunts are part of the culture of competitive insults characteristic of performances at weddings. The play of invective between umthimba and ikhetho dominates the proceedings. As if to meet their greeting, the leader of the ibandla rushes forward in his zebra skins to make a mock attack. He is immediately fended off—not by the ikhetho, but by the umakoti and her attendants, who hold him back. Unrepentant, he chants to the women of the umthimba, and they respond. This play between umthimba and ikhetho is laced with humorous rancor, indignation, and feigned confrontation.[23] In this it serves its purpose well: for each isizwe to assert its independence, pride, and power.

Inside the isibaya, the umthimba and the ikhetho are now separated by the umbogisi, the symbol of betrothal, at its center. The bridal party have gradually moved closer to the center of the isibaya and stand bent over, eyes downcast. The *umkhongi* (bridesgroom's man)[24] surveys from the right, and the umkhwenyana's *ummeleli* (advocate) is now approaching them. The ummeleli presides and delivers the official wedding contract on behalf of the umkhwenyana's family.

The men are armed with izinduku and *izinhawu* (shields), the young women groomed in colorful garments adorned with beads, streamers, an assortment

FIGURE 2.3 Ndlovu *umsindo* (marriage ceremony) at Ncunjane, December 29, 2011.

of jewelry, and izidwaba. The umthimba line the lower fence while the ikhetho are arrayed along the upper perimeter. The parties meet in the center where the umakoti and the umkhwenyana stand a few yards apart. The umakoti is partially obscured behind a line of her attendants, while instructions are called out by the ummeleli overseeing the proceedings.

umMeleli: Uyamthanda na?	Do you love him?
(waving induku)	[pause]
[pause]	Do you love him?
Uyamthanda na?	[pause]
(waving induku)	
[pause]	

At last, the umakoti steps forward and unfurls her *isicephu* (small grass sitting mat) on the raw earth between the parties. Her downcast eyes and bearing show extreme reticence, caution, and subservience. She must use the language of inhlonipho and custom toward her new family. Black, green, red, and blue V shapes are patterned into the mat. In the center is a white T shape. The umkhongi steps forward, picks up the mat and folds it into his hand. He is holding two sticks. One is a walking stick with a T-shaped head. The second is a much shorter dancing stick with a knobbed head and black leather handle. Contained within these items are his authority, his ancestry.

The umakoti's umkhwenyana now approaches, smiling.

umMeleli: Sondela   Come forward.

The umakoti is still reticent, bowed down between her retinue.

Women: uyamesaba?	She is afraid of him?
Assembly: Sondela, sondela.	Come forward.
Kiph' isandla.	Show your hands.
Sondela umkhwenyana.	Come closer groom.

The moment arrives: the umakoti and the umkhwenyana extend hands toward one another. The tips of their fingers embrace for the briefest of moments. The contract is complete.

———

With the rite completed, the dance continues. The men from Nkaseni begin moving up the slope to the top of the isibaya, and the Ncunjane men move down to take their place, both groups chanting amahubo.

iKhetho: Izo, insizwa webana?	These are the warriors you gathered?

This chanting is followed by an ihubo of the Thembu tribe.

iKhetho: Phulula, Phulula iyohlaba inyathi, iyophakamisa.	Gently, gently, the buffalo stabs you, lifts you up.[25]
Senqa umgwaqo, senqa umfulo.	We crossed the road; we crossed the river.

Following the ihubo is an umcushulo song:

iKhetho: Izozala inkonyane iyamabutho kaZulu.	The calf will beget Zulu regiments.

Now it is the turn of the Ncunjane men to giya. They kick up sand and dust, engaging in mock combat with their furious wielding of izinduku. Call-and-response chants overlap between the soloist and the group, and then another umcushulo song from the girls:

iKhetho: Nangu ethintha
    undlunkhulu.
Wathintha abafo, wathinta impi.

Here he touched the home of the
    main wife.
You touch brothers, you touch
    the army.

The umkhwenyana giyas as the umakoti and umthimba exit through the lower gate of the isibaya. There is much jubilation from the women. Men from the umthimba have gathered outside the umakoti's hut to which her belongings are now delivered. As the Nkaseni people parade out of the isibaya, they march to a Thembu ihubo:

umThimba: Siphethu ugodo
    olshunqa nthuthu.
Siphethe umangolongolo.

We are carrying firewood that
    makes smoke/fire.
We are carrying the machine
    gun/army rifle (R1).

This is a large circular *indlu* (room) with Western-style windows, air brick ventilation, and a thatched roof.

umThimba: Bosala bekhala.

We leave them crying.

In the isibaya the Ncunjane men are now preparing to leave too. There is much bugling and striking of shields.

iKhetho: Umtanami, umkhunz'
    umtanami.

My child, warn her my child (as
    in warn her to behave).

The Mchunu ihubo follows:

Thula uzoxosh' impi, impi
    yamabala.
Impi yenduku ngege
    ihlule thina.

Silence, the army will conquer
    you, the army of shadows.
The fighting stick has never
    conquered us.

Wensizwa uzoyidele
   inkani.
Wensizwa ungutshwala
   bakanyoko.

Young man will tire of being
   stubborn.
You are a man because of your
   mother's beer.

The amahubo in the isibaya is drowned out by bugling in addition to the singing of girls and men circling inside the umuzi. Now the ikhetho exit through the lower gate, and there is much jubilation and ululation from the elder women. The climax of the umsindo is registered in a polyvocality of sound, giving voice to each generation embedded in the next. AmaHubo are sung by the men entering through the main part of umuzi near the indlu enkhulu. The umthimba have separated so that the umakoti and her attendants have gathered in a circle next to the indlu enkhulu where they are singing and dancing, and taking turns for solo displays called "one-one." Young women in the umthimba come forward to dance in the central area between the izindlu, spectators lining the banks above, sitting on rocks, standing in a dense huddle. The married women arrive in regal attire carrying long staffs with red flags to match their izicholo. The umthimba women and the umakoti continue their celebrations in sound. But during their gentle tunes, the ikhetho men return through the umuzi stopping to sing in an adjacent space. As they approach the bridal party, the married women form a barrier secluding the umakoti from her husband and his men. The men sing an ihubo:

Angiboni intombi angiboni
   luthonje asiye she.

I don't see a girl, I don't see
   anything, let us all go.

And so, they move on, out through the main entrance. Their singing and chanting are very loud now, having peaked in intensity after their giya. The girls and umthimba are singing in call-and-response, dancing in a circle. It is time for the umakoti to take to the dance arena. The stamping dance begins with the dancers' ankle rattles accentuating an offbeat rhythm. The umakoti uses her whistle percussively in time with the beat. The joyous cries of married women ring out as they join in the dancing, ululating in high voice. The clapping increases in volume and patterns alternate and intersect. The umakoti raises her leg to stamp, but now she's impeded by her heavy isidwaba. Above the women's singing is the singing of the Ncunjane men who are now back in the isibaya chanting amahubo. The layering of sound resonates the entire umuzi, fulfilling the rites of marriage.

The umsindo continues into the afternoon and evening with cohorts singing,

FIGURE 2.4 iKhetho men singing amahubo and flanking the *umkhwenyana* (bridegroom) as married women cordon off his *umakoti* (wife) in the homestead.

dancing, and stick-fighting. Later there will be feasting and drinking. There are restrictions on the consumption of beer. Only men of the *isibongo* (of the sib) may consume *amasi* (curdled milk) together. Similarly, specific cuts of meat are reserved for different members of the family, with guests served separately and in a different indlu to the immediate family. The use of dedicated spaces is an important point of cultural contact. The afternoon is long, but it is to end abruptly for us. Zamani rushes to call me away. There is trouble between the amabutho. They have been stick-fighting in a nearby field and three men have suffered head injuries. Someone drew a gun. We must go.

TRANSITION

The umsindo choreographs a woman's transition from one lifeworld to another, from one space of belonging to another. The transport of the umbogisi from one ancestral and familial space to a new home symbolizes this transition. The relationship between these two spaces is homologous, and familiar to her through enculturation. Still, the specific expectations of her as a young bride will be quite different. The umshado thus serves a purpose in this reorientation. The rituals serve to connect two distinct lineages irrevocably. The immediacy of a love relationship is confirmed, ilobolo transferred and settled. The forging of new bonds is stressed in the negotiations, performances, and pageantry leading up to the ceremony, in the ceremony itself, and in the succeeding months. The ancestral spirits of one lineage must recognize the coexistence of a new lineage if the bride is to be accepted and to belong. Singing is one dimension to the performances that mediate relationships between lineages and their ancestral spirits. The singing of amahubo (anthems), izibongo, and other genres of song demonstrate the polyphony of the umsindo as event and spectacle. The combative relationship that characterizes the interaction between the umthimba and ikhetho demonstrates a principle of mutual respect.

At the heart of the umsindo is a competitive spirit manifested in the rivalries performed between the umthimba and the ikhetho. The umthimba perform specific categories of songs. Rosemary Joseph explains that "although male members of the umthimba may join in the singing of particularly the *inkondlo, umphendu,* and *ukugqumushela* categories of song, the sentiments being expressed are essentially those of the bride and her age-mates who form the core of the bridal party."[26] Some songs are performed at both weddings and umemulo, coming-of-age ceremonies, and form part of a larger repertory of ingoma songs. Most wedding songs are short, usually comprising only two or three phrases in duration and performed in call-and-response between a soloist and chorus. Specific events in the wedding ceremony are addressed, and some songs are educative. Others may be used to instruct a new bride on appropriate behavior. The transition to married life may be challenging, and so the bride is prepared. One example, recorded at Mashunka, is a song reminding her to obey the laws of the new umuzi. ◀))

uMakoti bayakusho bathi
    unolaka ubothobela umthetho.
	Bride, they say that you are a
	    difficult person, you must
	        respect the law.

Songs reinforce the morals of the community and its laws. The ordering of social life depends on kinship relations, and persons are treated differently depending on their relationship. Rosemary Joseph observes that "residence may be influenced by kinship affiliation and, where this is the case, the individual's major domestic, social and economic relations are typically kinship relations ordered by kinship principles."[27] It is customary for a woman to join her husband after marriage, and marriage always involves an exchange of bride wealth, generally in the form of cattle.[28] Entering into marriage partnerships in Zulu society is a protracted process of gamesmanship and negotiation. The exchange of bride wealth is an honest signal of worth and a reasonable guarantee of eligibility, and so it is taken very seriously by both parties' families, who generally assemble a group of elders to act on their behalf. The joining of genealogies and the recognition of a shared cosmology is ultimately of mutual benefit, and the exchange of gifts reinforces the goodwill between the families. The restrictions on marriages between sibs accords with this recognition of shared genealogy and ancestral belief. While the marriage does serve as a "*rite de passage* for the couple," it is a "double transition" for the bride, who must now be accepted into her husband's sib. Separation rites are important, and are similar in principle to those for the umemulo (see chapter 3) with a focus on seclusion, restraint, abstention, and respect.[29]

It may take years for a young bride to be fully accommodated into the husband's sib. The practice of inhlonipho, to "avoid in respect," acknowledges her intermediate position in relation to her husband's ancestral spirits and family. The gradual process of rapprochement serves to conjoin the two sibs with one another.[30] It is accompanied from the beginning of marriage negotiations by the practice of ilobolo in which the husband's family members deliver an agreed number of cattle to fulfill the principle of reciprocity inherent to the marriage ritual. The bond of trust and friendship established through this practice must be recognized before the ancestral spirits so that they know that a change has come about in the standing of the families and their relations. The marriage negotiations are often tense because the balance that must be struck is contested. This principle of contestation in these negotiations signals strength and mutual respect. Both parties insist on the exceptional qualities of their candidates. The antagonism expressed in performances at Ndlovu's wedding is indicative of this principle. The performance of anger and offense serves a purpose at the umsindo, but once the ceremony has been completed there is a sharing of beer and meat, and the families establish friendly relations, thus ending the antagonism performed with such ferocity in the preceding days and months. The practice of stick-fighting often serves to resolve pent up tensions, though risks of escalation persist.

THE POLITICS OF SONIC SPACE

The texture of the umsindo's polyphony articulates a phenomenology of space by marking others while conjoining kin. If the norms governing the relationships and coordination of performers were not widely recognized and respected, the entire event would quickly devolve into chaos. That these norms are sanctioned is thus a function of shared horizons of belief and understanding. It is this sense of social consciousness that is shared between and across groups at an umsindo that suspends discord and makes bonding possible. It also points to cultural norms shared across time and place. The umsindo, in short, is a relational sonic space and one fit to its purpose for a community. The Ndlovu's umsindo at Ncunjane demonstrates a principle that embodies the ritual rivalry embedded in the social relations between the umthimba and ikhetho, and how this is articulated in sonic space. The combination of groups singing, dancing, and gesticulating simultaneously but asynchronously, creates immense excitement. Each group performs a different ritual function, and their interaction is often competitive rather than cooperative. The resultant polyphony maps out the complex networks of relationships that exist between the families of the bride and bridegroom as the ceremonies proceed. The structuring of sonic spaces and their interrelationships as this process unfolds reinforces the norms of custom. The ways in which sonic spaces align, collapse, integrate, disintegrate, and overwhelm one another show how the politics of space is performed in sound. *umSindo* refers both to the totality of these sonic spaces and to their interaction for it is through this interaction that the ritual power of the ceremony is evinced.

THREE

Songs of Sacrifice
uMemulo and the Politics of Gender and Generation

DAKENI, JULY 10, 2012

A party of women and girls have congregated in the shade of an acacia tree some two hundred yards from the umuzi. The dwellings are set on a gentle incline within earshot of the Thukela River and just above the floodplain. Girls are singing "e-yay-eh!" in call-and-response as they march toward the isibaya in single file. Yesterday, three cows were sacrificed, one for each of the three izintombi emulayo, the girls for whom the umemulo is being performed. Each girl has the *umhlwehlwe* ("the caul, or net-like covering of fat over the entrails"[1]) of her sacrificial beast draped over her torso. The umhlwehlwe is the white film that envelops the beast's gall bladder. It is carefully removed the night before the celebration and stored in the umsamo, an inner sanctum where the amadlozi reside. This display of the umhlwehlwe is a pungent, visceral communication to the amadlozi that the girls will henceforth be marked as marriageable women. The izintombi emulayo and their attendants are singing and stamping out a rhythm with their heavy ankle rattles as they enter the outer fence of the umuzi, traversing up above it, then turning slowly in front of the indlu enkhulu. Having announced themselves and having had their presence recognized, they circle back down the hill and out through the main gate to a clearing in an open field nearby that serves as a space for dancing. There they form into a semicircular line and it is in this pattern that they will continue dancing and singing for much of the afternoon. The singing awakens the quiet of the valley and attracts the attention of the community. With the afternoon sun still high in the sky, groups of children and neighbors trickle down to the open field. The crisp quiet of a sunny midwinter's afternoon carries their voices across the isigodi. Young men arrive, including three suitors wearing hides and clutching izinduku (fighting sticks). The elder men seat themselves on chairs and stools fifty yards from the girls, also in a semicircular array. Women and children have congregated with gifts (*umakho*) that include blankets, bags, and household items. Bursts of spontaneous dancing erupt as the izintombi emulayo break the line. Now it is the elders' turn to come forward with umakho. Bills are affixed to the girls' *incema* grass headbands, and the afternoon's performances begin to fill the valley with song.

The umemulo is a ritual widely practiced in Zulu societies that signals the coming of age of a girl or young woman, and her readiness for marriage. She is taught about the maturation of her body as well as her role and responsibilities as a wife. In some cases, holding an umemulo allows for the ilobolo marriage negotiations to be completed. This is significant because marriage will accrue bride wealth for her father's family and will result in her transition to a new way of life.

FIGURE 3.1 uMemulo at Dakeni, July 10, 2012.

Performances of song and dance mark every stage in a weeklong series of events culminating in celebrations for the whole community at her father's homestead. The father-daughter relationship is affirmed by the umemulo and is thematic to the songs composed for it.[2] In the run-up to the celebration, the initiate's activities are undertaken in seclusion and cloaked in secrecy. In this way, the umemulo is an initiation rite in many southern African cultures.[3] This chapter explores the role of song, dance, and sound in umemulo ceremonies recorded between 2011 and 2017 in the izigodi (tribal districts) of Dakeni, Mazizini, Makhane, Mashunka, Ncunjane, and Nkaseni in the province of KwaZulu-Natal. Continuities and discontinuities in umemulo practices are examined in light of earlier reports.[4] Analysis of these rituals shows how intergenerational and ancestral bonds are affirmed through performance and sacrifice. The practice of ritual is fluid, not static.[5] Rituals change and are constructed to meet the demands, desires, and spiritual needs of a community.

What purposes do umemulo rituals serve in Zulu communities today, and is there consistency in how they are performed across izigodi in KwaZulu-Natal? In the first two chapters, I explained how forces of colonialism, missionization, urban-rural migration, and industrialization were decisive in reshaping Zulu lifeworlds in the nineteenth and twentieth centuries. Christian missions and educational institutions disrupted social norms by outlawing rituals that did not conform to their mores and beliefs, including practices associated with ancestral belief.[6] With the development of an industrial economy, South Africa transformed into a complex admixture of cultures in the twentieth century with the imposition of Western norms and laws. John Blacking has described an altered midcentury soundscape that alienated communities from their ancestors. The profound impact of Western culture and tourism on the initiation ceremonies of the Venda, and other cultures, was indicative of this shift in society at large.[7] Carol Muller's work on rituals of fertility in KwaZulu-Natal shows how Zulu society drew on indigenous and Christian cultures to preserve rituals sacred to both.[8] In the postapartheid era, improved communications, infrastructure, and services have transformed rural societies in unexpected ways. Some indigenous practices that were denigrated or prohibited under apartheid have since been rejuvenated. Rituals and initiations have been adapted to serve new social institutions in rural and urban locations. Initiation rites and rituals continue to take place through the life cycle, despite fundamental changes to the societies in which they are practiced.

ABSTINENCE AND SECLUSION

The umemulo is a ritual associated with sexual maturation and as such is characterized by periods of seclusion and intense instruction through music and dance. The spatial dynamics of the umemulo are marked by the physical and symbolic exclusion of the uninitiated female body from the adult homestead. iziNtombi emulayo are confined to a room or other small dwelling in the homestead for a week or more, and during their seclusion must abstain from drinking amasi. This practice of abstinence is recorded in the earliest written accounts, including the entry on the *omula* in Bishop Colenso's *Dictionary* of 1878:

> *Omula*, v. Begin to eat food, which has been hitherto or for some time abstained from; begin to work for the first time = *Emula*
>
> *N.B.* This word is used of a girl eating *amasi* after her first menstruation, when her father kills a beast for her, and she eats *amasi* freely for the first time in her life and henceforward, or of a bride, when she begins again to eat *amasi* after her marriage (at the end of two or three months), or of a woman, when she eats *amasi* for the first time seven days after menstruation.[9]

The umemulo is thus conceived as a cleansing ritual. A woman is "made clean" through sacrifice. The relationship between cattle, ancestral spirits, and women in Zulu culture is regulated by the incest taboo. Since cattle products are associated with the world of men, unmarried or unclean women may not consume these, including amasi, because of the association with kinship. Cattle are slaughtered for sacrifices but are otherwise kept for milking and as oxen for agriculture. W. D. Hammond-Tooke explains how amasi "could only be shared with kin members of the patriclan. To do so was to make a statement that one was related to the host. In a society preoccupied by fears of incest, sharing amasi had vital implications for social bonds, especially sexual relations. To drink sour milk with a woman was to acknowledge her as a relative and thus not a potential sexual partner."[10] A new wife brings a cow from her father's herd to provide for her first years of marriage. The violation of this taboo on the consumption of amasi is likely to bring ruination on the cattle of the kraal. Drinking amasi also signals to the amadlozi that a woman is now recognized as of marriageable status.

Eileen Krige explains how the *ukwomula* is "regarded as her father's tacit permission to her to look about for a husband."[11] Max Kohler affirms that the *ukwe-*

mula signifies that the girl has reached "marriageable age" and is ready to return to "normal life" following a period of abstinence from amasi.[12] The derivation from the root *-mula* points to the sense of beginning anew, the commencement of a new phase of life. Once the cattle sacrifice has been completed, she may consume amasi from the cattle of her own homestead.[13] Kohler reports that misfortunes would befall the family if this taboo were to be broken. The seclusion hut belonged to the girl's mother, writes Kohler, and had "a wicker-screen (*umGónqo*) some three feet high and closed all round, save at the posterior part," which was placed to envelop the girl.[14] She would be expected to stay there for weeks, "withdrawn from public view (*ukuGóya*), till ordered out. Whenever there was need to go outside, she had to do so covered, head and body (*ukuGúbuzela*), by her kaross."[15] The purpose of seclusion emphasized the sense of "coming out" and transitioning to a new life.[16] The girl's "sweetheart" would be invited to participate the day prior the celebration. These observations in the literature were made in the twentieth century. The ethnographic extracts and analysis that follow demonstrate some of the continuities and discontinuities with these practices.

MASHUNKA ISIGODI, JANUARY 5, 2012

The Dladla umuzi sits on a slope opposite Mashunka mountain with a view of the valley below. Overcast skies and blustering squalls, intermittent rain, and thunder punctuate the afternoon. Excitement registers in the rush of sounds and people. The izintombi emulayo and their retinue dance at a ground half a mile from the umuzi. The homestead belongs to Sthenjwa Dladla, and the girls dancing today are daughters of his sons, Phelelani and Ndididi. Mukelisiwe Dladla, Xolile Dladla, and Danadena Dladla are the three girls chosen for today's umemulo.[17] I set off up a steep hill to meet them near the entrance to the homestead. Pickup trucks have parked along the track. Young girls dressed in finery prepare themselves at the foot of the hill. They divide into two groups and march to the dancing ground in the valley, singing all the way.

The geography of Mashunka isigodi is significant because it draws people into relationships as neighbors and friends who over generations have developed bonds based on kinship and proximity, both here and in the cities far away. The isigodi itself is comprised of four main districts: uJolwayo, Gwajiza, ubuHaya, and Nyakwenthaba. Each one has its own *ibutho* (regiment) governed by an *iphini* (second-in-command). These men arrive near the start of the umemulo to form part of the ibutho who fetch the *ubaba wentombi* (senior father of the girls, or grandfather), Sthenjwa Dladla, and accompany him, the umnumzane of the isigodi, down to the dance ground. A tremendous commotion announces their arrival from afar. Fighting sticks, shields, and assorted weapons are trounced in the air as the men sing amahubo on their march down the hill. The umsindo created by their chanting and singing resonates in the low-hanging cloud that has descended on the isigodi. Women and girls await the amabutho. The izintombi emulayo dance and sing, unrushed, and seemingly unmoved by the fierceness of the approaching regiments. Their mothers and elders have congregated and are using special *umuthi* (medicinal herbs for healing) called *intelezi* (plant matter used for protection against witchcraft and misfortune) to calm down the amabutho who are now close at hand and are engaged in fierce marching, dancing, and war cries, driving their way across the ground. This interaction between men and women, contrasting aggression with conciliation, maintains a tension, and a call-and-response of its own. The interpolation of sonic space complicates the social dynamic, with the singing of men and women initially overlapping.

The practice of *umakho* (gift giving) has now begun. A girl will often have chosen a boyfriend prior to the umemulo, and he will be expected to bring gifts with his sisters. In the case of a married woman, it is her husband who bears the primary responsibility for gift giving. This practice follows the umcimelo, which takes place during the week leading up to the sacrifice and involves visits to family members and the community to invite them to the weekend celebration as well as to request gifts. Common gifts include *amacansi* (straw sleeping mats), *izivovo* (strainers for Zulu beer), *imali* (money), *imishanelo* (brooms), and *izingubo* (blankets). By the end of the afternoon, there is a huge pile of items in front of the young women, and rows of banknotes have been affixed to their heads.

The afternoon celebrations are preceded by the slaughter of cattle. One cow is slaughtered for each of the izintombi emulayo. Hide bangles are cut from the slaughtered animal and worn around the girl's wrists. The umhlwehlwe is removed and worn to indicate her status to the amadlozi. The girls are also smeared with *umadilika ibomvu* (red clay). Those who accompany the izintombi emulayo are the *izimpelesi* (bridesmaids). They wear grass headbands made from *incema* (*Juncus maritimus, J. effusis*).[18] The day reaches its conclusion when the induna is satisfied that all ritual elements are complete. As soon as this is indicated to the assembly, the young women run from the dance grounds and back to their place of seclusion. Back at the umuzi there may be some dancing and umcushulo songs sung (see chapter 1). But the main ingoma dancing will take place as a celebration on the second day when the ritual moves to the umuzi itself.

On the second day, dancing and singing commence in the afternoon. This time the ceremony takes place inside the isibaya of the Dladla homestead up on the hill to indicate to the amadlozi that an important change is taking place in the community. Ordinarily, women are not permitted inside the isibaya, but, as with weddings, this is allowed for ritual purposes involving the amadlozi. The practice of umakho continues with great excitement, and the singing and dancing goes on for three hours before Sthenjwa Dladla moves the festivities out of the isibaya. Unlike a wedding, there are no formal proceedings indicating passage or transition. Suitors, family, and friends come forward to offer their gifts, and sometimes to dance or giya in front of the izintombi emulayo and their retinue. Many bring bank notes, which they affix to the girls' incema headbands.

Once all gifts have been given, and the girls have sung and danced to their content, all move to another dance space immediately above the isibaya adjacent to the indlu enkhulu. This is the opportunity for recreational dancing. Everyone congregates at the dance arena where alcohol has been laid out. Meat is handed out to the *izibuki* (visitors from outside the isigodi), who are also given *umqombothi* (traditional beer) to share. There are crates of beer and spirits at the ready. The girls dance first, and with far greater freedom than before. Here at Mashunka the favorite dance is isishameni. The igoso of each district is different to the igoso of the ibutho from each sub-ward. At this umemulo there are several ranks of amagoso. Each ingoma team has its own distinct uniform: those with red and white shirts are "homeboys" from Mashunka;[19] those from uJolwayo wear police yellow, blue, and red with orange armbands. The dancers from iGwajiza have adopted a black shawl and ubuHaya wear blue trousers. Nomoya are izibuki from outside of Mashunka isigodi. The igoso for this group, uGuva, is a very tall man. "Bashisa mbawula" (the brazier/fire pot is hot),[20] he sings, calling dancers by name to come forward for one-one dancing. The return of men to their homes, and their dancing, is the height of the spectacle that is the umemulo even if it has no ritual significance to the transition of the izintombi emulayo. Bringing this community together binds them as a collective despite the permanent displacement that characterizes the lives of many living in a state of migrancy.

PURPOSES OF THE UMEMULO

Fathers are proud to host umemulo ceremonies to celebrate their daughters, and the event is understood as a public reward for a daughter's good behavior and chastity, thus indicating her value as a bride.[21] A young woman of good reputation is expected to accrue substantial bride wealth for her father, and so families are careful to instruct their daughters with care. Unlike many other initiations, the umemulo is not obligatory. It is held at the father's (or mother's) discretion.

Another purpose in hosting the event is to demonstrate the family's social status. The expense incurred is a sure sign of prosperity. At least two goats and one cow must be slaughtered in ritual sacrifices for each of the girls celebrated. There must be abundant food and drink provided for the entire extended family as well as large numbers of guests from the local community who will attend the feasting, dancing, singing, and drinking. An application must be made to the office of the inkosi for permission to host the event. A fee is paid so that an induna or other official is delegated by the inkosi to be present. His purpose is to ensure orderly conduct. The official register of umemulo ceremonies is kept by the secretary to the inkosi. In some communities the umemulo is also an indicator of social status organized to coincide with important life events such as graduations and birthdays. One such example was an umemulo that I attended at Shemula isigodi in the Jozini Local Municipality in northern KwaZulu-Natal at which the two izintombi emulayo danced very little. Instead, a hired team of dancers from a local primary school were responsible for the performances that day. This event was staged and recorded by a videographer, who directed the proceedings. Interestingly, some of the songs sung at this umemulo were also sung at Mashunka, Ncunjane, and Nkaseni. It turned out that many of the young women from these ceremonies would be attending the Mhlangeni, the umKhosi woMhlanga ceremony held at the royal residence of the Zulu King, Zwelithini kaBhekuzulu, at Nyokeni near Nongoma.

ISIKO

The umemulo marks a transition realized in songs of catharsis. A goat is slaughtered on the first day of activities to signal to the amadlozi that the ritual has begun. A period of ritual confinement follows. Relatives walk long distances to announce to family and friends in the district when the ceremony will take place. Gifts for the izintombi emulayo are expected and carried back. Boys from the extended family accompany the young women on these forays. At night, the initiate and her age-mates are secluded in a thatched indlu, or rondavel in her umuzi. At uMsinga, and elsewhere, this is called the *umgonqo* (the place of seclusion), the name used for the rite described by Kohler. Initiates are hidden behind a grass partition where they sing and take instruction from elders.[22] Their bodies are painted with umadilika ibomvu and they wrap themselves from head to toe in izingubo.[23] These will be shed only on the eve of the umemulo feast when the girls change into their izidwaba, beads, and ankle rattles for the dancing and festivities. They will also be draped with the umhlwehlwe. Only the peers of the intombi emulayo (singular) are permitted out during the day.[24] Visitors are not allowed, and family must bring gifts.

There are many restrictions on the intombi emulayo's behavior for she must observe similar taboos to that of a new wife. For instance, it is expected that she should be demure, should not raise her voice or laugh loudly, and should practice inhlonipho. A fire is made, and the ash used for ritual cleansing. The intombi emulayo drinks water with ash from this fire "to make her a good cook for her future husband; to boost her fertility, she eats bitter roots of the *impindisa* shrub and she avoids sour milk like a traditional married woman."[25] These customs are designed to steel a woman to the hardships of adult life and to prepare her for marriage as "an ideal wife in the eyes of her spouse and in-laws."[26] The umemulo songs may be taught to the girls prior to the commencement of the umemulo itself,[27] especially through participation at other umemulo ceremonies and practices. Nocturnal vigils in the umgonqo are used for instruction in the customs of adult life,[28] although these are not formalized. The girls also compose their own songs about love, relationships, anxieties, dreams, and desires. On their last evening together in the appointed room the girls will sing through the night. Dress and adornment are symbolic and prepare the transition to womanhood. Red ocher is commonly used on the face, torso, and legs of the izintombi emulayo, but not on the peers, who only use it only on their faces.[29] Men should avoid interaction with young women adorned with ocher because it signals seclusion and that they have been marked by the amadlozi.[30]

The last two days of the umemulo begin with the sacrifice of a cow. This act is usually carried out by the patriarch, or by one of the senior men in the family, in the presence of the ibandla. AmaHubo are sung and izibongo extolled during the sacrifice and butchery that follows. Soon afterward, dancing will take place outside of the umuzi in a nearby field or clearing. The importance of the amadlozi is reinforced in the sacrifices that take place during the umemulo, in the rituals that take place in the isibaya, and in the uses of ocher and gall to signal these rituals. The bladder is stored together with the rest of the carcass in the umsamo, a sacred space in the back of the indlu enkhulu. This must be protected from those who have bad intent for the gall is the most valuable part of the slaughtered beast. The umhlwehlwe is worn over the shoulders of the intombi emulayo. The father calls to the ancestors before moving to the *isigcawu* (clearing) where the community assembles. This is where the public performances of singing and dancing take place.

When the izintombi emulayo convene inside the isibaya on the final day of the umemulo, the occasion is marked by great excitement in the community. The girls sing and dance together with boys accompanying them. In some izigodi these dances are accompanied to the beat of cowhide drums. For instance, drums were used at Mazizini, Mnweni, and at Nkaseni and Makhane; but not at Mashunka, Ncunjane, or Dakeni. The initiates occasionally break the line to perform a short giya on their own, or to signal their affection for an accepted suitor by planting a spear in the ground before him.[31]

The performance of praises simultaneous to this act of anointing is essential to its efficacy in establishing the link with amadlozi. The amadlozi must be recognized and thanked for their role through praises and speeches by the initiate's father, or another senior family member who has powers to ukuthetha (speak sharply, scold) them. Once these acts of the amadlozi are complete, the ceremony can move out of the isibaya, the consecrated space of the ancestors, and into the homestead itself, the place of women. It is here that the girls will dance freely before the assembled crowd, and it is here that the men will dance ingoma in teams. Dance troupes from the surrounding izigodi use the opportunity to perform and compete before an audience.[32]

MAZIZINI, DECEMBER 12, 2015

Wiseman calls to say that they've already slaughtered one cow and are preparing for the second. I must hurry. Heavy rain and hail have delayed me in the mountains. The clouds have grown dark, hanging over the cliff faces. Off the tar and up the dirt track toward the little school I drive. When I get there it's already 5:15 p.m. The ibandla have congregated at Wiseman's umuzi. A small group is huddled in the isibaya. When I approach, I see a large beast butchered on its own skin; its entrails are unwound, intestines unbound. The flesh is neatly cut and separated into chunks. Tin roofing slats are placed on both sides as rough transport. There are ten men working on it now, including Wiseman, who is removing entrails. The process takes another twenty minutes or so, after which the meat is moved into the umsamo in the back of the indlu enkhulu. The meat is not put into the fridge. That will only happen tomorrow, says Wiseman. The next cow has been waiting not ten meters away and is visibly nervous, eyes darting. When I approach her, she gets up and snorts. The men have tied a noose around her neck and have bound her to a wooden pole in the isibaya. One of Wiseman's relatives approaches with a long blade. He must wield around her before thrusting the dagger into her spinal column, cracking the furrow in her neck. She screams in pain. Another jab, and another. But he's not succeeding. The beast is in agony. The next jab lifts her right foot into a spasm. The ibandla murmur their approval. Several more blows to the neck, and she falls to the ground, all four hoofs splayed out. Helpless and desperate, gradually giving in to her own death. This takes much longer than I expect: four to five minutes. To speed up the process, the knife is thrust into her chest cavity. Blood spews out of a gaping hole. But her legs are still kicking. The men move away again, having tried to subdue her. Her eyes are rolling in their sockets. Blood starts to ooze out of her mouth. More blows to the chest and a larger cavity. There is blood all over her front and nose now, pouring out her mouth. The pain must be extraordinary and unrelentingly horrific. I am horrified, numb. The butcher is at her head. He flicks her eyelids checking on her vital signs. Still there, still there, then, at last, gone. The body lies limp, and the men pile in with axes and knives, cutting off the skin, and laying it underneath the exposed carcass.

Wiseman says that everyone will share the meat, but that the legs are for the men only. The tail is for the family. It is the best meat, very expensive to buy. This has been accomplished with measured calm. It is the natural order of things. As I look on, one of the young men brings to me a strange object that appears to be a deformed hoof. It was found in the beast's intestines. Wiseman shows me that it is in fact a rubberized Disney toy! He says he knows this cow well, and that she would eat anything. His brother Vincent explains that it has been very dry and so the cattle fed on whatever they could find. A sheath of skin is removed from the intestines. This is the umhlwehlwe that will be worn by the intombi emulayo at the umemulo.

Once the remains of the two cows have been deposited in the indlu enkhulu, there is opportunity for dancing. Wiseman's daughters, Sanelisiwe and Nothethelelo, move with their retinue to an open area adjacent the indlu enkhulu above the isibaya. Thereafter, they proceed to a thatched rondavel in which all three are secluded behind a grass screen. This single-room rondavel is used by Wiseman for communing with amadlozi. It is his custom to make a fire on an open hearth, and to use the ashes to communicate with his amadlozi.[33] The izintombi emulayo spend the night in this rondavel where they prepare for the celebrations that will follow tomorrow. Their faces are painted in clay, and they are confined

FIGURE 3.2 *left* Siwakhe Wiseman Mbatha cutting the *umhlwehlwe* (caul) from the sacrificial beast, Mazizini, December 12, 2015.

FIGURE 3.3 *below* uMemulo ceremony at Mazizini, December 13, 2015. Notethelelo Mbatha (left), Siwakhe Wiseman Mbatha (center), and Sanelisiwe Mbatha (right). Both young women are draped in the umhlwehlwe.

behind a woven grass partition. Wiseman and the men of the homestead are not permitted to enter or to be present for the singing that takes place therein.

AMADLOZI

The amadlozi hold considerable influence over the well-being and prospects of the living. The umemulo is bound up with amadlozi at every stage. Clara Mbatha is grandmother to the izintombi emulayo at the Mbatha umemulo at Mazizini. She explains how on the first day of the umemulo the girls are taken to the "ancestors' house" where they are secluded. This dwelling is used by the family expressly for communing with the ancestral spirits. For the rest of the week, the daughters will not appear face to face with either parent. She and the children's mother then prepare umqombothi (traditional beer) for the celebrations over the weekend.

> It takes seven days to prepare umqombothi. Day one we start to cook, and we start to practice, and we improve until the final day. Before the final day we slaughter two goats. We slaughter on Saturday afternoon. Sunday, we eat them and finish them. After finishing them we slaughter two cows. We must finish the goats before we eat the cows. In this house we are not allowed to slaughter on Friday, so we only do it on Thursday or Saturday [because we are Christians]. . . . Only when the beer is ready can we slaughter. We take the beer onto the upper side of the house and tell the ancestors, and say no, the beer is ready now, and the cows are ready now, which means the game is on.[34]

Each intombi emulayo must eat the liver of the goat sacrificed for them, as well as the liver of their anointed cow. The cow is a powerful ancestral animal that is known to the amadlozi having spent its nights enclosed in the isibaya. The use of its gall to garland the intombi emulayo establishes a connection. The pungent scent of the gall draws the attention of the amadlozi. The principle of umsindo is evident here in the combination of singing, dancing, praising, and feasting, contributing to an immersive sensory experience. Sacrifice engages the senses. The umemulo is conceived as an *isiko* (ritual)[35] that serves to bind the community to their ancestral spirits and to one another. Monica Wilson describes this system of belief as a "cult of the shades" in which both the living and the dead take part in communal feasting.[36] The sacrifice at its center is meant to placate or satisfy the hunger of ancestral spirits and is designed to bring good fortune to those involved in the ritual.[37]

The consumption of beer and meat by all those who share in the meal is a feature of the umemulo. Wiseman explains that performing the umemulo will bring luck to his two daughters.

> I communicate with my ancestors, and God also. I say, "Please, God, give them luck, and please my ancestors"; I talk to my grandfather. There are ancestors—each and every one who passed away who belongs to this family, the Mbatha family, or their mom's family, Miya family; it is their ancestors. So, I'm also telling them [to] please come and give them their luck. They've got luck from their ancestors and their God, Shembe God.[38]

The ritual of sacrifice consecrates the body of the beast. The sharing of the consecrated meat reinforces the connection to amadlozi. Parts of the animal are worn to identify those for whom the ritual is performed. This marking in flesh signals transition and ensures both ancestral and public recognition for the new status of the initiates and their immediate family. Sacrifice is the most powerful mode of communicating with amadlozi. The summoning of spirits takes place during the slaughter of the beast, and in the consumption and adornment of its parts. The umhlwehlwe is taken from the sacrifice to link the living with their ancestral spirits.[39] The gall bladder is considered the most powerful token of ancestral recognition. Wearing the umhlwehlwe is important and must not be shared because it carries the girl's luck, and there is no use in sharing luck.[40]

The rituals demonstrate the dependencies that exist between kin, living, and dead, and may be interpreted as acts of reconciliation between parties within the community. This is where performance as reciprocity comes into its own. In these ways, the umemulo is used to teach the new lifeways and expectations of adulthood, to confer status and identity, and to instill communal values through ritualized performance. The umemulo temporarily suspends the taboos governing everyday social discourse and propriety, thus sanctioning modes of intergenerational communication otherwise considered inappropriate or disrespectful. Songs employ codes and secret languages that preserve the sanctity of the institution and mark a transition from one life phase to another.

uMemulo songs sung by the izintombi emulayo may include wedding and other recreational songs. In Shembe communities, the songs may also be borrowed from church. However, there are two categories that are specific to it: the *ukubhina* ("use language that modesty would ordinarily forbid") and *ingcekeza* songs. The lyrics to ukubhina songs are often sexually explicit and vulgar but coded so that the symbolism is understood only to peers. Krige describes the content of these songs in some detail.

> When sung out of context or heard by people for whom they are not intended [*ukubhina* songs] are regarded as obscene. The singing is called *ukubhina* which means to use abhorrent or obscene expressions which startle people. *Ukhubhina* also implies a threat as where, for example, a father utters a curse upon his son; once someone has *bhina*'d (sworn at) you, you will not do the thing he was objecting to. In these *bhina* songs the most vulgar words are always used in preference to more polite words.[41]

The vulgarity of the songs is often masked to the uninitiated.[42] The purposes of this vulgarity are contested, and some women deny any particular purpose. Rosemary Joseph claims that the ukubhina songs "serve as a form of sex education" and "serve to deter the girl from indulging in pre-marital sex."[43] This observation is consistent with contemporary umemulo practices in parts of KwaZulu-Natal. Among the Thembu and Mchunu tribes, the umemulo is associated with virginity testing. Well-being is established through the regulation of behaviors to adhere to societal norms and moral values, specifically in relation to the practice of safe sex. Singing is used in the context of the umemulo to educate and make young women (and men) aware of the dangers of unprotected sex, including awareness around the epidemic of HIV and AIDS in South Africa.[44] This ties the practice of umemulo in the isigodi to the politics of isizwe, and efforts by the royal house to forge a pan-Zulu identity in KwaZulu-Natal.

UMKHOSI WOMHLANGA

The women who participate in umemulo and virginity testing in izigodi are transported to the annual umKhosi woMhlanga (reed dance ceremony), which is hosted by the Zulu king in September each year. This ceremony was established by King Mpande in the nineteenth century but was not maintained following the fall of the Zulu monarchy. It was reintroduced by King Goodwill Zwelithini kaBhekuzulu in 1984 following his marriage into the Swazi royal family. King Mswati III was at that time practicing a similar *uMhlanga* at the Queen Mother's royal residence in Swaziland. The Zulu event takes place at the Enyokeni Royal Palace at Nongoma where tens of thousands of girls participate. A requirement for participants is that they be unmarried and childless. Virginity tests are undertaken by *abahloli* (elder women responsible for inspections).[45] This practice is also associated with the three-day ritual of appeasement known as *ukuhlolwa kwezintombi* (virginity testing), which is dedicated to the Zulu goddess Nomkhubulwana.[46]

At the uMkhosi woMhlanga I attended at the Enyokeni Royal Palace in KwaZulu-Natal in September 2013, there were an estimated forty thousand girls participating. Girls were organized in regiments by isigodi and would sing and dance together throughout the day accompanied by matrons. The procession began in the open fields at the lower reaches of the hill below the palace where the girls and young women collected their reeds. The procession then filed up to the isibaya where King Zwelithini and his entourage watched as they sang and danced for him and deposited their reeds inside the palace grounds. Many of the songs were umemulo songs that described similar virtues to those celebrated at the Mhlanga ceremony. In recent years, governmental and nongovernmental organizations have played an important role at this ceremony in efforts to educate girls and young women on the risks of unprotected sex, including HIV/AIDS and other communicable diseases.[47]

The ingcekeza songs are a category of umemulo songs sung at public events, like the umKhosi woMhlanga, and feature on the last two days of the umemulo. The following songs were sung by girls from Mashunka and Ncunjane.[48] The first of these describes relationship troubles. ◀))

Ngilinde ngalinda angimboni akabuyanga ngikhathele ukulahla umlenze. Uhambe nguJanuary. Nango December akabuyanga.	I have waited and waited, and I don't see him coming back. I am tired of throwing my legs [like a useless person]. He left in January. Now it's December and he's still not back.

This song describes the plight of a girl whose boyfriend or fiancé works in the city as a migrant worker. Men who leave for the cities may not return regularly, and

FIGURE 3.4 umKhosi woMhlanga ceremony, Enyokeni Royal Palace,
Nongoma, September 14, 2013.

so women are often left waiting in hope and despair. This is a common refrain in rural areas split by labor migrancy where young men seek work in the cities.

Songs of intergenerational communication are used to address topics otherwise forbidden. These include songs sung to fathers, and songs about the amadlozi. ◀⟩

Webaba omncane, ziphi izinkomo isibhemile? We baba omncane, mus'ukulokhu uyobayoba kade ungihlupha.	Small father, where are the cows everyone is expecting [you to bring]? Small father, don't hesitate, you've been annoying me.

This song is about the relationship of a girl to her "small father" (or uncle). *Baba omncane* (small father) refers to a girl's father's younger brother. In Zulu society your father's brothers are all considered fathers to you, and if your father passes away then these other fathers are called upon to take care of you. Furthermore, a younger brother is expected to look after a man's wife and children if the man passes on. In this case the younger brother is being called upon—in the absence of the girl's father—to produce cattle for the umemulo. Most young women desire an umemulo, but not all will be afforded one. The girls attending the novices may not have an umemulo of their own, and so they may use the opportunity to voice their dissatisfaction with their father for failing them. Such direct commentary is only possible in a sanctioned space and would not be tolerated otherwise.

Songs extolling the virtues of fathers are common because they emphasize the mutual respect between parent and child that is at the heart of the ritual. At every umemulo there must be at least one song praising the girl's father and his vital role in her upbringing.[49] Usually, these songs are led by an initiate rather than one of her attendants. Two such song texts follow here. ◀꙳

Ngibongeleni kubaba wami
    nangu esenzela into enhle
    esigodini.
Abanomona balayekile
    yeshe. Bebethi ubaba
    akanankomo wozani
    nizobona
    shindindiyeshe.
Wemama uzeungisize
    ungibongele ubaba ngento
    akanzele yona.
	I give thanks to my father for he
	    is doing good things for us in
	    this district.
	Those who have jealousy have
	    disappointed. They say my father
	    doesn't have cows, you come and
	    see [expressing happiness that
	    something has finally happened].
	My mother, please can you give
	    thanks to my father for the
	    things he has done for me.

Some of these songs are difficult to translate meaningfully. When I interviewed Ndididi Dladla about the initiation songs sung by his daughter at her umemulo,[50] he found it difficult to translate some of the meanings because the words are obscure or coded with ideophones.[51] His daughter, Landiwe Dladla, gave literal translations of the songs but did not explain the meaning of some lyrics.[52] Her reticence to divulge details of the songs may be attributed to the practice of inhlonipho.[53] The importance of preparations for marriage are also stressed in the need to understand the imithetho (laws; singular: umthetho) associated with the particular umuzi into which the young woman will be inducted, as demonstrated by the following two song lyrics. ◀꙳

| Ngisayozama we awungimele
    kancane ngisawozama icansi. | Wait for me a little, I'm trying to
    get a mat. [If a bride is going
    to be married, one must give
    a gift for the whole family; the
    mat is a gift to the family.] |
| Abawazi umthetho walomuzi. | They don't know the law of
    this homestead. [Neighbors
    witness what is happening,
    but they don't understand
    the laws.] |

These songs serve as commentaries on life in the homestead, and in a community governed by laws and customs that prescribe behaviors considered respectful and appropriate. The recognition of good conduct is of course best understood by the amadlozi. ◀))

| Mhlawumbe khuluma ingqikithi
    sisho ingqikithi isemtsamo
    ngangekho mina. | Maybe, on the day they were
    talking about the secret of the
    ancestors I was absent.[54] |

This last song is a reminder that the ancestral spirits are ever present in Zulu societies. It shows, once again, how a central purpose of umemulo songs is to facilitate intergenerational communication between fathers and daughters, mothers, grandmothers, and their ancestral spirits.

CONCLUSION

Performances facilitate and mediate the transfer of knowledge from one generation to the next. uMemulo songs composed during periods of ritual intensity bond novices and structure their social interactions into peer groups, or regiments, based on age and gender. Girls and boys in these peer groups develop close-knit, lifelong relationships grounded in mutual respect and trust. The initiated learn to call one another by special names and develop secret codes and languages that are remembered into old age. uMemulo songs are a technology used for intergenerational bonding. The restrictions on behavior conditioned by inhlonipho are relaxed in the sanctioned sonic spaces of the umemulo. This enables young women to be heard without interruption, or fear of reprisal. The annual umKhosi woMhlanga ceremony encourages umemulo performances to serve the interests of the Zulu royal house and is aligned with efforts to teach young women about sexual health and well-being.

Finally, songs of sacrifice have spiritual significance to communities of believers. The songs and praises that accompany the ritual use of the umhlwehlwe and gall to mark izintombi emulayo for their amadlozi are crucial to the transition that takes place in the lives of these women. The sonic spaces of the umemulo delineate roles along lines of gender, generation, and kinship that are consistent with the practices of the umsindo discussed in chapter 2. The next chapter explores this phenomenology of space in the analysis of ingoma dance among migrants who travel between their izigodi in KwaZulu-Natal and the metropolis of Johannesburg where they search for work.

FOUR

Phenomenology of iNgoma
isiShameni Dance and the Politics of Proximity

"La shon' ilanga!" (The sun is setting!) A crowd encircles the dancers, urging them on, baying for one more high kick to the day's denouement. The scene is chaotic. Blasts of ululation overlap the polyphonic thud of dangling feet. Cries of wild delight peter into the sunset. Dust billows into the lukewarm air, reverberating to its tender song. Children cling magnetically to elders, their eyes widened by the daze of spectacle. The dancers are in their element, their voices pitched with energies drawn deep from a year's tribulation. This is the moment to soar above what befell them. The swift approach of night rends at their sinews. A desperate and passionate agony is etched on their faces. These moments are last opportunities. The warmth of eager bodies unfolding in the amber glow casts flickering shadows in the half-light. A community encircled. All eyes upon them, all eyes beyond them. A lithe teenager writhes her way through, clutching at the sweat of the young men, embracing them, entreating them for favor. She dares not linger. The stage is not hers. The dancers have fixed their horizons and, enveloped in a steady chant, gesture toward the heavens as if propelled by the setting sun. The circle has permeated into the communal dance ground, and yet still the igoso commands us with a voice unwavering. Brandishing an induku, a young rogue cuts through the ranks, furiously declaiming his praises while scuffing the tufts of brittle grass under foot. His impassioned verse strikes a tenor at the very top of his voice. It's a fast move—too fast. The troupe is already in motion. "Phusha isitimela!" (Push the train!) A chorus of men chants the beat. Their slow, continuous clapping has modulated the tempo, calling all to measure. The beat becomes heavier with each swaggering kick, each lunge and fall, as if the very beings of these dancers have bonded together. The singing is inaudible above the shouts and gesticulations from the crowd. "'La shon' ilanga! 'La shon' ilanga!" (You must do it now!) Another soloist to the front of the line, shimmying forward, clutching his trousers at the waist, holding tight in preparation, then down, up, and whack! Fearless feet pummel the raw earth to their beat. At last, the men arise, ready, disciplined, and precise.

———

Dance is an art of proximity. Dance embodies ways of being-in-the-world and modes of action that articulate the experience of proximities simultaneously personal, interpersonal, and communal. This chapter explores the politics of proximity in the performances of Thembu migrants from uMsinga in KwaZulu-Natal who live at the Wolhuter men's hostel in Jeppestown, Johannesburg. 🔊 The hostel's location has fashioned its name, Jeppe, a place to which tens of thousands of men have trekked for nearly a century. Generations have used ingoma dance to negotiate conflicts over space. But in the postapartheid era, the efficacy of ingoma in defusing the violence associated with these conflicts has waned. The changed spatial dynamics of the city are no longer marked by intra-ethnic violence. Now it is the conflicts between citizens and noncitizens that are violent. The media labels attacks on African nationals as xenophobia, while the state insists that there is no hate; it is mere criminality. This violence has been perpetrated at least in part by hostel dwellers at Jeppe. What conditions give rise to it? How do hostel dwellers experience the politics of space in Jeppestown? This ethnography investigates the spatial dynamics of the hostel and city through the prism of performance, focusing on the role of isishameni, a genre of ingoma. Dance teams are cohesive social units that give cogent expression to the politics of the hostel as a frontier in the city. Negotiating hostel life in Johannesburg is about defining spaces and establishing normative relations within and across them. Dancers figure these spaces with familiar symbols, and in so doing establish strong bonds of community and allegiance. How does isishameni articulate a politics of proximity in the African city? What does isishameni tell us about the phenomenology of space and the projection of consciousness through movement?

Space may be imagined in several dimensions. For Maurice Merleau-Ponty, space is not an ordered setting but an agential mode; it is "the means whereby the position of things become possible. This means that instead of imagining it as a sort of ether in which all things float or conceiving it abstractly as a characteristic that they have in common, we must think of it as the universal power enabling them to be connected."[1] The situation of a person in space enables, constrains, and affords action. Paul Stoller writes that "in the phenomenological approach to spatial patterns, observers and/or social actors are no longer *in* space but constitute it through the dynamic actions of their consciousness."[2] Space is "a constituted conceptual force" used politically.[3] The territorialization of space by migrants in the inner city shows how competition over impoverished spaces may lead to violence and to expressions of hatred. The management of these spaces is an enduring challenge when the norms governing communities are degraded, or rendered obsolete, and where radically new ways must be found to contend with difference. isiShameni dance offers a window into the dynamics of a society shaped by these competing forces. This chapter studies the agency of dancers in constituting space as an extension of their social and political imaginaries inside and outside the hostel.

JEPPE, 2013

A white Toyota bakkie stops on Main Street. In the car, I am bundled in between the Dladla brothers; four of us are cramped into the front seat as we drive through the dilapidated gray warehousing and shuttered shops of Jeppestown to park opposite the iconic green gate of the hostel on Wolhuter Street (figure 4.1). The lettering is a relic: "Wolhuter Men's Hostel _____ Mans Koshuis Wolhuter." The lettering "Native" has been effaced, but the imprint remains. The Afrikaans word has been gouged entirely. Hostel security guards want to know what this *umlungu* (White man) is doing here. The Dladla brothers, whom I know from uMsinga, provide a brief explanation before leading me through the steel turnstiles. They are members of the Thembu tribe, and I have been invited to film their annual dances. Inside the hostel I sense the excitement of the day brewing in the long shadows. Hundreds of men are milling about in the high-walled courtyard between the brown-bricked blocks that enclose Jeppe's residences. Green Telkom telephone booths hang silent in the morning sun. Washing lines suspend over rank open drains coursing with black sludge. Tuck-shops, cell phone shacks, *shisa nyamas* (barbecue eateries), and laundries fill the inner sanctum. The air hums to the heavy beat of umaskandi music. To my astonishment there are

FIGURE 4.1 Entrance to Jeppe Hostel on Wolhuter Street
in Jeppestown, Johannesburg, June 4, 2017.

children wandering about; they stare up at me. "We are happy here," shouts a drunk. "There are no women!"[4]

Block 2 is our destination, a brown-bricked dormitory building on our right. We climb into the stairwell. The immediacy of the darkness disorients me. My head is spinning. There is no functional lighting. Ndididi's brother Sakhile guides my feet by shining the tiny luminous screen on his Nokia cell phone. I follow, bent double, trusting in each next step. The Dladlas' room is to the right of the landing on the second floor. A doorway to the right leads to a small room. The dimensions are roughly four by six meters. We sit sharing three beds and a bench. Two men are asleep, oblivious, on thin strips of foam set atop the one-meter-wide concrete slabs; they are working the night shift. I am handed a desk chair with a semiattached back rest. Most of the chairs have been decapitated and assembled amid a selection of tube televisions. The antique round glass globes suggest an anachronism to this insular chamber. Newspaper cuttings featuring soccer results line the walls. Ndididi studies these intently. He'd have won R6,850 had Poland not drawn with England in the World Cup qualifier last night.

"Who is your team?" Ndididi asks me cheerfully in his black and gold Amakhosi shirt.

"Sundowns," I say.

"Oh, yes, Patrice's team."

Patrice Motsepe is the billionaire businessman who owns the richest club in South Africa.

"But I also support Wits," I blurt out. "I studied there."

"Oh, the Clever Boys."

A pause.

"Ah, so you're Pule!" laughs Ndididi, referring to the former Chiefs legend Jabu Pule, whose surname is pronounced similarly to mine. I ask about Mashunka and the men's families back home. "How often do you get to see them?" Ndididi responds, "It's not like it used to be. Now, men go back not just twice a year but sometimes monthly. It is R170 to uMsinga direct from Jeppe, one way. But we must bring stuff, Danono, meat, nappies, otherwise there will be trouble from our wives!" So, the cost is more like R700 to R1,000, which is a lot of money when all you can get is "piece jobs"—that is, short-term employment, sometimes only for a day.

A single glass globe hangs in the Dladlas' room. There are live electrical wires protruding out in bunches, connections sprouting into the passage. We walk past the kitchen-dining room toward a distant emergency exit. I catch a glimpse of the smoke-black stovetops, men preparing luncheons in the half-light. Beside them a putrid mass of garbage is climbing to the ceiling. The corridor is seeping effluent. The door to the showers has been padlocked. There is no hot water. "It used to cost R27 a month to stay here, but now nobody pays, or maybe four out of a hundred," says Ndididi. "Things have changed a lot. There's no maintenance anymore. It is the ANC's fault.[5] They're always making promises." The posters pinned to Jeppe's walls feature only the face of Prince Mangosuthu Buthelezi, the leader of the Inkatha Freedom Party. Ndididi had plans to run as a councillor for the IFP in his ward at Mashunka. We inspected election results outside the courthouse at Mathintha back in 2012. The stakes are high; the difference between winning and losing an election equates to employment versus unemployment. It is time to go. We're heading for an exit like the end of a mine shaft.

———

The white-blue sky of a summer's day sings a gentle breeze. It is time for dancing. Hundreds of spectators are arriving on the lawns of Jeppe Park on Jules Street. Clumps of men deliberate their *stokvels* (savings societies). But some of the young dancers are already rearing to go. A large semicircle is forming in straggles. The tribal elders sit on stools directly opposite the dancers. They are fronted with bottles and boxes of alcohol, untouched. Soon a strong chorus is clapping and singing. It is a steady clap, clap, clap-clap, clap. No drums, no instruments, just voices and hands. The men dance singly and in pairs, presenting themselves in mock aggression, hands raised above their heads, feet falling to the beat and in syncopation against it. isiShameni dancers gather power in their thighs with legs lifted high in anticipation and release. The individual one-one dances are short and demonstrate speed and agility. *izimBadada* (special-purpose rubber-soled dancing shoes) are worn to cushion the blows and protect feet from the colossal impact of ingoma stamping. The thud of dancing feet mimics the heavy crushing of grains at a rural homestead. The afternoon begins with the younger, less experienced men who have yet to master the advanced, complex dance routines. One or two steps, stamp, and then the characteristic leap backward into the chorus of singers behind them. The more experienced dancers shimmy, adding nuanced and sometimes humorous gestures. A favorite is to adopt a series of poses, out of time to the beat, and in so doing to extract the mirth and approval of the crowd.

In troupes the dancing is different. Coordination is precise, exact, fine-tuned, and military. But the carefully practiced routines also build inevitably to the series of high leg lifts, and the almighty stamp and leap backward into a feigned death. The large, open grassed lawns in front of the dancers are hardly utilized. Instead, the dancers keep in proximity, often bumping against and leaping over one another. The isishameni pose is static and vertical. Timing is essential. Those who flounder are rooted out by the igoso who leads the troupe with his singing and gesticulations. He commands the dancers, instilling discipline, respect, and the law.

Msukelwa Mvelase's posture is balanced, confident, and composed. He dances with men from the Nomoya district. Their distinct uniform consists of white vests marked with red-crossed bands, dark trousers rolled up and tied with tasseled skins at the knee, orange armbands, and white izimbadada. I first filmed Sukelwa and his troupe dancing at Mashunka, uMsinga, in the midlands. Here on the lawns of Jeppestown the audience is different. Men from neighboring districts sing and clap along to the songs known to all, standing as an *impi* (army)

FIGURE 4.2 The uNomoya isigodi dance troupe congregated behind Msukelwa Mvelase (left) dancing at the Dladla homestead in Mashunka, January 6, 2012.

FIGURE 4.3 The Nomoya isigodi dance troupe with Msukelwa Mvelase (fifth from left) dancing in Jeppe Park, December 1, 2013.

flanking the *amasoja* (soldiers). They share the bonds of tribe and custom, of histories intertwined, rivalries made and unmade; and increasingly these men recognize kinship and friendship across divides. They dance together, and they identify with a common set of gestures and norms. Dances are measured to a common consciousness, and so, too, the merits of a troupe's choreography. When Msukelwa rises from his last dance, he does so as an *isoja*, as one who carries the determination of his fellows, as one who embodies the identity of a shared heritage by constituting space in their image.

THE POLITICS OF VIOLENCE

Jeppe is a world in flux. Home to more than ten thousand migrant men living out of thirty-two hundred rooms, Jeppe is one of the largest and most over-crowded migrant hostels in South Africa. Men sleep in shifts and share quarters on floors. In recent years the hostel has attracted media attention for criminal activities associated with its residents. Most outsiders despair at its violence. But hostel dwellers know differently. They express frustration, anger, and resentment at the politics of neglect that characterizes the administration of the hostels. Their narratives turn to violent crime and joblessness, to speculation on the slow grinding macroeconomics that is beyond their control and indifferent to their needs. At the heart of Jeppe's struggle is the decades-long decay of social norms and values that accompanies chronic unemployment. The normative experience of migrancy in twentieth-century South Africa rested on systems of support premised on employment among kin, as well as systems of order and discipline imposed through imithetho, inhlonipho, and the generational social stratifications governing home and family life.[6] These foundations have been eroded to such a degree that men find it difficult to orient themselves toward recognized norms. The bonds between generations have been loosed, the idea of the family dismantled. Factors external to the hostel have gradually degraded the integrity of life within its walls. The hostel space was designed to enclose, but this enclosure pushes back against its alienation, alienating those who would threaten its sovereignty.

The state of the hostels and the patterns of habitation that characterize them are the product of a complex history characterized by enforced alienation.[7] Successive colonial and apartheid governments imposed on Black South Africans a life of migrancy from rural homesteads to rapidly industrializing towns and cities.[8] This was accomplished through a series of dispossessions and enslavements that began in the seventeenth century. But the more immediate roots of the current situation of landlessness and segregation is to be found in the legislative agenda of the Union government established between the British and the Boers in 1910. As discussed in chapter 1, land was stolen en masse from indigenous South Africans with the passing of the Native Land Act of 1913. Black families were forced off the arable land to make way for White farmers, for mining, and for the general exploitation of natural resources.[9] This was but the culmination of centuries of colonial subjugation, and it only reinforced the racist agenda that White South Africa had guaranteed by excluding non-Whites from full participation in government. The acquisition of South Africa's natural resources and the indenture of Black labor had drastic consequences for the livelihoods and social dynamics of rural communities. Taxation of land, livestock, huts, and homes forced men, and later women, to work on the mines and in urban settings to earn wages. And so began patterns of migrancy that persist still today in the dynamics of joblessness, hopelessness, landlessness, and poverty experienced by a large cross section of South Africa's population. While millions of South Africans consider themselves urbanites, there are still millions more whose lives integrate the distant yet intimately connected spaces of metropolis and rural village. These migrants have imagined new forms of music, dance, and art that intersect and make sense of these realities, as has been widely documented for isicathamiya,[10] umaskandi,[11] ingoma,[12] aurality,[13] as well as many other genres and expressive forms.[14]

MABONENG

The economic outlook of Johannesburg's inner city has changed radically since the mid-twentieth century. Hostel dwellers at Jeppestown originally worked in the vibrant cultural and business districts downtown and in nearby Hillbrow. By the 1980s, however, some of the most popular neighborhoods had deteriorated and become dangerous. In the first decade or so of the twenty-first century, efforts were made to revitalize some of these places, as the following extract from a *Vogue* article explains.

> Around the time of the legislative end of apartheid in 1991, Johannesburg was falling apart from crime and urban blight, and the South African city became known as one of the most dangerous places on earth. But in recent years, with the stabilization and steady growth of Johannesburg's economy, crime has

tapered off and previously abandoned neighborhoods have once again begun to thrive. The perfect example of this is Maboneng, located on the eastern edge of Joburg's central business district. A handful of easily walkable blocks up, down, and around the main drag of Fox Street, Maboneng is South Africa's answer to Williamsburg, Brooklyn.[15]

Jonathan Liebmann and his company Propertuity established Maboneng as a hip location for artists and young professionals who frequent the arts district, mostly on weekends. Up-market studios and residential apartments are connected to food markets and designer shopping, restaurants, bars, and hotels. Since 2009 the Maboneng precinct has gentrified the inner city in a program of "renewal." The City of Johannesburg's tourism website credits the precinct with improving the inner city by transforming what were once "no-go zones as a result of urban decay and crime."[16] This sales pitch attracts both tourists and the middle class. "With a mix of restaurants, coffee shops, clothing boutiques, art galleries, and retail and studio space, the precinct draws the inner-city public as well as the chic, art-going crowd of the city's suburbs, bringing life back to this downtown Johannesburg neighborhood."[17] Efforts to "reclaim" the city by suburbanites, hipsters, and artists remain controversial. At the time, the city and many members of the middle class lauded the change. According to Shannon Walsh, "in Maboneng, the desire for centrality, to be *in* the city, has led to huge swathes of urban territory turned into privately controlled, individually conceptualized, and corporately branded urban enclaves. The vision of one young man, and the wealth of his international financier, have superimposed a new neighborhood, privately held and managed, over the history and geography of the city."[18] Walsh argues that "the precinct appeals to a kind of globally conscious urban hipster, out of touch with the suburbs, who feels the city is theirs to take."[19] In this analysis, Jeppestown's urban poor have little to offer in terms of investment and the development ideals of the city. Some consider their presence a risk rather than an opportunity. By contrast, wealthy consumers and investors bring with them the promise of a revitalized precinct with improved amenities.[20] But who are the users targeted here, and what benefit will these amenities and developments provide for residents such as those living at Jeppe?

The spatial dynamics of Jeppestown seem only to be compounded by this gentrification. Delia Ah Goo notes that "despite various attempts to counter the negative processes associated with gentrification in the Maboneng Precinct, it appears as though the people from the surrounding Jeppestown community

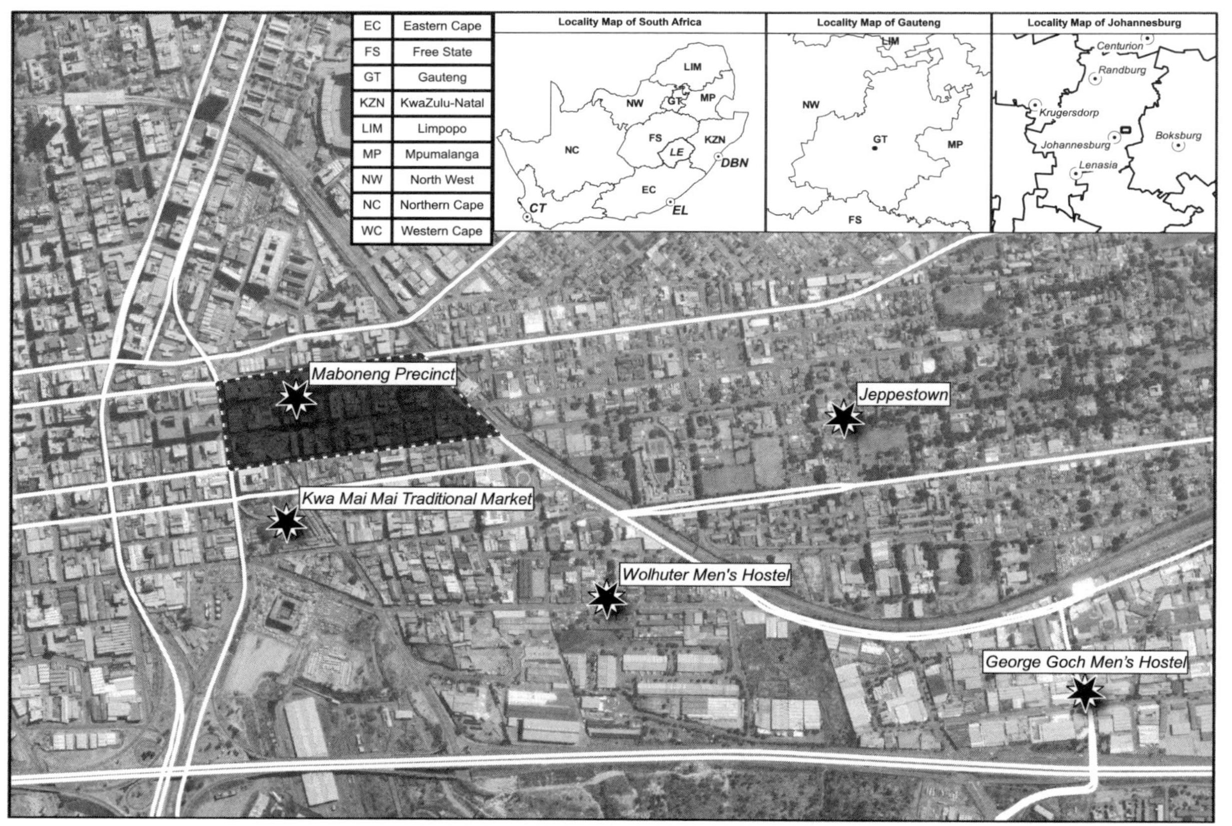

FIGURE 4.4 Map and imagery of Jeppestown, Johannesburg. Created by S3 Technologies.

are physically, socially, and economically excluded from the area."[21] The distinctions between communities are made visible and inaccessible through this commitment to the investment of outsiders rather than to an inclusive policy of development. The reality of the poor residents of Jeppestown is that they will gradually be forced out of homes they cannot afford. Melissa Mnyambo argues that this would lead to further alienation.

> Mr. Liebmann is correct that the area needs renovation, something that can be gained from hipsterfication, but when middle-class people move into all these "empty" buildings, less privileged Jeppestown residents who can no longer afford their rent as property values rise become victims of economic eviction but they also risk experiencing cultural alienation. They have not crossed a border but a border has crossed them as they are suddenly living in New York, in Johannesburg.[22]

The inequality registered in this juxtaposition of Jeppe and Maboneng points to the larger rifts and cracks in postapartheid society. Livelihoods fashioned in the vicinity of Jeppestown have changed since the mid-1970s, when the current induna, Manyathela Mvelase, arrived. In an interview, he recalled how at that time most men were employed on a permanent or semipermanent basis. But permanency is no more. The phrase that captures the postapartheid malaise is, in Mvelase's words, "piece jobs"; the best one can do is short-term, uncontracted, informal work. The stark reality of Jeppestown's fractured spaces shattered the illusion of a safe, gentrified space when violence broke out in August 2019, and videos emerged of looters ransacking shops and businesses and attacking foreign nationals who reside in downtown Johannesburg.

VIOLENCE IN JEPPESTOWN

A culture of violence persists in Jeppestown. The factors informing this violence are deeply rooted in the history of the community. During apartheid, the migration of rural disputes to the urban hostels fomented intra-ethnic tensions that were sustained by apartheid security forces who provided weapons and ammunition to warring factions.[23] Tensions were exacerbated by the removal of Black South Africans from their ancestral lands and their resettlement in confined spaces. Conflicts over land and resources resulted in bloody battles between neighboring communities. Stock theft and assassinations were commonplace in rural izigodi, and this violence spread to the homeboy networks of migrant workers in and around Johannesburg, Durban, and other industrial areas. A cycle of reprisals destabilized areas that had formerly been ordered by respected modes of governance and justice. The plight of these displaced communities was desperate: they were fighting for jobs, fighting for a place to live, fighting for ancestral land.

Political violence was stirred in the 1980s and became more intense through the transition period between 1990 and the first democratic elections in 1994 when it reached devastating levels in clashes between the African National Congress (ANC), the Inkatha Freedom Party (IFP), and the Azanian People's Organization (AZAPO). GG Alcock worked in the Johannesburg hostels and in the rural country districts at this time. "KZN was a complete warzone," says Alcock. "The violence was in essence tribal . . . The scale of it was unbelievable. When I arrived in Joburg [in the late 1980s], it was when they had this hectic fighting in KZN and it spread to the hostels."[24] The hostels became fortresses that were barricaded to the outside world, inhabitable only by family members and friends. Men did not interact with local communities for fear of death, and so the hostels became increasingly isolated even from their immediate surrounds. Jill Kelly has described the scale of violence in KwaZulu-Natal, and its extensions elsewhere, as "civil war."[25] She argues that this war was facilitated by the apartheid government arming the IFP against the ANC and using its "total strategy" to effect "an international proxy war" that lasted until as late as 1996.[26]

With the advent of democracy, tensions gradually subsided. In the late 1990s and early 2000s, the IFP lost considerable ground to the ANC. The rise to power of President Jacob Zuma (promotional T-shirts worn by Zuma's political supporters read "100% Zulu Boy") shifted the dynamics in the predominantly isiZulu-speaking country districts and in the hostels.[27] The violence did not disappear, but it was less deadly. At the same time, other new forces began to emerge in the postapartheid political economy that undermined the social structures governing hostel life. In the early 2000s, riots and looting in the Gauteng townships and hostels were labeled xenophobia by the media.[28] An influx of refugees and immigrants from Zimbabwe, Nigeria, Malawi, Mozambique, Sudan, Ethiopia, Congo, and elsewhere engulfed Jeppestown. Foreigners set up shop in dilapidated and abandoned buildings and created viable businesses. Hostel dwellers perceived these immigrants as competitors for jobs, and some resorted to looting and intimidation to force them out. There were also reports of assault and murder.[29]

Since this period, the state has done little to address the crisis in the hostels.

As illustrated in the opening of this chapter, when I visited in 2013 nearly all the sources of communal lighting were disconnected; there was no hot water, and raw sewage seeped in open drains. It was alleged that the suspension of services was part of an attempt by the City of Johannesburg to close the hostels by making them inhospitable. But would this solve the problems of crime and violence in Jeppestown? One of the residents, Mr. Mngomezulu, complained that the media "portrays us as angry mobsters that are about violence."[30] This reputation has been recognized by journalists. Nomsa Maseko wrote that "the hostels have always been dangerous places to visit, even for the police. As a crime reporter in the late 2000s, on at least four occasions I was present when officers who entered hostels were killed. Following the xenophobic attacks—in which seven people died—the police and army jointly raided some of these hostels. The Jeppestown Wolhuter men's hostel in Johannesburg was the first to be searched for weapons in April."[31] For some current and former hostel dwellers from uMsinga, crime ranks third on the list of potential "employment" options at Jeppe. Renowned dancer Sakephi Mbatha left for this very reason, saying that with so few opportunities for work he did not want to be tempted into a life of crime.[32]

Induna Manyathela Mvelase is the headman for Jeppe Hostel, and he is responsible for the welfare of its residents. Interviewed in 2017 about the violence and xenophobia in hostels, he said, "Police are discriminating against hostel dwellers; they keep saying criminals live here, but the truth is criminals live all over the country. We didn't start the violence." On the charge that hostel dwellers looted foreign-owned shops, Mvelase replied, "It's only because they're hungry. Many are unemployed."[33] The perception is that "foreigners," or outsiders, are being favored for jobs. They undercut South Africans by working for a lower wage and out of desperation are prepared to accept unfavorable conditions. "They must just go back to their countries, because they're taking our jobs," says another hostel dweller, Sibangani Langa.[34] Jeppe residents have demonstrated against the owners of car repair shops, grocers, and the like, accusing these "foreigners" of committing crimes, including human trafficking, drug dealing, and prostitution. Journalist Greg Nicolson reports on how "protestors point to issues such as struggles with employment and housing, but ostensibly their claim is that police have failed their neighborhoods and they need, as a community, to take up the fight against drugs and prostitution. Nigerians have been a key target and several homes have been torched and foreigners, from various African backgrounds, forced to flee."[35] The crisis around xenophobia is an escalating battle that threatens the safety and livelihoods of many residents in South Africa.

The mayor of Johannesburg at the time, Herman Mashaba of the Democratic Alliance, claimed that "undocumented migrants" were responsible for the crime epidemic in Johannesburg.[36] According to official statistics, there were eighty-eight murders committed in Jeppestown in 2016. In May 2017 Sizakele Nkosi-Malobane, the MEC for safety and security in the Gauteng province, described the policing challenges in Jeppestown as "horrific."[37] "The Gauteng Department of Community Safety has attributed the high levels of crime in Joburg's eastern suburbs to a lack of personnel and patrolling vehicles. Jeppe is the worst affected police station as it is short of 7 vehicles and 44 personnel, while also experiencing high levels of contact crime, including murder, assault and robbery."[38] To make sense of all this, I spoke with Induna Manyathela Mvelase (MM) and other hostel dwellers to get their side of the story. Fezela Zwane (FZ) used to live at Jeppe, and on a 2017 visit he accompanied me as translator.[39] The following is a transcript of our conversation.

MM: Eish, even when I open my Bible, I don't know where to open it to. We had jobs when there were White people leading the country. They closed the borders with other countries. The South Africans, even those who are not educated, they would be working if there were not so many people coming from outside the country. They are competing with the South Africans; they are taking everything from South Africans. Not Zimbabwe, all over.

TP: And they work for less?

MM: Yes, they take everything. And then the South Africans get nothing.

TP: So, the government needs to be stricter with the borders?

FZ: It did not used to be so easy for outsiders to get in. This means the law was stricter. You came for a reason. Same applies to us. If you go somewhere, you must go for a reason.

MM: Firstly, can I ask you a question? [directed at TP] Are you here in South Africa as a South African?

TP: Yes.

MM: Were you aware that in those days [i.e., during apartheid] women's body parts were cut up and sold? [pause] No, but now they are.

FZ: You hear it on every radio station.

MM: Secondly, since you are a South African. The body parts of cars that are at panel beaters. Are you aware of this?

FZ: What he means is that if you walk out and see these factories, you will see that most of them are full of car parts. Where are those cars coming from? People are stealing them. Foreigners. But during those times [during apartheid] there were not these problems. Even for body parts.

TP: Are there foreigners living here in Jeppestown?

MM: [Laughing.] All over. We don't even know where the accidents for these cars happen. It goes back to the borders.

TP: And the police are not doing anything?

MM: [Laughing. Coughing.] Yes, there are police, but they are confused about what to do.

TP: They told me that here in Jeppe there are more murders here than in Hillbrow. How is the crime here?

MM: It is confused because, here, the crime of hijacking is high, but you never know where it came from. Foreigners are involved, as well as South Africans.

TP: What about drugs? Is that a problem?

MM: The drugs issue, that you can't promote and say that it is a problem here. You can see there is drugs, but you can't point exactly where it is. Myself, I am a father. If I see children standing on the street selling prostitutes—it hurts me deeply. If you see a child, you want to see it do good things, not bad things. All this points to government, it is their responsibility. Prostitutes, drugs, car hijackings, jobs.

Msukelwa Mvelase, the induna's son, has lived in Block 2 for nearly twenty years and is a dancer for Nomoya isigodi. I ask him about living conditions in Jeppe and conflict in the surrounding suburb.[40]

MM: We are not sleeping here. But it is the people outside.

FZ: They are shooting.

MM: If someone goes out and gets shot, we go out and check if it's our friends and family. But it is safe inside.

FZ: There is security at the gate.

MM: The problem is that these criminals do things outside, then run here and hide from the police. This gives us a bad reputation.

FZ: There used to be a big problem with hijacking. Now the induna doesn't allow any cars inside Jeppe. I got special permission for you to park next to his place. They used to hijack cars and drive them into the hostel, and the police were too scared to come inside.

Fezela carries my bag and belongings through Block 2 of the hostel. I must not be seen concealing anything while walking through Jeppe. A stumbling man in green grabs hold of me. "R10, umlungu, give me R10." I say, "No, I'm not carrying money," but he persists in wrenching my wrist, pressing against me. I try to remain calm; he's drunk. Msukelwa and Fezela move quickly, urging him off without using force. He relents, grudgingly, chuckling under his breath. I'm hurried through the turnstiles and out onto the street, one man on either side of me, their guns concealed. "Don't worry," says Fezela, "everyone knows me. You will be safe." Sure enough, I hear men calling from the hostel above. "Hawu, Fezela, kunjani baba?" (Hey, Fezela, how are you, sir?) We walk briskly to a side street. We are close to the park now, still within sight of the hostel. On the pavement, we approach a car on a hoist, wheels removed. Men are sitting around drinking beer from green bottles. Some of the men stare blankly at me. We are being conscientiously ignored by others. Chickens run. For sale signs stand inside the adjacent warehouse. Its appearance is dilapidated and anonymous. In Jeppestown there are many such buildings. Most were factories or workshops that have been taken over by migrants seeking work or shelter, or by the families of men living in the hostel. The stench of sulfur is overpowering. I hold my breath and stoop through the makeshift doorway. Tiny wooden rooms line the darkness, padlocked and windowless. Many call these places *emkhukhuwini* (shacks).

Sizakele Zwane is a woman in her mid-forties from Nambithi in KwaZulu-Natal. She moved here in 1996 with her two children, looking for work. The government had promised family housing for the men of Jeppe that year, and the result was a surge of hopeful arrivals. "I have six children that I am looking after," says Sizakele.[41] "When their father passed away, I moved here looking for work to support them." More than twenty years later, she still lives in the single room she started with. There's no running water, no toilet—nothing besides a bed, cabinet, side table, and some photos on the wall. The unit is neat and tidy, clean.

"The problem here," she says, "is the criminals. Guns. There are too many."

"What about support from the municipality?" I ask feebly.

"There are no services here. But I do have child grants for two of my kids."

Sizakele's husband arrives. He's from Jeppe and sings isicathamiya with a group called Es'killer. They practice in the basement of Block 2 during the night. Sometimes they compete elsewhere when they can afford it. I am struggling to make sense of the place, of the rationale for the lives lived here. Why here? "I sell beer to support my children," explains Sizakele. "My friend sells chickens, and she kills them for the guys in Jeppe." Everyone is afraid of the dark, and of what happens at night with the guns, the drugs, the prostitutes, the police, the hijacking, the prostitutes. And all those people outside, those "foreigners"—what are they doing?

The collapse of the Thembu worlds at Jeppe is evident from the large number of men leaving the hostels, the reduction in elders, and the many deaths from tuberculosis and AIDS. I ask Induna Mvelase what has changed at Jeppe since he arrived forty years ago, in 1977, and he is studied in his answer:

<table>
<tr><td>Yabonake, kushintshile kakhulu.</td><td>You see, it has changed a lot.</td></tr>
<tr><td>　　Kushintshe inhlonipho,</td><td>　　Respect has changed, law has</td></tr>
<tr><td>　　kushintshe umthetho.</td><td>　　changed.</td></tr>
</table>

"Do you mean respect for elders?" I ask.

"Firstly," he says, emphasizing his point in English, "the elder people are still there, but they don't have respect from the younger generation. Secondly, the law was there, used by the elder people, but now there is no more of that law." The young men just will not take instruction. They no longer respect their elders and do as they please without consequence. The decline in the performance culture at Jeppe, which includes isicathamiya, isishameni, and umaskandi, is ascribed to financial constraints. Men cannot afford to travel between hostels, to competitions, and back home. GG Alcock suggests other reasons, pointing to a new, "urban" generation. He tells me, "Everyone's got a cell phone, they're more likely to listen to house music than maskandi. They're still into that, but it's not as big. I think there's a kind of cultural erosion, in a sense. You also have less and less big community events, even in December." Fewer communal ceremonies take place because these are expensive to organize. The opportunities for dancing and singing have dwindled, as GG continues.

Weddings are very rare because people can't afford lobola. People are lobaling for years. So people live apart, or they do *vat en sit*, which is living together illegally.[42] So the youth are exposed to less and less big events. If you go to an event even at uMsinga, you see all the young school-age kids watching the dancing. In the past, they would have been dancing. [Now] they're not even singing along because they don't know the words.[43]

The generational disconnect described by GG Alcock is evident in the ways performances of music and dance are increasingly practiced as extracurricular pursuits in rural schools rather than as events and rituals integral to community life (see chapter 6). Norms of respect and social conduct—of imithetho and inhlonipho—were perpetuated, and moderated, in performances that facilitated intergenerational communication (see chapter 3). This breakdown in intergenerational communication is evident at Jeppe, too, as Sakephi Mbatha points out. He is a renowned dancer who lived at Jeppe for years. I asked him why he returned home to uMsinga after living at Jeppe and Nancefield hostels. He recalled, "It was very, very difficult because I didn't find piece jobs, and nobody was going to look after me. I was scared that maybe I will be tempted into criminality, so maybe I must just go back. . . . Since the elders went home, it became difficult for us. The youngsters can't take care of each other. Most of the elders have come back [to uMsinga], many of them passed away. The youngsters are left there."[44] The decline has negatively impacted the homeboy networks and the practices of music and dance that sustained them. Induna Mvelase tells a similar story. "Izingili was finished long ago," he says. "And isicathamiya is going down slowly. Before, in those times, people who were working they were coming from the hall in the basement. They used to compete here, they put money for the winners. The judges decide number 1, 2, 3. All that goes down with the value of money." The cultures of performance recorded by scholars in the 1970s and 1980s have declined.[45] The consequences of poverty and joblessness have been detrimental to the once vibrant competitions in the hostels, says Mvelase.

> People are not working. They need money for competition, for traveling. Because those people performing there are living in Daveyton, Boxburg, deep Soweto, West Rand, and come together to make a group of song. Those things are now no longer there. Secondly, in isicathamiya, it cost because they wear same suits, same trousers, same tire, same shoes. Was expensive because they wear two-piece . . . Some other ingoma, like *izingili* [an acrobatic dance style from northeastern KwaZulu-Natal] and ishameni, there was that for happiness ingoma, not for competition, just to enjoy. But even that comes lower because there is no money to get that happiness anymore whereby, because of that time, dancing together they were drinking [with] each other to be happy. It goes back to traveling issues.

The wider social and economic malaise in Jeppestown is registered in performance. The stories told by Induna Mvelase, Ndididi Dladla, Sizakele Zwane, and Sakephi Mbatha embody the fundamental changes that have accompanied South Africa's transition from apartheid state to liberal democracy. But they also figure into broader geopolitical shifts that are continental in scope and consequence. The mass movement of migrants across Africa has given rise to the contested spatial dynamics of South Africa's cities. The xenophobic incidents of the past two decades demonstrate serious and violent enmity between migrants. In the context of these violent interactions, ethnic affiliations are affirmed. The practice of dance may once have been a means to quell such violence. But this was only possible when ingoma was itself a lingua franca.

In the 1970s isishameni came to replace stick-fighting contests known as umgangela that had been used in the past to resolve violent conflicts between izigodi. The homeboy networks who danced together in private and at community events came to function as fighting units.[46] The dynamics between factions were mediated through dance. Tensions over land tenure and skirmishes between families were defused through the practice of umgangela during the summer months when men returned to their rural homesteads. Stick-fighting contests were an important check on tensions and were regulated by strict rules overseen by the izinduna and tribal elders. Clegg describes how umgangela was "a means of expressing, actually being violent, but at the same time containing district opposition. You have these very strict rules—you may not hit a man when he's down, if he says 'Kumu' or 'Manutshe' you have to stop beating him."[47] The Thembu call stick-fighting of this nature *uphenge*. The practice of uphenge and its role in conflict was corrupted by various social factors, including competition over access to land and jobs on farms. By the 1980s it had taken on a negative connotation. Clegg's analysis of this change is startling:

> People now just want to win, to enforce their domination over other districts, and the ritual aspect of the *uphenge*, this inter-district stick fight, loses its cohesion. You have people being killed, hacked, people going to *uphenge* carrying *pangas*, choppers, and spears. Fighting sticks are weapons of playing. Men play with these things. If I hit a man and he dies, it's a mistake. These are not weapons of war. In *umgangela* to this day if you hit a man and he dies, there is no court case.[48]

When uphenge began to exacerbate violence and could no longer resolve the turmoil between districts in a peaceful fashion, an alternative was found: team dancing.[49] A culture of ingoma developed with sanctioned rules that restricted and controlled the performance of aggressive or threatening acts. This practice is still evident at Jeppe and in performances at uMsinga. Induna Mvelsa explains that in the isishameni the performers act as if they are fighting. "The *isishameni* they are doing like they were fighting—but they were not fighting, they were dancing,"[50] says Induna Mvelase. This aggressive dancing is carefully monitored by women. At weddings and umemulo ceremonies, married women use intelezi to calm the dancers (see chapter 3). It is also the role of the igoso to restrain his dancers and to ensure that things do not get out of control. Sakephi Mbatha explains that the igoso must have special vocal qualities and must enforce the law. He need not be a talented dancer; it is the qualities of leadership and creativity that are most prized.

> The igoso must have a nice voice. That's the main factor. He can make all these people come together and sing nicely. It is the main role. The igoso organizes the people. After you have been elected, you must pass your law. Then you say every weekend you must come here at about eight o'clock. It's all from the igoso, the igoso must pass the law. They are doing the rules in hostels. They just look for a big room in the hostels to practice.[51]

The principle of upholding customary law (umthetho) is a feature of the social structure of hostel life that isishameni embodies. Most of the dancers in a troupe will share a place of origin in KwaZulu-Natal, or a direct family connection. They dance as a team and practice on weeknights and weekends.[52] On Sundays, men gather to discuss business, to consult on their stokvel investments, to drink, and to dance. The dancing is a form of entertainment, but it also solidifies the bond between men by affirming rank and identity. At the end of the year, the dancers perform in an all-day display of inter-district dancing. These hostel dances serve as practice for the weddings, umemulo, and *imisebenzi* (return of the spirit) ceremonies that will take place over the Christmas holidays back in KwaZulu-Natal. The social structure of dance teams is homologous to that of the izigodi. Each isishameni dance team is coordinated by an igoso and an iphini. Their role is to schedule practice sessions, choose songs, and train the youngsters in the correct steps and gestures. Most teams consist of thirty to forty dancers called amasoja. The rank-and-file dancers are generally young men under the age of thirty. A similar hierarchy and regimentation are observed in other Zulu dance forms like umzansi.[53]

isiShameni is characterized by the alternation of two phases. One involves coordinated dancing in groups. This is contrasted with the alternation or sometimes simultaneous dancing of two individuals in competition, a practice termed "one-one." The texts of the songs may be about skirmishes in the home districts, love forsaken, and love begotten—or even about hostel gossip, an opportunity to spill the beans. Tensions between individuals are expressed, aired for all to hear, and are sometimes left unresolved. Once you have had your turn you must step aside, as it were. Tensions between groups are resolved in part through interactions with the audience members, who are interlocutors in the performances, responding to the gestures and feats of the dancers.

The stylistic features of isishameni are distinct from other forms of ingoma danced across much of southeast Africa.[54] In umzansi, a style common across the southern parts of KwaZulu-Natal, men move in lines and range the dance arena often in a militaristic fashion. When men dance individually or in unison, they move forward and back, using the space in a linear fashion. isiShameni is distinct in gesture and structure with its emphasis on the vertical.[55] A distinctive feature is the relatively static use of the dance space. Dancers use minimal lateral movement, emphasizing upward gestures with their arms with a characteristic vertical stamping motion. As the routine nears its end, there is dynamic movement, but still within the confines of a relatively small compass of no more than two to three meters in diameter.[56] These characteristics of isishameni are evident in performances by dancers from Nomoya, and Msukelwa Mvelase's style offers a case in point. He summons considerable power set on his haunches and holding his body firmly in place with arms raised to balance his low center of gravity. It is the strength of his core that enables him to reach upward with the stability needed to deliver a powerful stamping motion with his foot lifted, and then descended, from directly above his head. If dance is an art of proximity, then isishameni is an art of alignment. The balanced bodily axis is definitive of the isishameni ideal. Its qualities need to be understood not only in terms of the orientation of the solo dancer's body in space but in terms of the coordination of dancers' bodies in space and time.

THE AESTHETICS OF ENTRAINMENT

iNgoma team dancing depends for its force on the ability of dancers to coordinate themselves to a groove[57] and to articulate their movements to rhythm. The social dynamics of ingoma dance may be understood in terms of an aesthetics of entrainment. Gavin Steingo and Louise Meintjes have both invoked aesthetics as a vehicle for interpreting the social dynamics of performance in South Africa. Steingo's careful analysis of kwaito and the aesthetics of freedom points to the broader social implications of musical praxis,[58] whereas Meintjes offers a detailed study of ingoma.[59] Here I locate dance aesthetics in the realm of cognition. That is,

I interpret the expressive gestures and coordinated musical intentions of ingoma dance as a fashioning of mind and body to space and time.

Entrainment happens when we share attention with others and coordinate our attention and action to the same or interconnected collective tasks. "In musical usage," writes Gary Tomlinson, "entrainment names our capacity for 'beat-based processing' or 'beat induction'; our ability to perceive the regularity of an even or isochronous series of pulses, to predict the continuation of the series, and to coordinate our activities in advance to this continued regularity."[60] Choral singing and dancing in cyclical forms (like ingoma) engage this capacity for beat-based processing where singers pitch the same or harmonious notes to a rhythm while coordinating their movements to a beat. "Entrainment describes a process whereby two rhythmic processes interact with each other in such a way that they adjust towards and eventually 'lock in' to a common phase and/or periodicity."[61] Entrainment can only happen if the performers have internalized the beat or a sense of pulse or tactus against which their performance is measured. Their movements can then be in step with one another without having to react to a beat.[62] Entrainment underscores our capacity to dance, to sing together, and to perform in ensembles. Entrainment is a human universal. Music and dance require that we do things together simultaneously and in a highly coordinated fashion. These forms of entrainment are characterized by the ability to predict the timing of future events.

In ingoma, the metrical ground for entrainment is established by the singers who clap a pulse. The singers establish a tactus and basic rhythm against which the dancers articulate their own distinct rhythms, often in syncopation and cross-rhythm. Clapping is used to accent beats in the tactus and to create cross-rhythms that serve to propel the movements of the dancers. In isishameni, these rhythmic patterns must be memorized and coordinated in movements. Often, dancers will take no obvious heed of one another on the dance floor, fixing their gaze upward or turning to display their independence. And yet it is in these moments of independence that the synchrony of their entrained community is reinforced in performance.

Jonathan Clegg was himself a dancer of ingoma who performed regularly at the hostels in Jeppestown. He argues that dance is best conceived as "pure play."[63] In Clegg's analysis, "the dance dances the dancer." Dancers recognize a lore implicit in their performances. The rules of the dance are interpreted in accordance with the conventions of the community.[64] Clegg describes an "aesthetic reality which 'devours' the consciousness of the spectator and dancer and transports them into a 'new world.'"[65] This description accords with what Mihaly Csikszentmihalyi describes as the sense of "flow" that performers experience when they reach a heightened state of control, concentration, and mastery.[66] The idea of worlds of consciousness and the flow of these worlds as transcendental to the material lived reality of which they are an expression offers a lens for interpreting ingoma. Understanding the contexts for this lived reality, then, is essential for the interpretation of dance, and for making sense of its meanings in and for a community.[67] Dance transcends lifeworlds as an ideal expression of being. Play happens in this transcendental realm where mundane activities are suspended. But this play is considered a moral force, insists Clegg. "The dance is used as a means of communicating both general and special, sacred information from the social system to the individual. . . . The dance educates the individual in a subtle manner, the artistry and aesthetic being woven into a concept of the ideal society."[68] Dance as play enables individual expression within bounds. This embodies the aesthetics of entrainment in which the rhythms of sound and movement are used by individuals and troupes to articulate their identities against a common time.

THE PHENOMENOLOGY OF COLLAPSING WORLDS

When homeboys dance isishameni at Jeppe Park, it reinforces ties of identity and belonging that feel more urgent than ever. The spatial and social dynamics of dance point to the complex social imaginary out of which migrants fashion their worlds on the urban frontier. Dancers enact their realizations of space through play. Dance as play is used to territorialize space, to mark its boundaries, to condition its fields of interaction, and to assert ownership over its domains. But as social praxis it does more than this. It constitutes a structure for living a disciplined life in the city within a close network of kith and kin governed by imithetho and inhlonipho. The potential collapse of the dance world and of its laws and customs is evident in the behavior of thousands of hostel dwellers who raided downtown Johannesburg in August 2019.[69] This show of force by a generation asserting its independence from the traditional Zulu leadership offers the clearest indication yet of the collapse of custom, and of the fraught politics of proximity that now prevail in Johannesburg's contested inner-city spaces. This chapter has put forward the idea of an aesthetics of entrainment in ingoma dance, drawing on research in cognition to explain the politics of ingoma in time and space. The utility of entrainment as concept and ideal enables close analysis of the rhythms of dancers and their spatial interactions. In the next chapter, I discuss the politics and prosody of izibongo and how umaskandi artists use its prosodic dimensions to articulate their barbed political commentaries.

uMaskandi iziBongo
The Politics and Poetics
of Popular Praises

JANUARY 6, 2012

Zamani and I drive for Mashunka isigodi in Thembu country to meet umaskandi musicians Khonya had told me about and two men who can help me: Fezela Zwane and Ndididi Dladla. It's a short drive, about ten minutes along the road to Tugela Ferry, and when we arrive, I park on a verge at the foot of a steep climb. There are homesteads dotted amid grass, scrub, and aloes. The Thukela River makes a sharp turn in this neck of the valley before disappearing behind Mashunka mountain. Across the river is Nomoya isigodi. It is a warm day, but squalls suggest rain. While I take in the view, Zamani surveys the valley in search of our interlocutors. Then he shouts out to a homestead several hundred meters down the hill, and we set off on foot. Halfway there I see a man emerge from the shade of the tree line. Ndididi is wearing a black and gold Kaizer Chiefs football shirt, and he's walking over to meet us. He is a strong, powerfully built man with a broad smile and confident bearing. Zamani introduces me as Tom, and I'm met by a firm handshake. Ndididi grins and asks after my plans at uMsinga, then gestures to his umuzi where I can already hear guitar-playing outside.

Most of the *imizi* (homesteads) I have visited in the Thukela valley consist of four or five dwellings set atop a raised level platform in a circular pattern, usually with at least one rectangular shaped house in the center. Immediately below the platform is the isibaya, which is central to the spiritual life of the umuzi. Here at

FIGURE 5.1 Khonazugcina Dladla (left) at Mashunka.

the Dladla homestead, a few trees dot the platform, and underneath are benches, plastic drums, and assorted stools. Men in overalls, trousers, shirts, and vests sit drinking, laughing. The guitarist is a wiry thin, middle-aged man named Khonazugcina (Khona for short). He talks to Ndididi, who seems always to be jovial yet insistent. Khona asks me for a drink, meaning alcohol of some kind. I tell him that I have nothing on me. He frowns but goes on playing. A plastic *gogogo* (water drum) is brought for him to sit on. The top is crushed from use. He sits gingerly, appearing to balance his discomfort with the guitar. Khona battles to walk on one foot—an old injury, I am told, sustained while he was working in Joburg. Ndididi motions that he should play something. First, he wants a drink from the *umlungu* (White man), he says. I take out my recorder and microphone. Khona tunes the guitar. Attached to the index and ring fingers on his right hand are pieces of wire that he is using as plectrums to play chords two strings apart in parallel motion. The recorder loads the SD card, slowly; but there is no rush, I think. The song begins with the *intela* (introduction), much as I expect from an umaskandi, and, to my delight, he rattles off his *izibongo* (praises) at incredible, incomprehensible speed. ◀◈

Later, I ask him to tell me what the izibongo means. He seems not to comprehend and so I ask Ndididi. It turns out we are using different terminology for the same thing: he calls praising *ihhashi*, an alternate name. But he doesn't want to translate or slow down his ihhashi. He jokes around and avoids the topic; but Ndididi grows impatient, the broad smile peeling off. Eventually we convince Khona to repeat his ihhashi slowly, which he then does in a deliberately exaggerated fashion. "The men and women hate him here, and they can't wait for him to die," translates Ndididi. This causes some bemusement in the assembly of young men and boys who have now congregated.

EXAMPLE 5.1: "Sondela" (Come closer), Khonazugcina Dladla (2012)

'Skhulumanazi uhlalabemzonda
    abafazi namadoda uputhu
    oludliwangeplan.
umSindo wezinja zibanga imfene
    emvakwendlu kwagogo.
Khona phansi Mashunka
    lenkhona Corn Leaver 'sigodi.
Keli-kehle.
Seyikhala inkomishiwezi.
Wathi qheqhe, wathi mihli.
Wa-qheqhe, wathi mihli.
Wathi qheqhe, wathi mihli.

I say to you to the person who is
    hated by men and women, the
    man that is eating the pap with
    the plan.
The noise of dogs they are
    fighting over baboons behind
    the house of the grandmother.
I am down by Mashunka in Corn
    Leaver district.
[Imitating the sound of cups
    falling]
The cups are crying.
[Vocables]
[Vocables]
They say qheqhe, they say mihli.

Khona plays a few more songs between entreaties for beer. I ask him his name. Do I mean his umaskandi name or his "pass" name? he responds. I was often asked this question by performers, which is interesting because "pass" is the colloquial name for an identity document that has long since been discontinued. The pass system in South Africa was law from 1916 until 1986. Decades have passed since the system requiring Black persons to carry passes was abolished, but that memory is etched on generations who were subject to its dehumanizing consequences. Identity documents impose identities, while in song one can sing one's own identity into being.

———

iziBongo are declamatory praises used for dramatic effect in umaskandi music.[1] The practice of personal and popular praising is common across Zulu cultures in southern Africa. uMaskandi izibongo are distinct from praises in other genres due to the synthesis of elements. Rapid, tonally nuanced phrases of incisive social comment are set to instrumental music. The art of praising fashions narratives of experience, genealogy, and heritage that are replete with idioms and lyrical encodings intelligible only to those familiar with the contexts, symbols, and sounds specific to umaskandi lifeworlds.[2] Since the mid-twentieth century this combination of Zulu style and idiom has come to define the genre of umaskandi as a form of indigenous popular music. This chapter considers, in turn, the meanings embodied in performances by recording artists Phuzekhemisi and Mfaz' Omnyama, as well as group and individual umaskandi recorded during my fieldwork in KwaZulu-Natal. Khonazugcina and Mdidiyeli are from uMsinga, and Jonathan Mathenjwa is from Ndumo.

The first part of this chapter describes the relationship of umaskandi izibongo to genres of choral dance song, gourd bow music, and other forms of recited izibongo. In the second part, I discuss the social dimensions and the characteristics of umaskandi izibongo through textual exegesis. The third and final part examines the prosodic and musical dimensions of izibongo through transcription and analysis of performances by Phuzekhemisi and Jonathan Mathenjwa, the latter of whom I recorded in 2012. The combination of sonic and social perspectives on izibongo demonstrate the complex intertextuality of umaskandi as a genre embedded in the everyday that constantly engages with the symbolism and ritual of Zulu cosmology. iziBongo connects orators with listeners who share experiences of displacement and desire, of migrancy and marginality. By listening closely to the sounds of izibongo, we gain an understanding of the distinctly personal means by which umaskandi orators assert their agency by speaking to and for imagined communities across the rural-urban ethnoscape. The dual emphasis on semantic and prosodic elements in this chapter shows how social and sonic dimensions may be approached in a complementary fashion.

IZIBONGO

The term *izibongo* is used to describe the praises declaimed in oratory and in song for purposes of veneration, identification, and social comment. David Rycroft writes that "the Zulu term '*izibongo*' may either denote the plural of '*isibongo*' (meaning 'surname' of a clan or family) or, more commonly, a personal praise-

FIGURE 5.2 Jonathan Mathenjwa performing with Mqamuli Wezintambo
at Ndumo Hill, April 22, 2012.

name or a set of these, applying to an individual (or sometimes to an animal or an inanimate object)."[3] Izibongo contrasts with *izithakazelo*, which are the clan names or praises recited when men introduce themselves. These clan praises are brief, formulaic, and specific. iziBongo contain similar formulaic elements but are more complex in structure, more fluid in content, and are declaimed with greater expressive nuance.

The declamation of solitary izibongo is an art performed by *izimbongi* (praise poets), who serve to extol the virtues, foibles, and idiosyncrasies of kings, rulers, and other venerable personages in public. In formal contexts, izibongo serve to introduce dignitaries by reflecting on their exceptional achievements and characteristics using metaphoric language and ingenious narrative devices. The laudatory qualities of izibongo embody meanings associated with the related term *bonga* (to praise, laud, extol, or to give thanks and express gratitude). Izibongo praise poetry, then, is used not only to name and to identify but also to accord status and recognition, to thank and to celebrate, and as a vehicle for social and political comment. As with praise poetry and song in many other African cultures, the Zulu *imbongi* is granted license for public comment and criticism that would otherwise be restricted by virtue of rank and decorum. Citing nineteenth-century sources, Eileen Jensen Krige describes the imbongi in earlier times as a kind of "bard," or "praiser," in service of *izinduna* (headmen) and *amakhosi* (chiefs). Krige explains:

> Every headman in Zululand had an *imbongi*, and there was one at every military kraal besides the special *izimbongi* of the king, who lived at the royal kraal. Their function was to proclaim publicly the praises of their chief, or any notable visitor, at public festivals or grand occasions. For this they selected the most brilliant incidents in the career of their chief or the history of the nation, and composed praises that may be considered as the poetry of the Zulu nation, similar to the sagas or ballads of other races. The praises of the kings are handed down from generation to generation, and they are sung when the spirits of the chiefs of old are specially approached for their blessings. In singing praises, the object of the *izimbongi* is to chant them in as loud a voice as possible, and with as little regard for punctuation as the need for breathing will allow. The herald or *imbongi* was also a jester, and took part in all the dances at the royal kraal, disguised in some grotesque attire.[4]

Features of the izibongo recited by these izimbongi are retained in the practices of umaskandi musicians today, who, outside of the traditional court and kraal, have taken on the role of social critics. The sharp criticism, witticism, and satire characteristic of umaskandi izibongo address social issues of broad importance to urban and rural communities. A comparison with the izibongo declaimed by izimbongi demonstrates two important similarities: first, the performance of praises is characterized by very loud and rapid declamation inhibited only by "the need for breathing"; second, both the umaskandi and the imbongi occupy the role of jester. Audiences will expect artful and sometimes cutting humor.

The social contract implicit in izibongo enables this license and freedom of expression even in societies otherwise resistant to public dissent. To understand this, we need to figure izibongo within a larger practice that Leroy Vail and Landeg White describe as "public poetry." Vail and White explain, "The performers seek through poetic expression a language with the authority to marshal a public response, and the poetry confronts the changing panorama of African history with a stream of comment—heroic, celebratory, elegiac, satiric—always attempting to construct . . . 'a map of experience.'"[5] By speaking directly to people's lived experiences, izibongo may also be read as a genre of public theater and spectacle that engages with and demands a response from its subjects. This engagement is true also of the popular self-praises of which umaskandi is a subgenre; that is, izibongo that draw on the same structural conventions and range of expressive devices to serve different ends.

Popular praises are distinct from *izibongo zamakhosi* (the praises of kings).[6] The formal recitation of royal praises are lengthy, dignified, and sanctioned performances that employ a carefully measured style of vocal delivery with much closer attention to genealogy and history than the popular praises characteristic of umaskandi and other popular genres. The latter extend features of praising used in everyday social interactions. Adrian Koopman classifies the popular praises of young men into subcategories such as *izibongo zokushela* (courting praises), *izibongo zokulwa* (fighting praises), and *izibongo zokugiya* (dancing praises), and describes them as "the oral poetry of the common people as opposed to that of the professional bards." Koopman states that "they have a lively, earthy nature which reflects the characteristics of those who compose them; and they are still very much a feature of modern Zulu society."[7] The naming practices in these izibongo are used by umaskandi who describe themselves and one another using colorful imagery.

The borrowing of conventions and formulas makes izibongo an unusually broad category interjected into many song and dance genres, including isicathamiya, umshado, umakhweyana and ughubu bow music, and umaskandi. Liz Gunner and Mafika Gwala point to the "very close relation [of popular izibongo] to song and chant, particularly *izigiyo* which we translate as 'songs to go with the war dance.'" Gunner and Gwala explain that "izibongo are also closely related to dance, particularly but not only *ukugiya*, 'the war dance.' In popular performance, the three activities of praising, dancing, and calling out *izigiyo* fuse together."[8] These popular self-praises are an important part of everyday performances of self and society, a means of articulating one's identity and distinctiveness among friends and neighbors with ever more poignancy in a world of strangers. Popular self-praises became iconic to the minstrel art of umaskandi in the mid-twentieth century, and through subsequent convention they have become integral to the character and substance of the genre as an expression of Zulu identities. As umaskandi itself migrated from the art of itinerant street musicians who sang while they walked, to become a popular guitar, drum-and-bass style on radio, cassette, and compact disc, it retained these roots.

"*Umaskandi,*" writes the Zulu linguist D. B. Z. Ntuli, "stands out as the forerunner and initiator of a style that combines music and praise-poetry together in a unique fashion."[9] There are many features of umaskandi that extend principles of Zulu music that exist in other genres, including especially choral dance song and gourd bow music. The explanation for guitar styles as rooted in bow music is remarked on by many commentators, including scholars Tom Collins, David Coplan, Nollene Davies, Carol Muller, and Kathryn Olsen, who emphasize the relationship of *maskanda* (the Anglicized term for *umaskandi*) to bow music while recognizing the power of choral dance song in the rhythms and choruses that define several dance styles.[10] Writing in the 1970s about the rise of "township music," Rycroft observed that the guitar took on "almost exactly the functional role previously fulfilled by the *umakhweyana* gourd-bow (apart from the fact that it was also used by girls) in that it serves for self-accompaniment to solo singing. Also, as in former times, this kind of musical activity is frequently performed while out walking."[11] The practice of solo singing and praising that was initially performed to the accompaniment of single-string bows was transferred to the guitar. What made the guitar an ideal exponent for this tradition of minstrelsy was that its multiple voice parts could double as the customary choral response. The addition of voice parts in the guitar, according to Rycroft, "demonstrate a furtherance in the expression of Zulu musical principles that was formerly quite beyond the capacity of any form of traditional bow."[12]

Rosemary Joseph, writing of a similar fashioning of imported instruments to indigenous principles, describes "an active tradition of young men's topical songs and love songs performed to the accompaniment of the *udloko,* a single-stringed bowed instrument with tin resonator attached at the upper end of the stave."[13] During her fieldwork, Joseph documented "an active tradition of young men's topical songs and love songs performed to the accompaniment of the guitar and concertina which clearly reflects the principles of musical organization inherent in traditional bow music."[14] She remarks that "the guitar and concertina traditions would seem to stem ultimately from a male tradition of performance on indigenous string instruments such as the *ugubhu, umakhweyana, isithontolo,* and *udloko* although the more immediate stimulus may have come from the women's tradition of playing particularly the *umakhweyana* and *ugubhu* at a time when the male tradition of playing these bows had ceased to be active."[15] This evidence shows the strong continuities that existed between umaskandi and other forms of Zulu culture, and it explains how umaskandi itself became an indigenous music genre drawing on a wide range of cultural practices. Continuities with older forms of Zulu music are also evident in the practice of izibongo. The praises performed by Mntwan' Constance Magogo kaDinuzulu in several archival recordings are a testament to this.[16]

uMaskandi emerged from the experience of labor migrancy in South Africa whereby men and women took up jobs in urban areas and on mines to sustain families who remained in rural areas. The apartheid homeland system forced migrants to identify as noncitizens in cities and industrial complexes who had to carry passes identifying their place of origin and the nature of their employment. Most were employed in manual labor for corporations, or on the mines, and were often housed in all-male dormitories (hostels) and compounds. uMaskandi, isicathamiya, and other genres of song and dance became popular modes of expression in these hostels. iziBongo offer a critical response to these changing conditions, and the need to express, often in difficult and hostile environments, a sense of place and identity. Ntuli elaborates on this new function for izibongo, pointing to a transition period during which traditional practice was transformed as a response to new social contexts.

> When *maskandi* music was initiated, the tradition of praising was still very strong. Most of the *maskandi* musicians lived in compounds close to their places of employment. When one of them played and sang well, his colleagues praised him; otherwise he praised himself. His fans sometimes wanted him to demonstrate his skill to other groups. This eventually led to open contests which were held in the street, mainly at the weekends. Since the musician was a complete stranger to some of the members of his audience, he felt obliged to introduce himself. He would tell the people who he was, where he came from, which river or mountain was in the vicinity of his homestead, who his chief or headman was, and whatever information he could supply for the benefit of his audience. In between all this he would also recite his praises.[17]

Being "a complete stranger" in a foreign context created the need for a common mode of communication, and so developed the conventions of izibongo in which extended self-praises came to include standard features of geography, such as river, mountain, district, and inkosi. These served as social introductions that were imbued also with musical characteristics of emplacement like the umzansi and isiZulu regional dance rhythms used in guitar music.[18]

The language and gesture of these izibongo were shaped by experiences of encounter but drew upon familiar modalities to express and contend with these new challenges. Jonathan Clegg was immersed in these conditions during the 1970s as an anthropologist, dancer, and musician. His observations on the origins and practice of umaskandi in this period are invaluable because he became part of the tradition through his partnership with Sipho Mchunu and many other Zulu musicians from uMsinga, and in the migrant hostels of Johannesburg and Soweto.[19] Clegg locates the origins of the competitive element to umaskandi in the martial arts of Zulu stick-fighting. The following extract is from of a talk by Clegg in which he performs the persona of the umaskandi for an audience to explain the genre.

> The songs you choose to sing first are the kinds of blows and the metaphors you'll use—"Why did you choose that song first?" "*Bengifihla induku yami yokugcina*[.]" "I was hiding my best shot, because I want to play all my weak songs first," and get him to expose his best shot and block it with a good shot from my guitar, and the whole encounter is described in a martial metaphor because it is a martial tradition, it is a martial culture, and there is a set format around which you will play. You will begin with an introduction—the introduction you will play is what is known as *iihlabo, izihlabo* which are just little melody lines which give the person listening an idea of (a) the scale that you're playing on, (b) where you're going to start to play, and that will give him a very rough indication of, (c) the kind of song you're going to play. It also shows off your technique, and *izihlabo* is in fact related to *ukugiya*. "Before I fight with you and have my weapons, I will perform a series of movements with my stick and my shield just to show you how well I can do it, and then we'll fight, perhaps."[20]

The gestures, music, and language of umaskandi embody this aggression not only in the guitar work but also in physical exertions, gesticulations, and acrobatics of movement and dance. It is striking that words like *hlaba* (spear, or stab) and *shaya* (strike), among other threats, are seldom sung in umaskandi songs. These challenges are reserved instead for recitation in the izibongo. This indicates the power accorded izibongo and the license afforded umaskandi in ways that simulate the practice of izimbongi, though with far greater ferocity and often through direct confrontation.

The "martial" culture that Clegg has recorded in the uMsinga and Weenen districts of Natal, and to some extent in Johannesburg hostels (see chapter 4), may be read also as a response to the sense of vulnerability experienced in unfamiliar and hostile conditions. For Zulus working far from home outside of their homesteads and the familiarity of kith and kin, without the commensurate social standing, respect, and security of regulated lifestyles, in short, persons in a contested order of things, umaskandi offered and continues to offer a means by which to assert and define oneself as an independent subject where worlds and values collide. In such contexts, izibongo offered not only a mode of address but also an honest signal of social standing. To deliver izibongo while playing guitar or concertina in public demonstrates beyond doubt one's abilities and inclinations. To use the top of one's voice to call out one's genealogy, accomplishments, and social comment is more than mere braggadocio; it is a demand to be heard, recognized, and validated. It is not the truth content of izibongo that renders them valid but rather the valence of their symbols read into and against a shared set of experiences, anxieties, and ambitions. It is in these foreign contexts that the "Zuluness" of umaskandi took center stage. To be sure, the creation of a synthetic Zuluness in the recording studio,[21] on Radio Bantu,[22] and in apartheid policy and ideology[23] are important factors in making sense of this confluence of identities. What izibongo call attention to in the midst of all this, and what they implore still today, is that we listen to the humanity of persons at the very center of conditions of social inequality and deprivation whose voices are too often drowned out by the larger narratives of oppression and counter-oppression. The symbols recited in umaskandi izibongo share this experience with humor and wit, and transfer to an order of becoming the sense of dignity that has been denied them by circumstance.

The tension between rural and urban Zulu cultures, and the politics of dispossession and impoverishment, of the social fracture that apartheid policies enacted, is implicit in recordings from this era. The song "Imbizo" (1992) by the brothers Phuzekhemisi and Khethani is indicative of tensions resulting from the systems of land tenure and tribute required under apartheid.[24] This song caused outrage due to its strong criticism of the amakhosi who extracted taxes from their rural subjects, a practice instituted by British colonists in the late nineteenth century as an instrument to generate cheap migrant labor to fuel the industrial economy (see chapter 1). The apartheid government took advantage of this practice and used it to generate a degree of supplication from traditional leaders who benefited from hut taxes on rural homesteads. The song takes aim at the practice itself as well as the ways in which it was continually abused by chiefs and headmen to extract profit despite conditions of deprivation experienced by their subjects.

EXAMPLE 5.2: "Imbizo" (Gathering), Phuzekhemisi and Khethani (1992)

Solo and Chorus: Lo mhlaba uyathengwa, ungaboni s'hleli kuwona.
This land we pay for, even though you see us living in it.

Chorus: Njalo ngonyaka sikhokha imali yamasimu endunene.
Every year we pay tariffs for the fields to the chiefs.

Solo: Njalo njena kukhon' imbizo
There are always gatherings

Hawu, njalo kukhon' imbizo
Wow, there are always gatherings

Sihlala sibizwa emakhosini
We are being called by the chiefs

Sihlala sibizwa phezulu
We are being called from above [by the elders]

Sihlala sifunwa esikoleni
We are wanted at school

Bathi khona imbizo.
They say there is a gathering

Chorus: Ungaboni s'phila kulo mhlaba siyawukhokhela.
Even though you see us living in this land, we pay for.

Izibongo:
Wow, I really stabbed this time,

Awu, ngahlaba ngempela, uPhuzekhemisi no Khethani!
this is Phuzekhemisi and Khethani!

Madoda, khona phansi eMkhomazi
Men, from down there at uMkhomazi valley

S'buya khona kwaDumisa.
We come from kwaDumisa.

Hay' ngabatshela umfoka baba uKhethani
Hey, I told them it's my uncle Khethani

Ngathi bayo thintha imamba isemgodini
I said, they will touch a [mamba] snake in its hole

Ngathi hayi bafana yo'limaza meyike yaphum'
I said, "Hey boys, you'll get hurt when it comes out"

O'pasopa' insizw' uhamb' kwesgxabhane
Watch out, young men, if you go where it burns

Lesi esise enzansi siwisa amatshe.
It makes the rocks down there to fall.

Hoo!
Hoo!

Solo:

Hawu, njalo njena khon' imbizo	Wow, again and again there are gatherings
Njalo njena khon' imbizo	Again and again, there are gatherings
Ngithi sithathaphi imali?	Where will I get the money?
Sihlala sibizwa endunene	They're calling us to the chiefs
Sihlala sifunwa KwaMtholi.	They're looking for us at Mtholi.

The lyrics begin with measured outrage. Sarcastic remarks are leveled against the amakhosi, commenting on the extraordinary lengths they go to extract tariffs, even venturing so far as to disrupt children in classes at school. The izibongo begins with a boast. Phuzekhemisi jests at the boldness of their blunt criticism—criticism, it turns out, that had serious consequences for the artists. Although the album *Imbizo* sold over two hundred thousand copies,[25] Phuzekhemisi's rural homestead was allegedly burned down in retaliation for the sharp critique leveled at traditional leaders. This only reinforces the point that "ngahlaba ngemphela," they really did hit the mark this time!

"Imbizo" is fascinating, also, in the ways it rails against a leadership and system that are often taken to coexist with the nationalist Zulu identity portrayed in the music.[26] In fact, a careful reading of the song reveals that Phuzekhemisi and Khetani shatter the image of a mythic and unitary Zuluness beholden to a patriarchal authority. Instead we find in umaskandi a potent public critique of the institutions at the root of the rural-urban contradictions that came to define migrant life in the mid to late twentieth century. The "Imbizo" izibongo asserts an aggressive and defiant threat to those who would seek them out "down where it burns" for they shall meet with "a snake in its hole." This aggression is sharp and closer to izibongo zokulwa than izibongo zamakhosi. The style and structure of these praises warrant scrutiny for they speak of a musical practice that has achieved considerable sophistication in its range of expressive forms, and a practice that departs from the conventions used in other forms of izibongo discussed in this chapter.

STYLE AND STRUCTURE

The functions of the izibongo section in umaskandi music are laid bare in a structure that has become standardized over the past four decades on radio. Ordinarily songs begin with a brief solo flourish on the guitar or concertina known as the *izihlabo* (stabs) or *intela* (introduction). Alternations between the soloist and chorus in call-and-response follow before the izibongo are performed halfway into the song by the umaskandi. Nollene Davies outlined the structure of the izibongo section in research conducted in the early 1990s, and this structure is still utilized in many performances today, including those I recorded during fieldwork at Mazizini, uMsinga, Mnweni, Ndumo, Nkaseni, and Thukela Estates. Davies explains:

> The *izibongo* section [in umaskandi] consists of two distinctive portions. The first is relatively concrete and consists of personal praises. The maskandi identifies himself, his place of birth, chief, geographical locale, and other personal information in a rapid declamatory delivery. These praises are often highly idiomatic and thus replete with hidden meanings decipherable only to close friends and relations. The second part of the izibongo is more free and usually involves some form of social critique or narrative. The "message" of the song is most directly expressed in this section. Technical display must be of a standard with this message if the performance is to be deemed successful. . . . This could involve criticism, satire, advice, praise, fears, humour or almost anything. The meaning of, or story behind the lyrics is not always clear to listeners and often requires some further explanation. However, it would certainly be understood by the person at whom the song was directed.[27]

Major recording artists like iHashi Elimhlophe, Mfaz' Omnyama, and Phuzekhemisi sometimes omit portions of their personal praises and get straight to the point of their critique. But all refer in some shape or form to key markers of identity in their personal praises before turning to the more specific social comment. The umaskandi whom I recorded tended always to include the autobiographical information first, sometimes choosing to recite longer social commentaries than is customary in recorded umaskandi.

The structure identified by Davies is manifest in izibongo by Jonathan Mathenjwa, an umaskandi guitarist and vocalist from Ndumo in northern KwaZulu-Natal. I recorded nine songs by Mathenjwa and his group Mqamuli Wezintambo at a community hall on Ndumo Hill on April 30, 2012.[28] The izibongo he recites in these songs are nearly identical in respect of the personal praises; the themes of each song change but his praises include consistent references to his family, place of origin, river, and chief. In the song "Bafana Bafana" (Boys, boys), he sings about South Africa's national football team and the role that Nelson Mandela played in bringing the Soccer World Cup 2010 to South Africa. ◀ッ The izibongo laments the twenty-seven years Mandela spent "rotting" in prison as a political prisoner to the apartheid state, and thanks him for bringing to the nation an extraordinary triumph. Mathenjwa's izibongo demonstrates, in its thematic praise of Mandela, South Africa's first democratically elected president and principled leader, a close relation to the practice of the imbongi.

EXAMPLE 5.3: "Bafana Bafana" (Boys, boys), Jonathan Mathenjwa (2012)

Hawu ng'khuluma nazo majida
　　eMhlathuz' eMalambane.
Ngiphuma phansi ushay'eng im-
　　fula uphuza ushay' engiphum'
　　eNdumo la ngisuka khona
　　esitolo sakithi engithenga
　　kuso leso.
Yimina madoda umfana ongay-
　　idl' inyama yenkomo ngama-
　　phisisi.
Umfana kaKhila lo umahamba
　　ngendlela umuntu owazala
　　mina angimazi ngazi umuntu
　　owazala umah.
Induna yami engiphethe uN-
　　kosinathi, umfan' kankosi
　　umfo kaMathenjwa.
Ngaphezulu kamoya akukhanyi
　　la ngiphuma khona.
Ngithe hlupheka hluphekile uma
　　ngizonda wajabule' bangithan-
　　dayo.
Ngiyambonga mina uMandela
　　ubekhona kulomhlab' ukuba
　　akekho uMandela ukuba ayifi-
　　kanga indebe e-South Afrika.
Waboza uMadiba ujele izwe
　　Lethu uMandela.
ihoba ihaya ihoba ihaya [bridge]

Hey, I'm speaking to you guys in
　　Mhlathuzi Malambane.
I come from down there by the
　　river where I drink, I come
　　from Ndumo, that's where I
　　come from, that's the store
　　where I shop.
I, men, am the boy who does not
　　eat beef in small pieces.
I am the brother of Killer, the one
　　who walks alone on the path,
　　the person who created me I
　　do not know, I only know the
　　one who created my mother.
My headman, the one that I belong
　　to is Nkosinathi, son of the chief,
　　brother of Mathenjwa.
On top, where the wind does not
　　shine, that's where I come from.
I say those who suffer will suffer
　　more if they hate me. I will be
　　happy for those who love me.
I thank Mandela for being here in
　　this world, because if Mandela
　　was not here then the cup
　　would not have come to South
　　Africa.
Madiba rotted in jail. Mandela
　　rotted for our country.
[Vocables]

The meanings of several phrases in these izibongo are obscure. Mathenjwa claims, for instance, that he is "the brother of Killer." This could be read as a boast, or alternatively as an indication that he is not to be trifled with. A second phrase, "Ngaphezulu kamoya akukhanyi" (On top, where the wind does not shine), is difficult to interpret. "On top" refers perhaps to the high ground of Ndumo Hill where he lives. The peculiarities of "wind does not shine" suggest an idiomatic reading. Where words are indecipherable, it could be that their meanings are coded by the shape of the performance itself. Some words and syllables in "Bafana Bafana" are delivered too quickly for accurate transcription. This matter will be explored in more detail when the musical dimensions to izibongo and the role of speech tones are considered. It is common practice in izibongo for syllables to be concatenated and sometimes entirely omitted, just as Krige pointed out for izibongo zamakhosi. In such instances the tonal features of isiZulu are compromised, and meanings must be inferred based on context rather than articulation. This practice holds its own logic and could be read as a barrier to facile interpretations, an invitation instead for close listening, or an encoding that operates as an obstruction or deferral. The bravura of umaskandi takes on an elusive character, allowing the orator a further degree of license through ambiguity.

A third example further demonstrates the importance of prosodic features in the interpretation of izibongo. Mfaz' Omnyama was one of the most prolific professional musicians in South Africa during the early postapartheid period. In the izibongo to the song "Nay' inkinga," he invokes powers and asserts authority to an audience sensitive to a wide array of Zulu symbolism. He introduces himself as an *inyanga* (herbalist) and describes this close affinity for ancestral spirits as part of his lineage. To invoke spirits and divine powers in the most public of musical displays serves to intimidate competitors, and at the same time claims a spiritual authority that is very much in keeping with the institution of the imbongi.

EXAMPLE 5.4: "Nay' inkinga" (There is the problem) Mfaz' Omnyama (2000)[29]

Hha! Zash' mfana mshini	Ha! I say this is the boy who is
wezidalwa zabantu!	a machine manufacturing
We'Mfaz Omnyama nezingane	human beings!
zakho.	Mfaz' Omnyama and his children.
Nangu phela umfana ozalwa	Girls, I am dying with the insult
yinyanga.	of "mother."

Kanti naye uyinyanga
Futhi ugogo wakhe isangoma.
Kanti umfowabo ngumthakathi.
Khuphuka lapho dlala beyiduda
    beyithengela amasaka
Nguye uMaqhude njalo umfo
    kaSabelo
Ngimthatha le eStanger
Kanti naye uGeorgie, impunga!
Ikhona lapho ibhasi-ghita
    bomabili
We vuka!

There is the boy who is the child
    of an herbalist.
In fact, he is an herbalist too
And his grandmother is a diviner.
In fact, his brother is a wizard.
He has improved the one who
    enjoys playing who used to
    buy mealie pap.
He is Maqhude, this brother of
    Sabelo
I brought him from Stanger
And in fact, Georgie, grayed!
There are two bass guitars there
Wake up!

The proof of his powers is demonstrated in his success in umaskandi. After all, he has "improved" the lives of the musicians in his band. The personal praises in this song provide a context for interpreting others. In the song "uVelaphi wamashushu dali?" for instance, we find similar statements at the outset, but they are not fully developed. In this song, Mfaz' Omnyama sings about a lover whose suspicious and drunken behavior he treats with contempt. A comparison of the izibongo of the two songs "Nay' inkinga" and "uVelaphi wamashushu dali?" points to several consistencies in his practice.

EXAMPLE 5.5: "uVelaphi wamashushu dali?" (Where do you come from, restless darling?) Mfaz' Omnyama (1997),[30] solo and chorus

Solo: Uvelaphi dali? Uvelaphi
    unje?
Uvelaphi dali-we?
Chorus: Wemashushu njen'
Awu, we-dali
Solo: Uvelaphi?
Uvelaphi dali?
Wen' uyaphuza dali

Where do you come from,
    darling? Where do you come
    from looking like this?
Where do you come from, my
    darling?
Chorus: Why are you so restless?
Oh, my darling
Where do you come from?
Where do you come from, darling?
You drink, darling.

The izibongo broaden the narrative and comment as if in conversation with fellow band members and peers.

Ayi, zashi' uphela	Hey, I say to you,
Mbhobho womathambo.	A horn to blow the bones.
Bhensa maqina	He crouches hard
Mfaz' Omnyama nezingane zakhe.	Mfaz' Omnyama and his children.
Matshitshi qomane safa kanyoko inhlamba	Virgin girls agree to the courtship, we are tired of the "mother" insult.
Phezulu kwaNongoma lapho engiqhamuka khona.	On top of Nongoma, that's where I come from.
Kuphuma uGeorgie lomfana ngimlandele kanti	I brought this boy, Georgie, in fact
Uthini Sitayela lapho?	What do you say about this, Styler?
Uthini wemfana ziyavova?	What do you say, boy who makes beer?
Hheyi la, ngehlelwa inkinga ngelinyelanga	Eish, there I encountered a problem one day
Ngihlezi nomuntu kant' angimazi ukuthi isidakwa uyaphuza.	I am living with a person but I did not know [she] is an alcoholic who [still] drinks.
Ngathi ngiyabheka ngelinye ilanga.	I tell you I found out one day.
Hawu, phela kuyasha langaphansi kwesikhindi.	Eish, it's really burning down in those underpants
Kwavela kwaphela itrue love!	True love is over!

These izibongo include an extension of the praises from "Nay' inkinga." "Mbhobho womathambo" refers again to his status as an inyanga from the line "Nangu phela umfana ozalwa yinyanga." The "horn" is used in acts of divination to blow bones thrown by an *isangoma* (diviner) to determine an ailment or to establish a cause. Mfaz' Omnyama invokes the act to give power to his praises, and in homage to his ancestors. In "uVelaphi wamashushu dali?" he refers to his place of birth, Nongoma, and converses with his band mates, Georgie and Sitayela. It is only in the final third that he turns to address more directly the subject of the song itself: the drunk woman he has been living with and whom he is suspicious of. At this point in the izibongo, he slows down the rate of delivery considerably even while the tempo of the music remains steady. The opening lines are declaimed at maximum speed, with very rapid and almost incomprehensible self-praising. Then he takes time to draw out a sardonic reflection on his feelings and repressed anger at being misled. He takes a long breath before uttering the words "inkinga ngelinyelanga," and similarly at the beginning of each of the remaining phrases with a pitch accent placed on "angi-mâzi" (I did not *know*). It is this state of ignorance and suspicion that pervades the song and that is reinforced in the prosody. The use of pitch accent is crucial here to the tone of this commentary.

The sense of deception is made explicit in the reference to sexual infidelity and disease in the second to last line, "phela kuyasha langaphansi kwesikhindi" (it's really burning down in those underpants). This creates a point of narrative contrast following his request to "matshitshi" (virgin girls) to accept his courtship. References to sexual potency are thematic to Mfaz' Omnyama's izibongo. In perhaps his greatest hit "Tshitshi lami" (My girl), he makes a similar boast in the izibongo, where, as in the song "Nay' inkinga," he refers to himself as "mfana mshini wezidalwa zabantu" (the boy who is a machine manufacturing human beings). A further parallel extolled in both songs is the danger of alcohol. In "Tshitshi lami" he warns young men to beware of beer ("pasopa itshwala!"), perhaps also in view of its tendency to obscure judgment.

We see in these examples a combination of elements that accord with genre-specific features of umaskandi izibongo that are both semantic and prosodic. Mfaz' Omnyama relies on patterns of alliteration, assonance, repetition, and concatenation of words and vocables to achieve a convincing performance. These articulatory features are their own music. They simultaneously conceal the meaning of the lyrics, which employ imagery that is aphoristic, obscure, or even deliberate gobbledygook. In these ways, izibongo place considerable cognitive demands not only on the performer but on listeners too. This elusive quality is part of an aesthetic of concealment and ambiguity used to similar effect in Jonathan Mathenjwa's izibongo.

There are also supra-textual elements specific to the mode of delivery that must factor into our interpretation. The speed, control, percussive articulation, and carefully weighted phrasing of Mfaz' Omnyama's performance displays considerable bravura comparable perhaps only to iHashi Elimhlophe among contemporary umaskandi in the sophistication of the praising. These technical attributes facilitate several expressive purposes, including, crucially, a dramatic posturing by the songster: elements of display, self-parody, play, and humor alternate rapidly and are actively engaged with and enjoyed by listeners who applaud the characteristic jest of the imbongi. It is this play of prosody and gesture that conveys with communicative force the drama of umaskandi over and above its strictly semantic dimensions, some of which, by virtue of their articulation, are lost. The analysis of these prosodic dimensions requires the introduction of a technical apparatus and language for it to be described adequately. Before prosodic features are considered in more detail, it is necessary to attend to the contexts for analysis, and to a broader range of scholarship on umaskandi that has sought to link social and musical factors to one another.

ANALYTICAL APPROACHES TO UMASKANDI

Scholarship on maskanda has to date focused on structural features of the guitar styles[31] and on the content and social commentary of the lyrics.[32] Kathryn Olsen and Barbara Titus have continued this tradition in work that takes a more reflexive turn than their progenitors, Rycroft, Clegg, and Davies.[33] Titus foregrounds what she describes as her "Eurogenic" hearings of maskanda using transcriptions in staff notation. She points out that "music analysis is a culturally specific social practice rather than a transcendental capacity to objectively dissect a unit into parts."[34] This truism of critical musicology folds neatly onto a body of maskanda scholarship that is increasingly homogeneous in scope and insight, written as a framing of Zulu music that feeds into global discourses of power and appropriation as well as local discourses of ethnicity and identity politics.

That music analysis is a function of the tools it employs is self-evident. Staff notation prescribes the categories of a tonal system even before we have understood the nature of that system for a particular culture. Its limitations therefore need to be stressed; otherwise, what we take as fact are the characteristic features of a culture's tonal structure, harmonic practice, or rhythmic dimensions even where this emphasis is unwarranted or irrelevant to the expressive demands of the culture. In short, what we take to be normative about a musical practice is too often limited by the inappropriate application of tools prescribed for the analysis of Western art music. In the analysis of maskanda, these tools are still those of Western staff notation—or at least this is so for Rycroft, Davies, and Titus. It should not be surprising therefore that Titus and Davies reach similar findings to Rycroft. His analytic reduction of tonal systems in the pitch patterning of Princess Magogo's ughubu bow music is a classic instance of the reductive impulse,[35] and it is carried over in subsequent theories of Zulu tonal systems that are satisfied with triadic explanations at the expense of a practice more variegated in its gradience and asymmetry.

To take account of elements of gradience and variation, I choose to depart from staff notation because the uses of pitch in song and izibongo, or to put it in less prescriptive terms, in vocal musicking all told, cannot be defined by the range and structure of musical instruments tuned to a well-tempered system. The voice is an instrument of its own. I use the software application Praat as an alternative to staff notation to show how the pitch contours of izibongo are inflected by factors of speech tone, intonation, and melody.[36] The advantage of these analytical pitch reductions is that the details of pitch production are not reduced to categories of perception. It is for us to make sense of what these categories may be, and to establish how they function. We need ask: why should we find it necessary, as music scholars, always to invoke common practice tonality as a frame of reference? If the answer is mere convenience, then we need to work harder at making sense of sounds that do not conform to Western norms.

To use technological innovations for pitch analysis is not new.[37] It is common practice in linguistics to use fundamental frequency pitch-tracking software to analyze tone and intonation, and I employ similar methods here using the software application Praat, which is designed for linguistic research. This is not to claim for these methods any more distance or objectivity than others. It is to simply to recognize in this an alternative that does not reify categories of pitch and duration unique to umaskandi.

In the following transcriptions, pitch is graphed from low to high using a measure of frequency in hertz. The range for these recordings is 50–550 Hz. The gradience of pitch is retained in this linear analysis, which provides a clear indication of the curvature of intonation gradients. The articulation of consonants and fricatives give rise to brief lapses in these gradients, which appear blank on the transcription, but these spaces are usually filled in by our auditory system.[38] The use of digital recording technologies is not without complication. Sampling errors must be carefully checked. I have edited the pitch contours by removing octave jumps or other clear and obvious errors in sampling, and I have used my ear to transcribe sections that are indeterminate to Praat but that have a distinctly falling [\], rising [/], falling-rising [↓], rising-falling [↑], or level [_] pitch contour (tone is transcribed as phonetic here). I have chosen to indicate pitch movement rather than individual high or low tone contrasts. This is to indicate the ways in which microprosodic elements condition melody. Prosodic features will remain invisible and inaudible to us until we have a technical vocabulary for describing them and a set of tools for depicting them. The prosodic dimensions of izibongo distinguish them from both song and speech. The analysis that follows enables us to recognize the factors of tone, intonation, rhythm, and rate that are distinctive of umaskandi izibongo. To understand how these fit together means taking account of prosodic features as well as considering how these have been approached in music and linguistic theory.

PROSODIC FEATURES AND STRUCTURE

Prosody refers to suprasegmental features, or "those aspects of speech that involve more than single consonants or vowels. The principal suprasegmental features are stress, length, tone, and intonation."[39] Features of tone and intonation are conditioned by the manipulation of pitch to convey both lexical and grammatical meanings. In isiZulu, semantic tone is limited to a contrastive high versus low pitch relation between adjacent word segments. The pitch height of speech tone is relative rather than absolute, as is the case for melody. Intonation refers to the gradation of pitch contours over the course of an utterance. Fluctuations in pitch are used to signal prominence and to convey paralinguistic meanings and affective states. In izibongo, where conventions of speech prosody are sometimes ignored, there is substantial play with prosodic elements of tone and intonation.

The importance of speech tone and intonation in African song has been recognized by many scholars, and not least because most African languages are tone languages. For instance, J. H. Kwabena Nketia observes that "music and language are not only parallel . . . but also that text-tune relations are integral."[40] Arthur Morris Jones and Kofi Agawu provide detailed insight into the features and function of speech tone and its relationship to melody.[41] John Blacking's classic text *Venda Children's Songs*[42] is perhaps the most detailed account of an African tone system with transcription and analysis of some fifty songs. An important feature of this study is the way in which Blacking links social dimensions to musical practice without reifying an "objective" pitch structure. Thomas F. Johnston on Tsonga music, Deirdre Hansen on Xhosa music,[43] and David Rycroft on Zulu music have explained similar principles in Nguni and closely related language groups.[44] To date, this body of research on pitch prosody has focused on establishing the "rules" and formal function of speech tone as well as its interaction in the ordering of melody in "traditional" music. Discussion of intonation is generally restricted to the observation that downdrift plays a major role in the structure of melodic contour. None of these studies have yet dealt with the tonal features of izibongo in umaskandi, with only Rycroft contributing to the study of izibongo in Nguni song. In his paper "Zulu Melodic and Non-Melodic Vocal Styles," Rycroft compares *ukubonga* (praising) to *ukuhlabelela* (song) and makes the following remarks: "Regarding pitch usage, definite levels of stable pitch recur to some extent, and certainly to a greater extent than is the case either in 'non-melodic' song items . . . or in speech."[45] He also points to differences in duration; for ukubonga, "natural speech rhythm is given a free rein, often at a very rapid tempo. The only rhythmic distortion—or perhaps stylization, in this case—involves prolongation of stanza-initial vowels, and even greater prolongation of stanza-penultimate vowels than occurs in normal speech."[46]

The following analyses focus on features of speech tone and intonation in izibongo. The goal here is to theorize the relations between prosody, melody, and semantics. Consideration of these prosodic dimensions provides a sonic complement to the interpretation of izibongo texts. isiZulu is a tone language in which semantic tone plays a crucial role in distinguishing the meaning of otherwise identical words. High versus low tone contrast is used. In some instances, its realization is complicated by various forms of assimilation and concatenation, and by the action of depressor consonants in addition to downdrift intonation. Depressor consonants include "all voiced fricatives, clicks, and plosives (excepting implosive *b*), and all compounds containing these sounds."[47] The action of these consonants results in a drastic lowering of pitch in the following syllable. We see this often in speech and song where these consonants result in a sharp decline in pitch. "High-toned syllables beginning with such consonants commence with a brief rising on-glide (or the high tone may be displaced to the next syllable in some cases if this has a non-lowering consonant . . .). Likewise, descending off-glides from high tones are conditioned by a succeeding consonant of this type."[48] These "depression" features seem also to influence an overall downdrift in intonation for both song and speech.[49]

The action of depressors in izibongo is less clear than for speech. Rycroft describes a finite arrangement of just four pitch levels in izibongo.[50] In a later study based on the analysis of *Izibongo zikaDingana* (The praises of Dingane),[51] Rycroft and A. Bhekabantu Ngcobo transcribed Princess Magogo's rendition of King Dingane's izibongo (as recorded by Jeff Opland in 1974), and discovered that the tonal and durational features contrasted markedly with the renditions by James Stuart and John Mngadi recorded for Rycroft's earlier study.[52] Unlike the prior examples, Princess Magogo retains the downdrift intonation characteristic of spoken and sung utterances in isiZulu. Nollene Davies observes a similar patterning in umaskandi, stating that "the overall movement of melodic patterns here and in the rest of the song, is descending. Thus, it appears that maskanda musicians regard their scales as beginning with the highest frequency and then descending. . . . The izibongo are recited with a slight fall in pitch in each section."[53] It appears, then, that Rycroft's early results are anomalous and that downdrift intonation is characteristic of many izibongo.[54]

CASE STUDIES IN ANALYSIS

Two examples of umaskandi izibongo are analyzed here as case studies. These are not representative or distinctive of umaskandi since its exponents adopt widely divergent styles and modes of delivery, many of which are highly unconventional. It is a genre that has developed in multiple directions for several decades, and with increasing technological sophistication in the postapartheid era. The early practice of minstrels accompanied on guitar and concertina gradually gave way to bands, small ensembles with vocal accompaniment, groups inclusive of male and female umaskandi, and to various forms of backing in dance and song. I know of several contemporary groups in which the dancers perform to backing tracks and have only limited involvement in the singing and composition of songs. All these forms of umaskandi coexist.

Since the introduction of drum machines, synthesizers, and digital effects in studio work, there has been a great deal of electronic experimentation in umaskandi, even if basic structural features, including izibongo, remain intact. This modernization or rather commercialization process has to some degree resulted in a disjuncture in the previously strong rural-urban interface of the genre and its newer "world music" character. Some of the umaskandi whom I record in rural areas request that I add drum-and-bass backing tracks to their records. This professional quality is thought to enhance the songs' popularity and their potential for radio play. The lyrics to these songs remain rooted in experience, in local features of place and identity that tend not to take on the broader social themes and commentaries characteristic of professional artists like Phuzekhemisi. It is therefore erroneous to consider the performances of a handful of professionals as characteristic of the genre. Most performers are amateurs, and yet very little research has been documented on their musical practices to date. For these and other reasons, this chapter is not intended as a survey. Instead, it offers a close reading of two texts to demonstrate the utility of new ways of listening to and representing African music using digital technologies. The transcription and analysis of pitch and durational patterning in the songs "Imbizo" by Phuzekhemisi and Khethani, and "Bafana Bafana" by Jonathan Mathenjwa, enable us to carefully examine the prosodic structure of umaskandi izibongo, and more specifically the action or suppression of speech tones, the role of downdrift intonation, as well as the rate and articulation of individual syllables. This shows how izibongo are a product of semantic and prosodic complements.

A note on method: pitch tracks were extracted from each of the two recordings using Praat. "Imbizo" is a commercial recording, and so it was not possible to extract the pitch from only the lead vocal track. The song has a steady and deliberate duple time beat overlaid with guitar and concertina riffs that repeat as a ground for the verse/chorus and izibongo (see the lyrics for an outline of the structure). The "Bafana Bafana" pitch track is more accurate because I used a multitrack recording technique to isolate the lead vocals using a head-mounted condenser microphone with a flat frequency response. The graphs generated for both pitch tracks are organized paradigmatically in terms of pitch profiles drawn from the fundamental frequency and measured in Hz on the y axis from 50 to 550 Hz; syllables of the text; and pitch movements of the individual segments represented as symbols. The syntagmatic dimension is structured according to the segmentation of individual syllables in time. These correspond to pitch movements and indicate the rate of utterance measured in seconds on the x axis.

"Imbizo"

Figure 5.3 is a transcription of the izibongo from the song "Imbizo" by Phuzekhemisi and Khethani. This is a classic instance of early '90s umaskandi. Phuzekhemisi performs the izibongo in this song in a fashion that contrasts with the styles of iHashi Elimhlophe and Mfaz' Omnyama, both of whom have a much faster rate of delivery, higher pitched vocals, and a more variegated range of expression. As Kathryn Olsen points out,[55] Phuzekhemisi's style was influenced by the pioneering umaskandi of the previous generation, Phuzushukela, whose declamation of izibongo fluctuated between the liquid and the languorous.

Figure 5.3 shows characteristic features of intonation, speech tone, and melody as described by Rycroft, Davies, and several others. The depressor action of consonants results in rapid lowering of pitch on several syllables. The articulation of fricatives, clicks, and plosives has a consistent pitch-lowering effect, which is

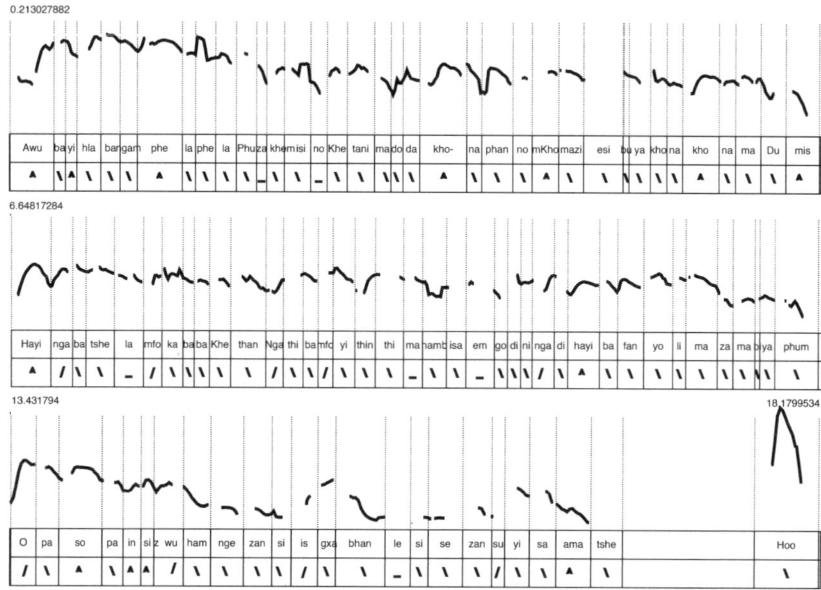

FIGURE 5.3 Analytical pitch reduction of izibongo from the song "Imbizo" by Phuzekhemisi and Khethani. Created by Thomas Pooley.

noticeable also in the on-glides to high tones. Sixty-seven of the ninety-nine segments have a descending pitch contour [\], and eleven have a rising-falling pitch contour [↑]. These depressor features seem also to factor in the gradual lowering of pitch across the course of the utterance. This downdrift intonation is a feature of spoken isiZulu. There are very few instances of level pitch. It is difficult to see how staff notation could be used to accurately represent these pitch movements, considering the extent of variation in the pitch categories used. This does not mean that umaskandi musicians do not use what I call "pitch targets" to orient and structure pitch relations. On the contrary, pitch targets play a crucial role in structuring the pitch space of Zulu songs where there is considerable gradience in the structure of pitch contours.

As shown in figure 5.3, the tonal features of izibongo are represented in descriptive form by the pitch track in the upper system. The overall pattern of the intonational contour shows a gradual descent or downdrift. The pitch patterns are broken up into phrases so that each line indicates a single breath group. Breaks in the pitch pattern indicate stronger consonantal articulations, although the line is often perceived to be entirely continuous. The text in the middle system is divided into syllables to show how pitch categories are rendered in relation to the action of articulators. The pitch categories in the lower system indicate the direction of pitch movement and are used to measure and compare the action of depressor consonants. The action of these consonants has pitch-lowering effects, such as at segments twelve and twenty-three. There are also numerous on-glides. The division of syllables also indicates the rate of utterance measured in syllables per second.

The action of depressor features also influences length. Vowels in syllables without these consonants are often longer and are used for expressive purposes, including pitch bends, such as "Awu" [1] and "Hayi" [37]. The action of depressor consonants is prevalent and is seldom violated since it is a phonetic feature of vocal production. Each of the three breath groups beginning at [1], [37], and [75] show a distinct downward trend from high to low. Where the rate of utterance is high, such as in the first two breath groups, there is an initial high point reached, followed by a relatively monotonic declamation ending in a short downward glide. Where the rate decreases in the final breath group, there is more variation in pitch, outlining a quasi-melodic mode of declamation closer to song. It appears, then, that the complexity of pitch renderings is to some extent dependent on the pressure gradient in the airflow mechanism.

The rate of utterance is fast, at roughly six syllables per second with frequent concatenation. This leads to ambiguity for two reasons. In the first instance, words and syllables are lost or blended into one another and crucial concords are omitted, leaving the listener without the necessary grammatical cues. In the second instance, the speed of utterance does not allow the listener sufficient time to make meaningful sense of the words uttered. Idiomatic language runs by too quickly to facilitate comprehension. Even the attentive listener struggles to anchor a listening without proper contextual information. This is not the case for all izibongo, and it is also not consistently the case even within a single performed izibongo. This is a musical strategy on the part of the umaskandi, who must decide when and where to use speed and lyrical ambiguity for dramatic purposes. Speed and ambiguity figure most prominently where messages are deliberately coded or elusive, and they result in a distinctive prosodic profile. Usually, this profile is characterized by a drifting intonation curve that supersedes individual speech tone requirements, and by a rapid rate of delivery and concomitant concatenation of syllables.

Finally, we need to recognize that there is a musical rationale to the structure of izibongo. The declamation of izibongo must entrain to their musical ground.

In "Imbizo," the phrasing of each of the three breath groups are structured according to the cycles of the call-and-response guitar-concertina accompaniment to which Phuzekhemisi entrains his vocals. The izibongo are not declaimed in free rhythm but are carefully attenuated to the meter of the musical accompaniment, defined as it is by the proportions of cyclical melodic and rhythmic riffs.[56] Figure 5.4 provides similar evidence of these prosodic trends.

"Bafana Bafana"

"Bafana Bafana" conforms to the conventional izibongo form outlined by Davies,[57] perhaps more so than Phuzekhemisi's praises, which are shorter. Figure 5.4 shows distinct downdrift intonation for all the izibongo breath groups with a penultimate low tone or very low finalis. This cadential low supersedes inherent speech tone requirements. The action of depressor consonants is especially noticeable on stops such as "du" [15, 38] and "phu" [31], although phrase-initial "phum" rises to a primary high point. This structural cue is characteristic of most izibongo. The intonation of each breath group tends to flatten out toward the end, suggesting a physiological constraint that is perhaps a consequence of the very high rate of vocal declamation. Figure 5.4 contains within it a phrase of the vocalized component of the song. This is extracted from immediately after the izibongo [212–235] and provides a useful point of comparison for features of izibongo and song. The sung portion consists of two sub-phrases with the second sub-phrase divided again in two. This explains the occurrence of secondary high points at [226] and [232], where the singer takes additional breaths.

The overall pattern of the intonational contour indicates downdrift declination.[58] The pitch pattern is broken up into phrases so that each line indicates a single breath group. The action of depressor consonants has pitch-lowering effects evident at [15] and [78]. Sometimes this pitch-lowering effect is overridden by other expressive needs, such as [36] at the very beginning of a breath group. On-glides, such as at [151], show this depressor function too. In "Bafana Bafana" the rate of utterance is extremely fast at nearly seven syllables per second. This makes it exceedingly difficult for the listener to make sense of the lyrics in real time. The consequence of such speed is that the umaskandi must concatenate or leave out words and syllables to fit the izibongo to the accompaniment. It is the musical phrase structure, not the izibongo, that defines the period.

The depressor action of speech tones, and their consequent on- and off-glides are conditioned by several factors. For instance, Mathenjwa tends toward less

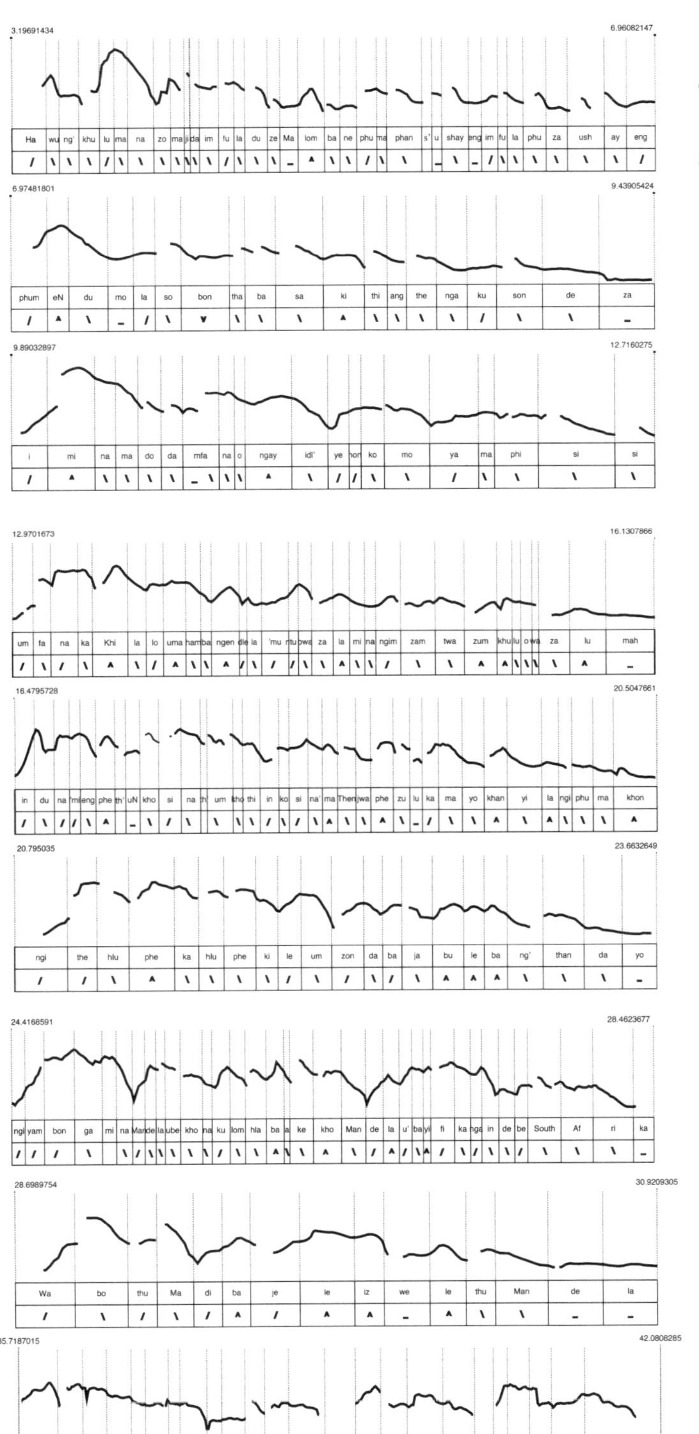

FIGURE 5.4 Analytical pitch reduction of izibongo from the song "Bafana Bafana" by Jonathan Mathenjwa. Created by Thomas Pooley.

precipitous and more rounded pitch-height adjustments. This leads to a measure of ambiguity in the interpretation of the lyrics that is a consequence of two prosodic factors: rate of delivery and downdrift intonation. Just as in the "Imbizo" example, a compromise is reached for musical reasons. The umaskandi must fit his izibongo to the cycles of the guitar accompaniment. Not all these syllables are clearly articulated, and so the analyst must infer meanings from close and repeated listening. A comparison with the sung portion of the song makes this point. Singing happens at a rate of 3.65 syllables per second, or at roughly half the speed of the izibongo. This is significant for two reasons: the lyrics are easily comprehended because the articulation is clear, and the umaskandi has time to engage in expressive melodic fluctuations. In other words, expressive melody is a function of time and breath. This is evident, also, in the recordings by Mfaz' Omnyama, who tends to engage in melodic play when he slows the pace of his recitations.

Why do some umaskandi insist on such fast izibongo? It would be much simpler to compose shorter lines and fit these to the accompaniment with ample time to spare. The answer points perhaps in two directions. On the one hand, there is the competitive element to the declamation of umaskandi izibongo: the fighter in martial combat with his or her rivals and foes. On the other hand, there are aesthetic considerations involving poetry and play. The meanings of izibongo—as with many other Zulu idioms and stories—remain resistant to simplistic interpretation, thus allowing for creative individual responses to complex social phenomena through performance. The umaskandi treats the izibongo very often as the pinnacle of their art, as the distinctive signature of their person, and as the measure of their artistic achievement. Artists are measured in relation to a set of conventions that for umaskandi izibongo have solidified into a critical practice.

Features of duration have been discussed only briefly in this chapter because the focus here is on pitch as an expressive device. Even so, there is a close relation between pitch and rhythm in song and speech. This is evident in cases where a relatively free rhythm is adopted, such as at the very beginning of the izibongo, and the vocalist must still abide by the underlying pulse in his or her segmentation of syllables and breath groups. The tonal features of the melodies provide structure and inspiration for the melodic intonational structure of the izibongo. Breath control conditions tone. Where speed takes precedence over intelligibility, or rather, where musical fit trumps semantics, as it does in Mathenjwa's izibongo, speech tone requirements are superseded by the logic of melody and meter. The consequence is a surplus of meaning characteristic of umaskandi izibongo.

This chapter offers contextualized readings of umaskandi izibongo as social texts of time and place, in addition to close analysis of their prosodic features. The reification of fixed rules of practice, of distinct levels and combinations of tones and intonational features, does not fit this broad interpretation of umaskandi izibongo, but it does provide a framework for interpreting details of prosodic structure that illuminate the performative and dramatic dimensions of umaskandi. The violations of linguistic conventions so characteristic of umaskandi izibongo display a bravura and uncompromising directness that is very much a part of the martial tradition from which these popular praises originated. The analysis of prosodic pitch movements in the izibongo of Phuzekhemisi and Jonathan Mathenjwa shows how pitch is conditioned by a range of cognitive factors, including deliberate acts of manipulation, to create dramatically satisfying performances. The desire by umaskandi to perform their praises at the top of their voices and as fast as possible explains some of the ambiguity and complexity in these praises. This social-aesthetic dimension to the practice of praising suggests that we locate it within a broader realm of sociocultural signification that is musical to the core.

In these myriad ways, we find that umaskandi izibongo blur the lines between song and speech to create a paralanguage that superimposes and impinges upon semantic readings of the music. The appreciation of umaskandi artistry is best figured then through a "thick" interpretation of its simultaneous semantic, prosodic, and paramusical dimensions. The ambiguity and elusiveness of umaskandi texts emerge from the frenetic renderings of their idiomatic and obscure uses of language and imagery. This coded aesthetic is consistent with the practice of the imbongi praise singers from which their practice emerged in the mid-twentieth century, and against and into which it may be read, but the dimensions of umaskandi izibongo are nevertheless unique in form and structure, virtuosity, and humor, and in the audacious response they continue to present to forces of oppression and colonialism. This is a minstrel art of telling and untelling, of paralinguistic and paramusical communication, and of musicking par excellence. We are invited to listen closely. The sharp social and political commentary offered by umaskandi is created in a richly symbolic language that displays fitness, skill, and standing in a community, and it renders humane the experiences of dispossession, alienation, and inequality that are the everyday reality for South Africa's urban and rural poor. *Hawu, ng'khuluma naz'!*[59]

SIX

Inscribing Tradition

Poverty, Inequality, and the Politics of Performance in Schools

SKHEMELELE COMMUNITY HALL, AUGUST 30, 2012

I clink two rand into a margarine tin brimful of coin as we surge through the doors of the Skhemelele Community Hall. Today's competition is the community event of the season. The Ingwavuma Circuit schools championships. Inside, enthused supporters have packed out the venue. The excited audience members, fashioned in a mix of traditional and smart attire, are brandishing sloganed placards of support. Ululation rings out in choruses. Outside, the tarmac is a chaotic stretch of overloaded taxis, emptied *bakkies* (vans), arrivals and departures. The adjacent patchwork field is littered with broken glass, squashed Coca-Cola tins, and crumpled candy wrappers. Barefoot dancers are matched in short skirts and *amabheshu* (buttock-covering skins), plastic-beaded outfits, smart waistcoats, and ties. Barebacked dancers congregate in long shivering lines, covering their chests with arms and shawls, waiting. Parents and friends pose, animated in conversation. Inside, a raucous throng of song bursts out with joyous energy. The steel-corrugated roof is the diaphragm for a sweep of sound punctuated only by ear-splittingly-amped announcements on the PA system. A sparkling array of plastic trophies fronts the leopard-skin print of the stage drapes. Light pours in from a cavity above, illuminating a dusty halo over the dancers who kick their feet high into the air before thudding down in concrete cadence. Boys wave *sjamboks* (long, stiff whip made from hide) to discipline their troupes. Girls assemble with long Shembe trumpets that splutter in guttural bursts. The quiet, close harmonies of isicathamiya are followed by izibongo praise poetry, the reverent hymnody of amahubo anthems, bright gospel, and frenetic disco dancing. Excitement builds to crescendo with the crowd favorite: ingoma dance. The emcee's pleas for order are drowned out in the delirium. Adjudicators sit, brows furrowed, seated at discrete intervals along white-bedecked trestle tables, now, to deliver the winners. Keyboards, mixing desks, DJs, and dignitaries line the walls. Children disappear, reappear leaping, peering in through tightly shut windows above, anxious to see all that transpires. Unionists look on. Today's winners will take home the glory, respect, and story for many a year to come.

———

Inequality defines the postapartheid condition. Twenty-one years after South Africa's first democratic elections in 1994, the nation has moved to radical levels of socioeconomic polarization considered among the worst in the world. Poverty, unemployment, and lack of opportunity are the consuming reality for millions of South Africans. The education sector was identified as key to socioeconomic

FIGURE 6.1 Ingwavuma Circuit Arts and Cultural Activities Competition
at Skhemelele Community Hall, August 30, 2012.

empowerment for the poor and the working class, and expenditure on education now amounts to nearly 20 percent of the national budget.[1] But the impact of policy reforms and broad spending has been blunted by poor service delivery, inefficiency, corruption, as well as limited skills and capacity in government. The financial constraints on poor families continue to limit access to quality education at all levels. The crisis reached breaking point with the "Fees Must Fall" campaigns at universities across South Africa in 2015. These protests were a long time coming and reflect on a myriad of challenges in the higher education sector, including the unequal status of students from poor communities. Rajendra Chetty observes this problem in South African schools in an essay on class.

> The limited number of black students who are able to secure scholarships, are the privileged ones with good matriculation results from advantaged schools where parents are able to afford high fees. The opportunities for poor and working-class students from townships, informal settlements and dysfunctional schools, who are in far greater financial need, are limited when the key factor for funding is merit, as opposed to poverty, class and need. The interests of the poor and marginalized are unfortunately not the foundation on which the post-apartheid educational system is built (since the advent of democracy in 1994), although there are constitutional and other imperatives to achieve a just, fair, equitable and humane social order with the mélange of official policy that only looks impressive at face value.[2]

The bifurcation of the education sector in South Africa into its public and private dimensions has only exacerbated inequality, and this trend shows no sign of abating. Over the past two decades, quality education has become increasingly unaffordable to all but the middle class and the rich.[3] Those who can afford it opt for well-resourced private and public schools that employ skilled teachers. By contrast, many of the public schools to which the working class and poor are sent must make do with limited resources for teaching and learning. In rural areas there are still schools without basic services like electricity, running water, and functional utilities. These straitened conditions are compounded by other factors, including a shortage of instructors, regular and protracted strike action by teachers, minimal oversight or regulation of teaching and administration, a paucity of textbooks and specialized learning materials, overcrowded classrooms, and a curriculum that is complexly ordered and difficult to implement.[4] In a specialized field like music, there is inadequate training of teachers and little to no funding for materials, instruments, and venues. How are teachers and students in rural areas managing these challenges? Where do indigenous music traditions fit into spaces such as these?

This chapter surveys performances of Zulu music and dance in rural schools in the northern reaches of the uMkhanyakude District of northeastern KwaZulu-Natal, focusing on inequality and exclusion in indigenous musicking, and the reinvention of tradition through the efforts of the provincial Department of Arts and Culture. Education is a site at which inequality is reproduced. The contexts for music making in rural schools need to be understood. South Africa's private schools are well-resourced and offer music as a subject up to grade 12. This is not so for most public schools, which do not possess the facilities, nor the trained teachers, to implement music in the higher grades. This in turn perpetuates an inequality marked by dimensions of race and class. State policy and practice are to blame, but so are the distinctive regimes that perpetuate them. The status of music and dance in the Jozini Local Municipality shows how the teaching of music outside of the curriculum is popular, but extracurricular, and so poses barriers to careers in music and the creative arts, as well as to higher education. The internal dynamics of the field of music teaching, as well as the larger social factors impinging on its autonomy, bear scrutiny.

POSTAPARTHEID POLICY AND PRACTICE

In 1994 the priorities of the newly elected Government of National Unity were to address issues of poverty and inequality through the Reconstruction and Development Plan (RDP).[5] The RDP became the rationale for policy reforms right across the postapartheid landscape and was first applied to the education sector with the 1995 publication of the White Paper on Education and Training. Recognizing imbalances in access to and quality of education, government promoted democratic ideals in the national interest: "Our message is that education and training must change. It cannot be business as usual in our schools, colleges, technikons and universities. The national project of reconstruction and development compels everyone in education and training to accept the challenge of creating a system which cultivates and liberates the talents of all our people without exception."[6] The immediate challenge was to dismantle the existing segregationist architecture, and to rebuild and revitalize it with new ways of thinking and doing to "liberate the talent" of all South Africans.

The denigration of non-Western values and indigenous knowledge systems under apartheid had to be addressed and reconciled with the experiences and expertise of most of the population. On a grand scale, the government was tasked with decommissioning the system of "Bantu education" implemented by the apartheid government in the 1950s, a system that had stratified education as ideology.[7] The Bantu Education Act of 1953, and a slew of legislation thereafter, segregated education according to racial and ethnic classifications. A system of Christian National Education was implemented for Whites while Blacks were taught a substandard set of skills to prepare them only for service to their "own communities." Access to higher education for Blacks was curtailed and the training of teachers controlled. These measures were designed to ensure the superiority of Whites in the workforce, and their culture in society. In the process, Black South Africans were denuded of their culture and identity, their indigeneity exoticized and stigmatized as inferior and "primitive."

The White Paper on Arts, Culture and Heritage of 1996 outlined how the arts would be funded for a multiracial South Africa founded on democratic principles. The arts should contribute to the alleviation of poverty and to nation building (reconciliation). As Doreen Nteta, chair of the National Arts Council, explained, "the majority of South Africans did not until 1994 have the freedom to study where and what they wanted. As a result, not many of them studied the arts such as music, dance, theatre, and visual arts. They could not find employment through these disciplines. This has resulted in museums and galleries, theatres and orchestras having no professional black employees."[8] Policies drafted in early postapartheid era insisted on redress and access. Schools and universities were encouraged to rethink their admission policies and to introduce bridging programs for disadvantaged learners.

In 1997 the Department of Education implemented a system of "outcomes-based education" (OBE). Urvi Drummond reports that "the broad imperative for the main policy shifts in education was driven by a political agenda of social transformation and reconciliation and music education [was] thus being shaped more by values . . . than content."[9] The emphasis on values added a new dimension to the nation-building project, but African musical arts remained peripheral in the curriculum. In OBE, citizens were taught not only the mechanical skills to build a nation but also the democratic principles enshrined in the Constitution of 1996. The aims of this policy, writes Drummond, were specific: "massification of music education through the inclusion of many more learners in the music classroom; promoting the study of diverse musics that were previously marginalized; removing 'artificial barriers' to learning and providing a framework for music education that allowed learners to progress at their own pace and placing an emphasis on the group over the individual."[10] Not all these ideals were practical. For instance, massification leads directly to the overburdening of educators, and diversity can only be implemented where sufficient resources and training are available to teachers. This did not happen even after the initial policy document was reviewed in 2000, resulting in the Revised National Curriculum Statement (2002). In this policy, music was contained within the Arts and Culture learning area in a curriculum that also included dance, drama and visual arts, the same basic blueprint in use today.

The implementation of OBE was not successful. One obstacle was the government's decision to shut down teacher training colleges. The integrated approach to teaching through music, rather than specialized teaching of music, was impractical. "The South African Department of Education expects general class teachers, who have no or little specialized music training, not only to teach musical concepts to their classes but also to integrate the expressive arts into other non-music learning areas such as 'numeracy' and 'literacy.'"[11] A survey of teachers in the Western Cape province by Anri Herbst and colleagues demonstrated that many teachers, and especially those without prior training, had considerable difficulty implementing music as part of this new integrated curriculum. The survey authors explained:

> Our research shows that the teacher training that is provided is inadequate and cannot support the expectations of the curriculum now in use. Since 1994, the Department of Education's rationalization scheme has severely reduced the number of teachers training colleges. Many colleges have been closed completely, while others have been amalgamated with either universities or technikons. Where there were once fairly large music departments, now there remain one or two lecturers who are expected to implement the entire syllabus for Arts and Culture.[12]

The entire music education system had been stripped bare. New graduates entered the profession without even elementary knowledge of music. Since music literacy is knowledge of a highly technical nature and takes years to acquire, it is unsurprising that musical arts education is in disarray. Teachers cannot be expected to learn advanced musical skills and knowledge on their own and without support.

The new syllabus sought to counteract the accent on notated traditions prior to 1994, and the exclusion of African indigenous knowledge.[13] This was in theory a welcome move, but its implementation proved difficult. Anri Herbst, Jacques de Wet, and Susan Rijsdijk observe that "the lack of performance-based skills has a disastrous impact on promoting the praxial philosophy of indigenous Africa. Apart from this, very few teachers can improvise and compose music—a core characteristic of the performance-based musical arts in sub-Saharan Africa."[14] Genuine epistemological and pedagogical challenges could not be ignored. Meki Nzewi points out that musical arts education in Africa is holistic and communal rather than individualistic.[15] How are such African musical arts to be taught and examined in a system that privileges individual skill and assessment? The shift from focused instrumental or vocal practice to music as dance, song, and movement require an entirely different skill set, especially where teachers now must think in terms of larger groups and troupes. With limited training and teaching materials, even experienced teachers were not ready to implement the new curriculum. By the time OBE was jettisoned, the damage had already been done.

The revised and almost entirely new National Curriculum and Policy Statement (CAPS) for Grades R–12 was published in 2012. The CAPS document emphasizes diversity and allows students specializing in music the option of three streams: "Western Art Music," "Indigenous African Music," and "Jazz." The goal is to make music education more accessible and relevant in schools, as well as to preserve and revitalize indigenous knowledge systems. The democratic values of earlier policies are reiterated: "This curriculum aims to ensure that children acquire and apply knowledge and skills *in ways that are meaningful to their own lives*. In this regard, the curriculum promotes knowledge in local contexts, while being sensitive to global imperatives."[16] The need for "social transformation" is also recognized in the attempt to redress the educational imbalances of the past. The validation of "indigenous knowledge systems" and the values of the Constitution are prioritized and given expression in various ways in the curriculum for creative arts (Grades R–9) and music (Grades 10–12). It is with these factors in mind that I turn now to a case study that highlights both the opportunities and the challenges associated with the teaching of indigenous African music in KwaZulu-Natal schools. I have experienced firsthand the difficulties encountered by teachers and students. This case study of music education in the Jozini Municipality highlights the vitality of indigenous music practices and the shortcomings of the creative arts system in finding a place for them.

PERFORMANCE IN SCHOOLS

The Jozini Local Municipality of Maputaland is a region in which many families are dependent on relatives who work as migrants in towns and cities. The town of Jozini is the regional hub and mayoral seat, but most adults find work in the industries at Richards Bay, eMpangeni, eThekwini (Durban), and, of course, eGoli (Johannesburg). Thulani Gumede accompanied me as a research assistant and translator (see chapter 1) on visits to schools in the district. Very few had active class music teachers. We also conducted a broader survey of music in the surrounding communities but were frustrated in our efforts because, as Thulani explained it to me, so many households in this part of Maputaland are headed by grandparents and adolescents. The few adults who do remain in these villages work hard to sustain themselves in an unforgiving land. There is little time for musicking as entertainment. Music practices have changed irrevocably with the concomitant breakdown in the structure of communities. Youth enjoy house, hip hop, and rap, which they listen to on their phones, on television, and on radio. Music making in school is different, with children encouraged to perform indigenous and choral musics. In the years we spent researching music in schools, from 2012 to 2017 we attended many choral and dance performances, including regional competitions. Teachers explained to us some of their challenges, and in many ways, it is remarkable the degree to which local communities have integrated their indigenous practices into music making at school.[17]

The conditioning of the body and mind from an early age is what enables the expression of advanced musical skills in all cultures. At Jozini, the indigenous musical practices range from ingoma dance to indlamu, amahubo, amakhwaya, Afro-gospel, and isicathamiya, among several others. iNgoma (danced by girls) and indlamu (danced by boys) are arguably the least syncretic of these dances and are often the highlight of music competitions and festivals. The terms *ingoma* and *indlamu* are inclusive of a wide range of dance styles with their associated rhythms and songs.[18] How to integrate these forms as music and/or dance is a challenge for teachers of the creative arts curriculum because the distinction "music/dance" is borne of epistemologies of sound and meaning into which these indigenous arts do not easily cohere. The dissociation of the body from sound and event is evident most tellingly in the primacy afforded literacy as a measure of value in CAPS. Movement is intrinsic to the practice of indigenous song. Dancers are singers and circuits to the musical pulse, moving in relation to and against the beat, and creating rhythm with their bodies through clapping, stamping, striking, and gesticulating. The aestheticization of indigenous music and dance through the imposition of "universal" concepts and literacies, or its shift to the autonomous sphere of theory, results in a conceptual dissonance the music curriculum has yet to resolve. For as long as these tensions remain unresolved, the practice of musical arts in and outside of schools will struggle to take root because it does not speak to and of the cultures who perform it.

Schools in the Jozini Local Municipality range in size from around two hundred fifty to over fifteen hundred pupils. At least five new schools have been built along the main road between Makhane and Ndumo in the period 2011 to 2021, indicating rapid population expansion. Communities have integrated their indigenous practices into school music. Despite the variety and intensity of indigenous musical arts practices in Jozini, the nine schools we visited did not teach music literacy formally. "Music literacy" is defined here as the practice of reading and writing music using tonic solfa and staff notation. Of course, literacy need not be defined in such exclusive terms, but these are the terms used in South Africa's music education curriculum, and they are considered the sine qua non of musicianship. Schools at Jozini had no textbooks on staff notation, no ruled staves on classroom walls, nor were there chromatic marimbas, pianos, or organs available in assembly room stalls. In fact, most schools had only cowhide drums used for ingoma and indlamu. These are not instruments designed for the teaching of tonic solfa or the grand staff.

Interviews with teachers and principals made clear to me that very few students are directly involved in music activities. These activities usually take place after hours or within clubs and societies. Creative arts teachers are few and far between, and only one whom I met had been trained in music literacy. This was a shock to me at the time, but it has since transpired that very similar conditions exist right across the Gauteng province where music is taught in only a small proportion of schools.[19] At Jozini this reflects a shortage of skills rather than enthusiasm. Music and dance are popular extracurricular activities performed in the buildup to Heritage Month (September). In fact, I was dissuaded from visiting schools outside of the period from July to September because these are the months of the competition season during which learners practice, perform, and compete.

The competitions that begin midyear are highly anticipated events for schools across KwaZulu-Natal. Choirs and dance troupes prepare prescribed and original songs that include indigenous genres, as well as modern dance (disco) and izibongo (praise poetry). I interviewed principals and teachers involved with music to learn more about these events and soon discovered a vibrant community of song and dance. Schools prepared performances for me to record on video and audio, and I attended a two-day circuit competition at Skhemelele Community Hall on July 28 and July 29, 2012.[20] Primary and high schools from the circuit competed from early in the morning through into the evening. These school competitions are supported by the Department of Arts and Culture, and their vibrancy should continue to be supported and celebrated because they mark an exceptional display of skill and flare in indigenous idioms. These skills should be nurtured and developed as a route to further education and training at the tertiary level, as well as into the cultural industries thereafter. The reinvigoration of African creative arts is only possible if the logistic and epistemological challenges of forging an inclusive, holistic, and pragmatic curriculum can be achieved. This means addressing the problem of music literacy in the African context rather than returning to a concept of literacy based on Western notations alone.

At the rural schools I visited, committed teachers volunteer to conduct and instruct choirs and troupes after hours and on weekends. Sometimes, community members also step up to assist. At Entokozweni Primary School in Skhemelele, for instance, Sibusiso Khumalo coached the indlamu team to a provincial victory at the 2011 KwaZulu-Natal championships. I observed him instructing youngsters who practiced for long hours working on choreography and song. Khumalo, unemployed at the time, would walk many miles to work after hours with his enthusiastic young dancers, and the efforts of his young troupe became widely known. Their victory was a major source of pride for the school, and not least because of the large cash prize that came with the title of provincial champions. This shows how there are both material and symbolic interests at stake in the performance of musical arts in schools. Performers, teachers, and instructors compete for incentives. Schools attract talented musicians, dancers, and instructors to enhance their reputations. Individuals find meaning and fulfillment in the practice of these arts. The musical arts promote health. This creative space extends the community and provides inclusive linkages with parents and caregivers.

Arts and Culture Activities (ACA) are organized by the Department of Basic Education (DBE) and are coordinated at the provincial level to take account of regional cultural and linguistic differences. Music, dance, drama, and visual arts are all represented in ACA and are coordinated by the schools' Enrichment Directorate of DBE. Themes for ACA focus on health, wellness, and the social good, as well as on South African history and culture. Singing is the dominant mode of indigenous musical practice, and it is usually combined with dance and movement. The most popular ACA events in KwaZulu-Natal are ingoma and indlamu. Dance competitions draw large crowds. This contrasts with South African Schools Choral Eisteddfod, a major choir event. At Jozini, the audience was mostly made up of the participants who attended the circuit-level contests. By contrast, ACA events are generally sold out and last two full days with high participation from circuit schools. An indication of the scope and content of the ACA events is evident in the wide range of genres prescribed by the province of KwaZulu-Natal in 2017. Example 6.1 indicates the prescribed texts for genres of music and dance performance with their emphasis on matters of social importance to learners.

EXAMPLE 6.1: Prescribed Texts for Cultural Activities in 2017

isiCathamiya:	My future, my responsibility: Phansi nama "blesser" [Down with "blessers"]
uMaskandi:	Inhlonipho nokubekezelelana emaqenjini ezepolitiki [Respect and tolerance for political parties]
amaHubo:	[traditional hymns]:
Primary (Boys):	Sangena ngomnyama kwamthashana
Primary (Girls):	Saze sabulawa KwaZulu ◀))
Secondary (Boys):	Bayamqal' okaNdaba
Secondary (Girls):	Wen'okwanodwengu

The themes prescribed for the genres of isicathamiya, umaskandi, and amahubo enable students to engage with and create important social messages without using notation. The ACA competitions are undoubtedly some of the most vibrant singing competitions in South Africa today. This music is not based on the requirements of CAPS but could make an enormous contribution to the IAM curriculum. Community members often teach singing and dancing for indigenous genres like indlamu and ingoma because educators are not familiar with local cultural practices or simply do not have the training. These instructors could provide valuable practical insights so that the curriculum has local impact and currency. At the present time, an effective rubric for the assessment of indigenous folklore, music, and dance has not been established,[21] and this could play an important role here too. A major challenge for this rapidly expanding field of indigenous song and dance is to find ways of retaining the diversity and distinctness of cultural expression while formalizing it for inclusion in the school curriculum. The DBE has implemented a curriculum and a set of co-curricular activities that highlight the rich choral traditions of the country across a wide range of languages and cultures. These efforts are to be celebrated and improved on; singing is a major force for social good in South Africa, and its continued vitality must be fostered for generations to come.

CHALLENGES TO THE IMPLEMENTATION OF A TRANSFORMED MUSICAL ARTS CURRICULUM

Socioeconomic conditions in rural areas need to be factored into the assessment of the education system. Schools are entirely dependent on the state for resources because many parents and legal guardians do not earn enough to supplement fees. Most parents in these rural areas work as migrant laborers, and families must rely on subsistence farming, social grants, and informal employment to get by. There are few parents who reside with their children at home, and so grandparents and siblings are often children's primary caregivers. With no public transport available, many children walk more than ten kilometers per day to attend school—this in addition to household chores like fetching drinking water fit for consumption. These socioeconomic factors impact on learner support, too, because caregivers may not have the know-how or capacity to assist their children. In South Africa today, teachers cannot carry the responsibility of education without communities of support. In classes of fifty to eighty learners, it is difficult for teachers to develop close-knit bonds with their students or to nurture those who fall behind. Teachers are in short supply for schools in remote areas, and recruitment is a major challenge when salaries are low, social activities limited, and communities isolated. This is not a healthy mix for learners living in poverty whose everyday hardships overshadow their academic studies. It is difficult to see how policy reforms in the creative arts will achieve meaningful change without a broader response to rural socioeconomic development.

There are internal curricular challenges to musical arts education that must also be addressed. It is now the case throughout South Africa that the teaching of creative arts is secondary to the mandated focus on literacy, mathematics, and science education sanctioned by the provincial and national education departments. There is pressure put on principals and teachers to prioritize and to dedicate additional teaching time to these learning areas over others. There is also the perception that the creative arts are the station of last resort for teachers. The ideology that science and mathematics are progressive and the arts are optional instrumentalizes knowledge at the expense of values. The creative arts and music curricula are distinctive in their focus on values of collaboration, communication, and creativity. Considering South Africa's long history of discrimination and oppression, and specifically in view of current social ills—including racism, sexism, xenophobia, and corruption—repairing the social fabric of society through creative education and the performance of indigenous arts is an urgent project. The musical arts contribute to the health of society by developing coordinated social activities for the mutual benefit of diverse communities. Communication and cooperation are the measure of success that can only be achieved through rigorous practice, patience, and perseverance. The skills, knowledge, and values embedded in musical arts education are transferred across learning areas to develop healthy minds and bodies as well as to reinforce bonds of respect and dignity in communities.

PRIVATE EDUCATION

The chief alternative to public school education in music is the system of graded music examinations offered by the Associated Board of the Royal Schools of Music (ABRSM), Trinity College London (TCL), and the University of South Africa (Unisa). These graded examinations continue to set the standard for university entrance and contrast in fundamental ways with the indigenous practices outlined previously. Most private schools have used these examinations since the nineteenth century as benchmarks for their students' instrumental and vocal training, and thousands of students are enrolled in these activities each year. In fact, despite the much wider reach of music education in public schools, this system of private music education remains the primary route to tertiary education in music in South Africa.

The curricula for the three main examination boards are based on Western art music composition, performance, and literacy. The ABRSM theory syllabi aim to provide students with "knowledge of the notation of western music, including the signs and terminology commonly employed; an understanding of fundamental musical elements such as intervals, keys, scales and chords; skill in constructing balanced rhythmic patterns or completing given melodic or harmonic structures; an ability to apply theoretical knowledge and understanding to score analysis."[22] Similarly, for TCL the Grade 5 Theory of Music syllabus focuses on proficiency in Western staff notation, harmony, melody writing, in addition to various other terms and composition techniques.[23] Unisa's Grade 5 curriculum emphasizes the same rudiments: clefs; note values and rests; time signatures and grouping; key signatures and scales; intervals; terms and ornaments (Italian and French); harmony inclusive of four-part writing (SATB on two staves); completion of an eight-bar melody; as well as form analysis, including chord progressions, keys, phrases, cadences, and structure. There is also a history component that previously focused on the names, dates, and musical works of Western composers, but has recently been expanded to include South African composers and musical genres.[24]

Christine Lucia's study of the examination boards locates them within the broad colonial project of South African music education. Lucia argues that

> the hegemony of theory of music's influence in South Africa relies on the power of the (colonial) system behind it and on that system's wide dissemination through hundreds of textbooks and workbooks. The latter are overwhelmingly important (as important as, and similar to, bibles and catechisms), presenting a body of knowable facts in various ways and testing that knowledge through exercises. Such texts are almost all from North America and Britain (there are few indigenous examples) and for decades they have found their way to South Africa.[25]

The fact that these systems have "remained critically unchallenged" in postcolonial South Africa speaks to the dominance and elitism of private music education, in addition to its validation of Western art music *as* music, and largely to the exclusion of other musics. "The case of the Associated Board and similar external examining bodies in South Africa is an extreme example," writes Lucia, "of what the Comaroffs have shown as the colonization of consciousness in South Africa."[26] Education enables social stratification through the promotion of values, beliefs, and knowledge. This agenda creates a dissonance with postapartheid policy as conceived in CAPS, and with the remarkable syncretism of many postapartheid music cultures. It is also dissonant to the new generations of students who, after 1994, "have not already absorbed certain assumptions of value or systems of control through theory of music. Thus, employing its hegemonic norms uncritically is not only problematic but increasingly anachronistic."[27] Lucia's study shows how the theory of music has established itself as the true measure of music literacy. To read music is to be literate. But this hegemony does not extend to Jozini, nor to many thousands of schools across South Africa that do not possess the textbooks and workbooks that have enabled its hegemony elsewhere. Lucia's textbook *Music Notation* possesses many of the same rudiments included in the textbooks she cites, but with transcriptions and arrangements of South African music, and with principles of African musical systems added in separate chapters. This text normalizes the practice of music literacy as a South African institution. What other options are there for schools practicing indigenous musical arts that do not conform to such literacies?

Musical art works are too often defined as texted commodities. In education it is through scripture, not performance, that music is validated. Artworks are made manifest through notation. Without its canonic texts the history and theory of Western art music loses its intellectual authority. Indigenous musical arts rely primarily on objects and artifacts made meaningful through co-presence. The commodification of the musical score embodies modernity's battle with sound, with feeling, and those visceral powers that contorted music's relationship with modernity. The imposition of Western music education, and the hegemony of theory of music through staff notation, reinforces this dichotomy of sound and feeling by objectifying such experiences as literate acts. The major challenge facing teachers and theorists of African music is to bridge epistemological difference to recognize music as performance—and musical acts as irreducible statements, questions, and answers—and not to continue to fix sounds and movements as objects determined by properties of inscription, time, and space. Indigenous African musics occupy a very different literate realm to Western art music. These musics should be validated on their own terms, independently, comparatively, and coextensively with Western theories of music and music literacy.

INDIGENOUS MUSIC AND DANCE AT JOZINI

The enduring vitality of indigenous music and dance in the Jozini Local Municipality is evident in performances such as those described at the beginning of this chapter. Even so, the challenges faced by teachers and pupils are fundamental. Teachers in public schools lack basic knowledge of their subject. This fact is consistent across provinces in South Africa owing to changes in the curriculum, and because of the changing approach to educating teachers with the closure of education colleges postapartheid, which have impacted specialized subjects like music and dance. Societal challenges to the implementation of creative arts education in South Africa include factors of governance, corruption, underdevelopment, and class. Enver Motala and Salim Vally point out that many studies focus on the effects of education on class formation rather than on "why such *effects* or processes of social reproduction are visited on some social classes more than on others in the first place and whether this is related in any way to the even more fundamental structural and relational attributes of capitalist societies."[28] South African public school education reproduces inequality as a result of policy failures, practical challenges, and class domination by elites. Eurocentric arts and arts epistemologies are resilient sites of domination. Policy reforms have failed in practice and remain hamstrung by theories of music literacy alien to African indigenous arts. The policies of transformation instituted postapartheid will continue to fail for as long as the constraints imposed by the field of production remain structured by the imperatives of a minority elite. The accumulation of cultural and symbolic capital informs the ways in which class validation and aspiration continue to shape policy and practice in education.[29] Economic factors—inclusive of a deep-rooted network of teachers, schools, retailers, and examination bodies—must be understood in relation to the distinctive regimes of the elites for whom "classical music" remains the foundation of musical achievement and status.

Indigenous African musics are set to remain extracurricular activities until teachers are given the educational tools and support needed to teach them effectively; that is, flexibly, and in ways that articulate with the diverse realities of musical communities in contemporary South Africa. If musical arts education is to become an egalitarian practice, then it must reconcile with the full range of indigenous musical practices on offer, and these must be taught in recognized learning areas. There is a need to rethink the domination of Western musical arts over African ones and to seek alternatives to music-theoretical paradigms that entrench Western music literacy as normative. The teaching of indigenous African musical arts in theory and practice must render legitimate the surpluses of African musics without contorting their vocabularies to alien literacies. At the same time, schools in rural parts of KwaZulu-Natal like Jozini need to be properly resourced to educate learners in the arts of music and dance if these disciplines are to be effective parts of the curriculum, and of society.

SEVEN

Sounds of Tongaland
Environmental Justice at Ndumo Game Reserve

Cicadas sing a late summer chorus in the deep pitch of night. Their high-frequency buzz resonates a shimmering consonance through the humid air. *Too-whee-koo-whirrr* sing two fiery-necked nightjars in a hauntingly beautiful refrain to the new moon. Listening to the dark, I am surrounded by thickets of thorny *Acacia nigrescens* (*umKhaya*) and tall, waving grasses. This last steep of Ndumo Hill reaches down to the Phongolo floodplain where the guttural rumblings of a hippopotamus can be heard a mile from its narrow, fig-treed watercourse. There is disturbance in the bush. The cicadas scream a wall of sound. Honking blue wildebeest unsettle the undergrowth. Tongue and nostril have caught my scent. Sitting alone in the night, my ears wired to a microphone, I hear the far-off cry of fishing owls. The ellipse of their hooting signs the fragility of this unquiet hamlet. Attending keenly to the stark digital resonance, I hear a sound all too familiar. Dogs barking. Whose place *is* this? I listen again. Fiery darkness engulfs me. Anxious creatures trample the brambles. Then footsteps, and a rusted door creaking open, its key chafing in the lock. My own disembodiment heard again and again. In fits and starts, the undergrowth begins to move, crushed under hoof and paw. In this rush of night, adrenaline speeds my heart in wild meter. Yet still I hear no voices, only the whining mosquitoes who caress the blood out of my bare neck. I search for reflected light, not daring to disturb the equilibrium. But the moon is hidden away. ◀)

Nestled in the bush off a track strewn with rocks, boulders, and coarse brush

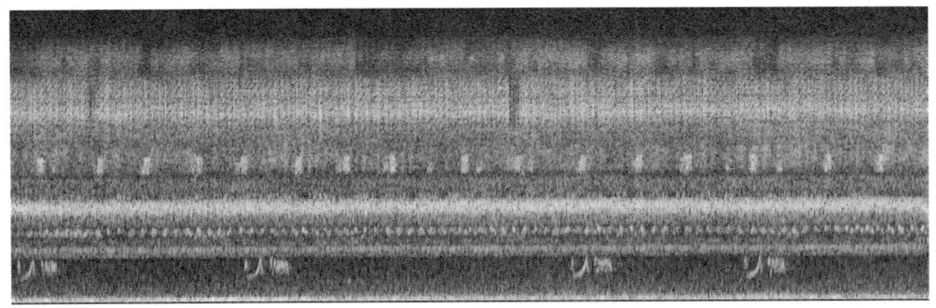

FIGURE 7.1 Spectrogram representation of fiery-necked nightjar call under a blaze of cicadas, April 2012. Created by Thomas Pooley.

is a green-walled cottage. The surrounding veld is scattered with thorny *Vachellia tortilis*, and dense scrub consisting of *Dichrostachys cinerea* and *Croton meny-hartii*.[1] A dilapidated signpost covered in brambles reads "Croc Farm." I swim through memory in search of this place. I faintly recall walking here as a child. It was my father, Tony Pooley, who built this outpost in 1966. Originally designed as a crocodile research station, the first of its kind in Africa, the building was surrounded by purpose-fitted pens close to the Phongolo River.[2] At Ndumo, my father was known as Mashesha, "he who hurries and takes."[3] During his first years at the reserve, it was open to the public only in the cooler autumn and winter months. His principal duties were in nature conservation, which included the protection of wildlife. Recognizing the superb natural beauty and diversity of the reserve, he saved up and eventually purchased a video camera to make wildlife documentary films. But on his first trip out on the Banzi pan, his boat was capsized by a hippopotamus, and the equipment was lost. Next, he acquired sound recording devices. He recalled, "In January 1962 I purchased a small Phillips battery operated reel to reel tape recorder, one of the first models to appear on the market. With half a dozen tapes, splicing tape and two sets of spare batteries it cost me very nearly my month's salary, which in 1963 was R98 per month! I had resolved to build up a library of sound."[4] He was to become a pioneer in recording wildlife sounds in southern Africa. His first wildlife recordings were released on the album *Wildlife Calls of Africa*, and most of these were made at Ndumo. *Sounds of the Bushveld* was made in collaboration with Dick Reucassel and was released in 1968. He worked with Tony Henley on *Birds of the Drakensberg*, which was released in 1969. Then in 1970 he released *Sounds of Tongaland*, which moved away from the documentary format of the earlier voice-over albums. This record gives "a brief impression in sound of the moods of Tongaland."[5] Side A includes sounds from Ndumo Game Reserve depicting the passage from morning until night in a condensed sixteen minutes. This record of bird and animal calls drew on the new possibilities of magnetic tape, which enabled him to combine recorded sounds into a structured composition.[6] The recordings on Side B consist of music and dance layered over the sounds of the environment in which they were recorded.

The relational moment in which representations of sound and sounds themselves commingled to unsettle our subjectivities as authors, listeners, and sounding objects gave rise to radical new experiments in sound. The use of sound as music was pioneered in twentieth-century compositions by John Cage, in the musique concrète practice of Pierre Schaefer, and in the sound design of R. Murray Schafer, among others.[7] Schafer's concept of "schizophonia," the denaturing and recombination of sounds from their source, has been influential in ethnomusicology and sound studies.[8] Colin Turnbull's work on the Mbuti influenced the young Steven Feld, who has written about a conjunction of new techniques that included musique concrète practice, tape editing, and electroacoustic synthesis.[9]

My father's wildlife recordings and sound compositions from the 1950s through the 1970s emerged in conjunction with these midcentury technological inventions and applications, and explored the possibilities for sound art that magnetic tape afforded.[10] Directed listening and the creation of an encompassing sound world were two goals of this work. The wall of sound that meets the ear in Ndumo's deepest forested glades is recorded in such a way that it gives presence to place. *Wildlife Calls of Africa* was a first step in this direction, but the effect was limited by the voice-over dialogue, which serves a documentary purpose. The emphasis on identifying species, some rare, some iconic, was the imperative on this album. For many listeners, including ornithologists and wildlife enthusiasts, listening to these records was their first and possibly only encounter with some of these animals. Later, he turned to the idea of recording an album of wildlife sounds without voice-over explanation and identification. This enabled a certain degree of freedom in the composition of the sonic spaces, too, for it afforded a different structure and range of sounds. The record *Sounds of Tongaland* is composed of a combination of human and wildlife sounds. Side A charts the passage of day in a sequence of sound events that capture birds and animals in their natural habitats. Side B is a record of songs, dances, and instruments made with communities in the immediate vicinity of the reserve and layered with the sounds of the forest at night. This album documents a time and place in ways that enable comparison. It was with this in mind that I made my own recordings of wildlife and music at Ndumo. The clarion calls of the fish eagle and the gentle hoots of fishing owls in the night echo across the decades in call-and-response.

Figure 7.2 depicts a spectrogram of fish eagle calls and responses. The freedom with which these birds call out across the expanse of the Nyamithi pan is iconic to a wilderness expressive and free. These are honest signals of wilderness. What I discovered upon my return to Ndumo was a quite different sense of sonic emplacement. The encroachment of hunting, snaring, and the illegal occupation of the reserve had resulted in a haunting disquiet. When I recorded in the bush, beginning in 2012, I perceived a heightened sense of anxiety among the animals. At other times, music could be heard from miles away and right across the Nyamithi floodplain from the town above. What do these fractures to sonic space mean for the ecosystems at Ndumo? I argue that sound is a barometer of an ecosystem's well-being, and that measuring these sound changes over time enables us to assess human impact. One measure of this impact at Ndumo is the diversity and ebullience of birdsong for which the reserve is justly famous.

Birdsong is a keynote in the Ndumo experience. The guides who take visitors on walks around the pans and onto the Phongolo floodplain are among the most experienced and astute birders in South Africa. Their ability to identify, imitate, and explain the behavior of birds demonstrates a passion for wildlife that underscores a deeper relationship with animals. This practice has been passed on from one generation of guides and guards to the next. In *Mashesha*, my father remarks on the importance of developing an appreciation for sound: "My Zulu game guard tutors impressed upon me the importance of listening to the sounds of the bush. To learn to identify and memorize sounds and to interpret their significance. There are times when this knowledge is not only

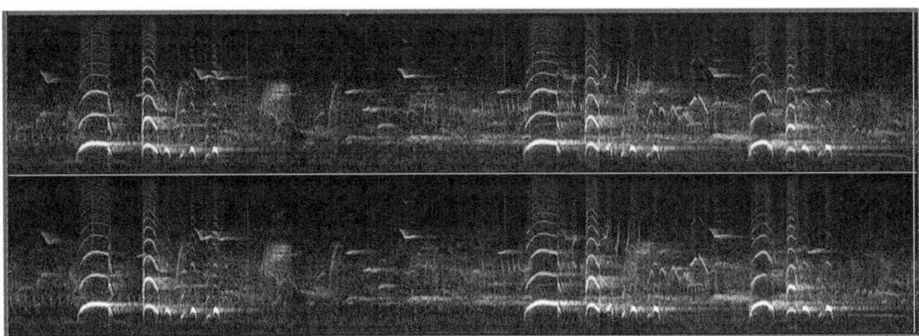

FIGURE 7.2 Spectrogram of African fish eagles calling at the Nyamithi pan, Ndumo Game Reserve, 1964. Created by Thomas Pooley; original recording by Tony Pooley.

useful in the course of daily work, but on occasion one's life could depend upon this knowledge."[11] For those working and living in this community, the sounds of animals communicate danger and serve as protection. Among the residents of Ndumo, there is also a deep spiritual connection to birds and animals. Specialist hunters search out birds and other animals for use as *umuthi* (medicinal herbs for healing).[12] Bones, teeth, skins, nails, talons, and other parts are used for divination, to diagnose physical and mental illness, and to ward off spirits.[13] Communities rely on the land for diverse food sources, including fruits, nuts, seeds, roots, leaves, fungi, insects, and larvae. The preservation of their natural ecosystem is thus important to a sustainable habitus, and its well-being is evident in the diversity and intensity of its sounds.

Ndumo was to have unexpected impact on my research. Sula Ngwenya had remarked on my father's skill in communicating with birds, and the memory of him lived on in the community (see introduction). It was in this context that I was identified with this place as his son. But in venturing here fifty years on, I set out to make my own record. Being in the reserve reoriented my senses and outlook through an immersion in the spaces occupied by creatures around me. This chapter reflects on the challenge of human-wildlife conflict in the reserve and its surrounds and on how this registers in the experience of sonic space as an embodiment of place at Ndumo.

NDUMO GAME RESERVE

The history of the 10,140 hectares sanctioned for conservation at Ndumo Game Reserve has been the site of struggle for centuries. The competing interests of land tenants, hunters, nature conservation officers, and health officials figure a complex history.[14] Human habitation in the area is ancient.[15] Before the influx of hunters and guns in the 1850s, this land was an ecosystem constituted by a wide range of animals, including lions, leopards, cheetahs, elephants, buffalos, spotted hyaenas, white rhinos, wild dogs, and many other species. The influx of hunters resulted in a drastic reduction in some species and the extermination of others.[16] An outbreak of rinderpest further depleted the broader animal population between 1895 and 1903, and in 1905 an ordinance was issued for the destruction of game. Commercial agriculture was attempted in the early twentieth century but failed because of low-quality soils and an arid climate with limited access to water resources. Another ordinance was issued in 1923, which resulted in authorities issuing additional permits for the extermination of animals considered vermin,

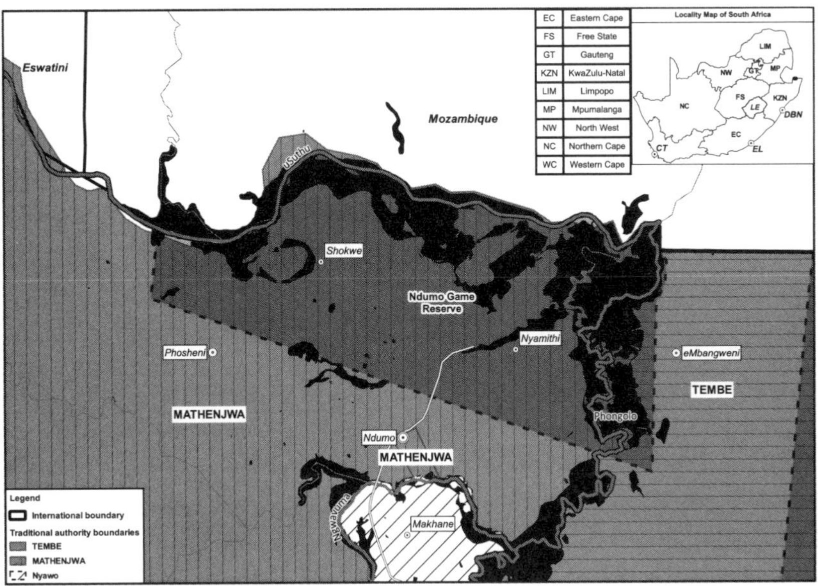

FIGURE 7.3 Map of Ndumo Game Reserve. Created by S3 Technologies.

including monkeys, baboons, lions, cheetahs, hyenas, leopards, civets, jackals, warthogs, bushpigs, wild dogs, and crocodiles.[17] When the lawyer and member of parliament Deneys Reitz visited Ndumo in 1921 and 1923, he recognized the unique biodiversity of the area and proclaimed it a game reserve on April 16, 1924, principally for the protection of hippopotamus.[18]

Despite these efforts, the eradication of wildlife throughout Tongaland was unrelenting and was exacerbated by *nagana* (sleeping sickness). Reitz had foreseen the value of Ndumo as a sanctuary for wildlife, but the proclamation of the reserve had limited impact because there was no fence or official guardian to oversee conservation efforts. That came later when Sergeant Game Guard Catuane was appointed to control poaching. Catuane was a local inkosi and so had some authority in the area, but he was unable to control the encroachment of people and livestock without clear boundaries drawn.[19] Tom Elphick took charge on October 13, 1951, and he established the first boundary fences and roads. Ian Player succeeded him in 1954 and began to keep records. He established that there were 1,466 persons, 740 head of cattle, 1,384 goats, 8 donkeys, 3 sheep, 64 dogs, and 37 cats residing in the game reserve. Player and Tony Pooley write that "at this time, it was rare to see game other than hippo and the occasional nyala, except for red duiker that were so common that the rangers were permitted to shoot them for rations."[20] There was a public road through the reserve linking stores at Catuane in Mozambique with Ndumo. This allowed for daily traffic between the two countries.[21] Foot-and-mouth disease was, and remains, a serious threat to livestock. A fence was erected by the Department of Veterinary Services in 1955 to prevent the spread of the disease from Mozambique to South Africa. Livestock were removed from the game reserve to establish a buffer zone, and some residents moved out with their cattle, settling on nearby land controlled by the Mathenjwa inkosi (figure 7.3). The fencing of the reserve was completed by Boy Hancock in 1955, except for the northern boundary marked by the uSuthu River, which has never been fenced. A small rest camp was opened in 1957, and tourists were permitted during limited holiday periods. In the late 1950s and early 1960s, the parks board restricted hunting by residents and those caught were removed with their families. My father witnessed this firsthand and wrote with concern about the potential consequences of dispossession resulting from racial politics under apartheid. He argued that the forced removal of families from the game reserve would ultimately betray the purposes of conservation. After witnessing the removal of a family from the reserve, he remembered, with a sense of exasperation, the ultimate frustration of this act.

> I felt a strange anger deep inside of me. A sense of injustice and also sadness. Here was this pathetic group of humans being punished for the misdeed of one of them [poaching animals]. Women and children who for many years had lived in the area, had tilled the soil, planted and reaped their crops, had known lean times, and times of plenty. Had laughed and played in the sunshine and at other times had lain desperately ill with fever. And now, they were being ejected from their home in the cause of nature conservation. Would these children grow up believing that to the white man, animals and game reserves were more important than they were? They had every reason to believe so![22]

The rationale for these removals was both political and environmental. First, it involved the racial geography of apartheid, which prohibited Black South Africans from residence in White-controlled areas, including game reserves. The second factor was conservation. During the 1950s and 1960s, rangers and game guards patrolled the game reserve to avert poaching. The sale of hides and horns was a profitable business then as now, and it threatened dwindling populations of crocodiles, rhinos, and other animals driven to extinction in Tongaland. A community of several hundred persons resided in the reserve, and these individuals cultivated crops on the floodplains of the uSuthu and Pongola Rivers. The government's forced removals program resulted in the last community members being moved out of the reserve in 1966. The Natal Parks Board reintroduced white and black rhinos, impalas, and warthogs in 1967, and the populations of game soon recovered, as did the plant life.[23] In the 1970s and 1980s, the reserve was managed by the Natal Parks Board before being transferred to the KwaZulu Bureau of Natural Resources in 1988.[24] By 1995 the fauna and flora in the reserve had reached a high point.[25] These areas were flooded during the summer months, but with the establishment of the Pongolapoort Dam at Jozini in 1973, these seasonal floods ceased and the water levels of the Phongolo River were radically altered, to the detriment of community and wildlife.[26] Elsa Pooley described an additional negative impact of farmland adjacent the reserve in a report noting the use of insecticides that drained into the stream feeding the Nyamithi pan.[27] These impacts motivate the need for environmental protections. The reserve was eventually proclaimed a Ramsar-protected site for its wetlands.[28] Its status is now under threat.

LAND CLAIMS

The communities living in the game reserve who were forcibly removed in the 1960s have reportedly filed land claims. The first claim was filed in 1992 and settled in 2001. The outcome of the second claim is not publicly known, but it is reported that this claim involving the community at Mbangweni is unresolved. The promise of transfrontier parks and large-scale tourism ventures have not materialized. Instead, Ndumo remains a government-managed reserve offering basic accommodation and camping facilities. It has no game lodge or luxury accommodation. The community at Mbangweni have destroyed the fence to the reserve and are occupying large tracts of the reserve. Evidence of large-scale clearing, planting, and grazing in the reserve can be seen on Google Earth, in numerous press clippings, and on social media. This has become a rancorous affair. Reports of violence emanating from the Mbangweni community intensified in the 2010s. The game fence was destroyed along the eastern perimeter, and threats against staff and visitors escalated with robberies and assault inflicted at gunpoint. Police and the army were called in at various points to safeguard tourists and Ezemvelo KZN Wildlife staff. In 2010 the reserve was attacked by a seventy-member mob that "destroyed a guard outpost, swing bridge close to the camp and threatened tourists and game rangers."[29] Much of this incident was covered on national media, with the Bhekabantu and Mbangweni communities demanding access to the land for agriculture and occupying large parts of the most sensitive areas in the reserve. Yolandi Groenewald describes how the troops patrolling the border did little to prevent "land invaders [who] continue to practice slash-and-burn cultivation, destroying large areas of mature riverine fig forest . . . Even more damaging is the rampant poaching and illegal fishing. Poaching of fauna, including the use of cable snares, has already killed one white rhino, and seriously injured another, the reports show."[30] Jeff Gaisford, spokesperson for Ezemvelo KZN Wildlife, commented on these incidents in 2010: "There are various risks to the people and the animals in that area if the community continues to invade the land. By cutting down important border fences, they are opening up the corridor to buffalo, which carry dangerous diseases. The disease could be a danger to domestic cattle and to people. It could also lead to increased rhino poaching."[31] The destruction continued in ensuing years with Tim Condon, Zululand Wildlife forum coordinator, stating that the population of rhinos had decreased to only six in 2014. All were removed in 2017 to another place of safety. A spokesperson for the reserve, Musa Mntambo, explained that "there is no fence because any fence erected is stolen by the community."[32] Richard Penn Sawers, Ezemvelo KZN Wildlife manager for northern protected areas, wrote that "the integrity of the game reserve is at stake."[33] There were reports of hunting for bushmeat, including hippo and buffalo.

Visitor walks to the eastern areas and along the Phongolo floodplain have been suspended, as it is no longer safe to visit parts of the reserve. In some areas, the project of wildlife conservation appears to have been abandoned altogether. Cultivation of large tracts of land continue unabated by Ezemvelo KZN Wildlife, and the reserve's fences have not been repaired. The southern and western fences also show signs of disrepair with missing strands and large holes. Most of the game reserve land is not suitable for agriculture and so the land occupation is mostly along the floodplains. This area appears to have been surrendered by the reserve's authorities, which means that the reserve has effectively been reduced in size by around 14 percent. It is now dangerously vulnerable to poaching and encroachment. On a visit to Ndumo in October 2019, I could see where large tracts of the reserve had been planted with mielies. Vehicles were being driven on makeshift roads, pumps were installed for irrigation, and cattle were grazing on the floodplain. All of this was clearly visible from the camp. No comment was made by game reserve staff who had been threatened and attacked in previous years. I tried to contact the reserve in 2021 to visit, but the phone lines were dead. Ezemvelo KZN Wildlife central reservations informed me that the reserve is closed until December due to a water shortage and problems with the utilities. I visited again in May 2022 only to be told that the camp was officially closed. This suggests turmoil in the management of the reserve and its ecosystems. The autonomy of the reserve as a protected area for wildlife conservation, education, and tourism has been jeopardized for over a decade with no sign of resolution. The failure to properly manage land claims and to enforce the law seems to be inflaming hostilities. By contrast, the communities in the Mathenjwa Tribal Authority to the southwest of the reserve continue to live in peace with conservation staff and contribute to education and conservation efforts. These communities have cemented partnerships like the Working for Water program and have made long-term connections with staff in the reserve.[34] It appears that the failure of governance in this remote region has resulted in a breakdown of the delicate balance that makes environmental justice possible. In this context, the future of the reserve and the well-being of its ecosystems is at stake not only as a conservation resource but as a resource for communities who subsist on its diversity. The story of this diversity involves the preservation of wildlife and endangered species, including the crocodiles that my father worked so hard to protect in the 1960s and 1970s, but also, more recently, the rhinos who have inhabited the reserve for decades.

ENDANGERED SPECIES

The first white rhino was (re)introduced at Ndumo on December 9, 1961,[35] and the first black rhino on September 21, 1962. Eight black and sixteen white rhinos were moved to Ndumo by 1965. The Natal Parks Board's Operation Rhino was conducted under the leadership of Ian Player, who worked with a team of rangers, guards, and veterinarians in Zululand to replenish a dwindling and threatened rhino population in South Africa. This is one of the outstanding success stories of conservation in Africa. Ndumo was part of this effort to grow and sustain rhino populations, and progress was measured systematically. Anthony Conway and Peter Goodman found that by June 1986 there were an estimated forty-two black rhinos (10 percent juveniles) and fifty-seven white rhinos (14 percent juveniles) in the game reserve.[36] "Because of the rhino's successful breeding in this small reserve, the KwaZulu Bureau of Natural Resources (who inherited control of Ndumu from the Natal Parks Board) in conjunction with the National Parks Board, were able to translocate ten black rhinos to the Kruger National Park in September 1989. In doing so, they took another important step in the conservation of these endangered animals."[37] This effort was part of a generally positive trend in southern and east Africa with populations of both black and white rhinos growing steadily through the 1980s and 1990s. But the trend changed course in the first decade of the twenty-first century with an uptick in poaching. Clive and Anton Walker describe how this developed into a battle to save the rhino from extinction.

> We are in fact fighting two battles: the battle on the ground, which is costly, dangerous and problematic in terms of sustainability; and a second more insidious one within South Africa at a state level, which appears to be in terminal decline linked to the socio-economic situation prevailing today. Even with the finest fighting force on the ground in the struggle, if the levers of power in high office don't function or don't care, the ongoing war will be a bloody one. There is, however, some hope, for South Africa is unique in that it has a citizenry that has shown it can stand alone at great cost and dedication and this provides the hope for the rhinoceros.[38]

The seriousness of this war is told in the rhino-poaching statistics: In 2013 there were 1,004 rhinos poached with 1,215 in 2014 and 1,175 in 2015. "At the end of 2016, the recorded number of both black and white rhino poached since 2008 stands at 7,137."[39] I experienced this war firsthand during my time at Ndumo. While driving to and from camp, I would occasionally hear heavy gunfire. This piercing of Ndumo's acoustemology was among the most frightening and unsettling experiences I have had in a game reserve, which is generally considered a place of peace. On one occasion the guards were searching vehicles for rifles, and I was escorted to the main gate by a military officer. Ndumo is exposed to threat partly because of its porous boundaries. The reserve's northern boundary is the uSuthu River, which is easy to cross, especially when water levels are low. At Red Cliffs there are often people fishing in the river, collecting firewood, and walking across the beaches. And then of course there is the problem of the eastern boundary fence at Mbangweni, which has been down for years. The decimation of game in that region is a concern.

FIGURE 7.4 Cultivated fields on the Phongolo floodplain inside Ndumo
Game Reserve, October 24, 2019.

SHOKWE PAN, NDUMO GAME RESERVE, AUGUST 30, 2012

Sonto Tembe and I make an early sunrise start on a guided walk to the Shokwe
pan. This ox-bow lake has been removed from its river by the tides of time. It
is fed intermittently by flood waters from the uSuthu River, a kilometer distant.
I am excited to record the birds and animals, and I hope there will be good
activity at the pan. On our last visit the water had been low, and I expected it
to be even lower this time around since there have been no rains for months.
We must first drive through the reserve from the camp into the Mahemane.
Our journey is delayed by a short stop at a bataleur's nest where the parents are
feeding their young.

The Opel Meriva I'm driving struggles with ground clearance, so we must
take the road along the boundary fence instead of through the Mahemane. We
arrive in the thicket just before 7 a.m. and park the car on the Red Cliffs Road.
The sun is already well up and the birds are in full chorus. Sonto loads his regu-

lation .375 shotgun in readiness for any trouble, human or animal. I ready my Zoom HD recorder, joking that the shotgun microphone with pistol grip will offer similar protection. I fit a wind shield. Our route takes us along the road for a few hundred meters before meandering off on a path through the bush and down to the forested edge of the pan. As the scrub gives way to the fig trees, we spot a brown-hooded kingfisher perched above the canopy. Last time I walked here with Sonto he called birds to us, as he always does, including his "friend" the golden-rumped tinker barbet.[40] Its three-to-nine-note repetitious call gives the bushveld in Zululand its distinctive sound together with the purple-crested turaco and the emerald-spotted wood dove.[41] I realized then how fond Sonto was of the bush and how important it was to him that it be protected.

The raucous cry of trumpeter hornbills echoes across the pan. Sonto cups his hands around his mouth and blows loudly in imitation. This act of imitation is also an act of communication, of human-creature recognition and husbandry, making sense and marking affiliation and friendship across species. But this time the birds keep their distance. I laugh, telling him that he's scaring them off. They'll think it's a huge bird making this sound! The fish eagles are out of sight. We walk down through the trees to the waterline. It is still very dry and there are no animals in sight. Birdsong is subdued. I clutch at my recording equipment training the camera through the reed beds, my headphones bumping along. This is the first time we have circumnavigated the pan. The standard route is to walk along the road arriving at the opposite end of the pan. Sonto suggests we turn back onto the shoreline. There he stops, abruptly. "Hawu, shame. Shame, shame, shame," he says. He points toward a large object lying on the edge of the pan. I use my camera to zoom in. A rhino. Dead. Three shots to the chest. The blood is still oozing from her wounds. Her horn has been sawn off. Droppings lie at her rear end, a visceral record of the shock and pain of her final moments.

Sonto initially thought it was an *ubejane* (black rhino) because of her size. But on closer inspection we see that it is a *umkhumbe umkhomazi* (female white rhino). Sonto does not want to approach; instead, he radios for assistance. This takes quite some time. Eventually he gets a response. I cannot make out what they are saying because he has walked off some distance from me, asking me to keep away from the dead animal. We wait. After what seems like an eternity, a call eventually comes through asking for our whereabouts. "Shokwe, on the road to Red Cliffs. You will see the car parked in the clearing," he says. At last, three uniformed men appear on the opposite end of the pan. They are jogging toward us carrying heavy automatic weapons. I recognize one of the men. Back

FIGURE 7.5 Sonto Tembe at Nyamithi pan, Ndumo Game Reserve, July 29, 2012.

in April, he had stopped me just as I was leaving the reserve office. He asked me where I was going and if he could have a lift. I said yes. Then, on my way out, he told me no, he couldn't go because they'd heard gunshots—an R4 assault rifle.

Walking back through the fig forest, I was distraught. I wasn't much interested in anything. Sonto, as if by habit, continued pointing out items of interest: a porcupine quill, a red duiker scurrying away, white-faced duck. But I was numb. As we walked along the path back to the car, we came across droppings. Rhino, said Sonto, fresh from this morning. There may have been two of them. On the drive back to camp, Sonto was preoccupied. How many rhinos had been killed so far? I asked. He said he thought five over the past two years—perhaps three this year already.

When I discussed the rhino killing with the community, I was surprised by the responses. I was told about locals who hunt in the game reserve for bushmeat and umuthi. I was told about witchcraft, about how locals needed specific animal parts for their practices. Cheryl Ogilvie's longitudinal research in the Ndumo area over the past two decades confirms this. She highlights serious environmental challenges around land use, deforestation, poaching, pollution, and what she describes as "traditional beliefs." The clearing of forests for firewood (the chief source of fuel in the area), farming, and harvesting medicines is taking place at a rapid rate.[42] Many homesteads in this area rely on subsistence farming. "The poaching of game (animals or birds), is considered a significant threat to conservation of biodiversity," she writes. "One third of all mammals and birds are threatened with extinction due to illegal hunting by humans."[43] According to regional ecologist Catherine Hanekom, poaching is performed by communities on both sides of the border and has some commercial value because bushmeat is sold at local markets.[44] Former rangers report that the poaching of hippo and buffalo has become a serious problem in the reserve because the meat is sold cheaply to the community, thus creating a reliance on this protein source. Still, subsistence hunters are not known to shoot rhinos. "But did they take meat?" I was asked, pointedly. Rhino horns, it seems, serve a different market entirely to those selling cheap bushmeat on the Phongolo floodplain.

JUSTICE FOR THE ENVIRONMENT

Ndumo is recognized as a key location for biodiversity in southern Africa. This biodiversity is rightly celebrated, and it is protected in the Constitution of the Republic of South Africa. The Bill of Rights, Section 24, states:

Everyone has the right:

to an environment that is not harmful to their health or well-being; and
to have the environment protected, for the benefit of present and future generations through reasonable legislative and other measures that
prevent pollution and ecological degradation;
promote conservation; and
secure ecologically sustainable development and use of natural resources while promoting justifiable economic and social development.

The Constitution of 1996 was designed to address the ills of apartheid and prevent its recurrence. Wildlife conservation had been legislated to exclude Black persons from fair participation in all sectors of society. Access to conservation areas was limited and Blacks were excluded from most of their benefits.[45] How should such disparities be addressed in the postapartheid era? The need to address the legacies of apartheid-era conservation policies and the displacement of communities has led to debates on the value and importance of conservation, on land restitution, and on how communities should be included as stakeholders and beneficiaries. Ndumo is a case in point with two land claims on the reserve. The subsequent destruction of boundary fences and the occupation of the reserve by a group at Mbangweni has resulted in the decimation of wildlife. The hunting and snaring of animals and the plundering of forests are endangering species. This has gone largely unchecked for more than a decade despite widespread reporting in the press, on social media, and with increasing desperation by shocked visitors to the reserve. Ndumo presents important issues that require principled action. What is the nature of environmental justice and what is its measure at Ndumo?

Embedded in many formulations of environmental justice is an insistence on the primacy of human needs. Humans are a part of nature as much as they are a dominating force whose very presence threatens that of other beings. Places set aside for conservation are thus marked separate from those inhabited by humans. Formulations of environmental justice tend to focus on how humans can and should benefit from the environment rather than on justice for our fellow creatures. For instance, Michelle Toxopeüs and Louis Kotzé explain how

> at a minimum, environmental justice relates to the equitable distribution of environmental benefits and burdens; to the recognition of group identities and differences within society and how these play into peoples' relationship with the environment; to specific environment-related needs of people differently situated on the socio-economic ladder; and to ways through which people can obtain maximum benefits from life-sustaining resources in an equitable way that also promotes justice in its broadest sense.[46]

Conservationists emphasize the needs of organisms living independently of both direct and indirect human influence; that is, the need for organisms to live in relative autonomy from the impactful presence of humans as well as human products and pollution. The scale of impact can be measured in different ways. For instance, the unlawful destruction of habitat in parts of Ndumo Game Reserve can be quantified in terms of gross habitat loss. The unrestricted use of fertilizers, insecticides, and poisons by subsistence farmers have the potential to destroy the ecosystem. The Phongolo and uSuthu Rivers and the pans they feed are essential breeding grounds for aquatic life. The introduction of pathogens

FIGURE 7.6 Shokwe pan at Ndumo Game Reserve, August 30, 2012.

is catastrophic for fish and other aquatic and amphibious species, as well as for the birds and reptiles that depend on them for life. In the absence of published scientific studies measuring the impact of human habitation inside Ndumo Game Reserve, and with visitors now prevented from walking close to the areas of occupation along the Phongolo floodplain, it is difficult to establish the nature and extent of the impact.

The ethical questions framing the study of sound at Ndumo need to be understood in the context of competing claims by anthropologists, conservationists, and local communities. The question of justice for Ndumo Game Reserve must contend with the fact that some of the families now living outside of its boundaries once lived inside and were forcibly removed during the 1950s and 1960s. The government recognized this injustice and awarded settlements on land claims to the Mathenjwa community in the Usuthu gorge area and the Tembe community at Mbangweni. Tony Carnie explains how "this was done with the condition that the land would remain a protected game reserve in perpetuity."[47] The complication is that the terms of both agreements are not publicly known, writes Simon Pooley. "Apparently, compensation remains unpaid. Exacerbated

by poor relations between conservation authorities and communities—causes
of which include historical evictions and violent encounters in poaching incidents—agreement on co-management has proved elusive."[48] The Mathenjwa community continues to play an active role in managing the reserve, and residents of
ePhosheni isigodi were employed to clear invasive species. But the relationship
between Ezemvelo KZN Wildlife officials and the Mbangweni community turned
hostile after a series of land invasions and attacks. The failure of their agreement
is cited as the main reason for continued tensions between conservation authorities and community members. It is unclear what role law enforcement is playing
in managing the ongoing crisis, but the plunder of natural resources continues,
and this sets a dangerous precedent for other protected areas in South Africa.
The growing literature on the politics of land and the environment at Ndumo
demonstrates a complexity that has no immediate solution and remains an
open-ended dilemma.[49]

A reciprocity of means exists between humans and their environments that
is tacit but fundamental to the survival of our species. The global challenges of
our time—climate change and mass extinction, among them—require us to rethink our relationship to our fellow creatures. I argue that environmental justice
means finding solutions not only for humans but for the creatures with whom
we share this Earth. This means recognizing our obligations to these creatures
on whom we are dependent for our own survival. Establishing the nature and
meaning of this reciprocity is explored here through reflections on the sounds
of Ndumo. It would be a mistake, then, a false dichotomy, to construct a binary
opposition between the environment and the community in the immediate
vicinity of the reserve.

Talk of environmental justice must recognize voices for the environment. The
loss of biodiversity at Ndumo is a deeply troubling symptom of a wider malaise.
The fact is that humans are responsible for the sixth mass extinction on the
planet.[50] As Gerardo Ceballos and coauthors argue,

> the loss of biodiversity is one of the most critical current environmental prob-
> lems, threatening valuable ecosystem services and human wellbeing. A growing
> body of evidence indicates that current species extinction rates are higher than
> the pre-human background rate with hundreds of anthropogenic vertebrate
> extinctions documented in prehistoric and historic times. . . . Population-level
> extinction directly threatens ecosystem services and is the prelude to species-
> level extinction.[51]

Leading scientists of climate change and habitat loss show that the consequences of extinction are catastrophic. The loss of biodiversity will have an irreversible detrimental effect on ecosystems because, as James Estes and colleagues explain, "extinctions are by their very nature perpetual, whereas most other environmental impacts are potentially reversible on decadal to millennial time scales."[52] The impact on humans will be felt "with far-reaching effects on processes as diverse as the dynamics of disease; fire; carbon sequestration; invasive species; and biogeochemical exchanges among Earth's soil, water, and atmosphere."[53] The loss of our fellow creatures will forever change this world, and this will be to our own detriment.[54]

The deterioration of Ndumo Game Reserve as a protected reserve for critical ecosystems and species under threat, in violation of law and treaty, calls attention to the failure of governance in South Africa, but also to our collective failure to recognize the existential threat posed by the loss of biodiversity. It is our collective responsibility to manage Planet Earth in a sustainable way. The subsistence farming taking place inside the game reserve is not profit-driven agriculture. Perhaps it is a means of survival in a place with few job opportunities and resources. A dependency on bushmeat and plants in the communities around Ndumo shows that poverty is a factor in the invasion. But it is not sustainable to cut down trees, pollute rivers and lakes, and hunt to extinction the resources that do exist.

There are at least two important reasons to find a balance at Ndumo and places like it. First is that the threat humans pose to ecosystems is ultimately a threat to our own species. The effects of environmental degradation are often irreparable and catastrophic, particularly when this involves the extinction of other species. A second argument is that we have a moral duty to our fellow creatures. The principle of reciprocity that underscores moral action in Zulu societies resonates here with work in ethics and moral philosophy on our obligations to animals, plants, and the ecosystems of which we are an integral part. Christine Korsgaard points to the dangers of speciesism and anthropocentrism in emphasizing our obligations to other animals.[55]

> It is almost a necessary truth that for an animal who functions by taking her own well-functioning as an end, her life itself is a good for her, her very existence is a good for her, so long as she is well-functioning, and *in* good enough condition to keep herself that way. The reason is simple: to be well-functioning is also simply to be alive, and in reasonably good health, in the manner char-

acteristic of your kind. So life itself is a good for almost any animal who is in reasonably good shape.[56]

That animals possess lives of significance to themselves and to others of their kind is undisputed. Memory and history are relevant to rhinos, crocodiles, eagle owls, and the many other inhabitants of Ndumo Game Reserve, some of whom have lived in the reserve for more than half a century. "Any sentient animal has good experiences and bad ones. But the more that experience accumulates, the more it makes sense to think that the animal, like a human being, can have a good or a bad life, where a life is not just a string of good or bad experiences, but a kind of whole with an overall character of its own. This is because it becomes true that there is something it is like to live that life."[57] Rhinos may not possess the same capacity for self-consciousness or reason that humans do. Yet they experience pain, suffering, anxiety, fear, sadness, hunger, thirst, desire, and so many of the drives and emotions that make us human. The expression of emotions in animals is to be found in their vocalizing, their singing, their gestures, and the beating of their wings. The birds at Ndumo return year upon year to this place, and this place alone. It is not a disconnected reality, a place of mere opportunity. It is a place that is their home, a home disturbed, a home exposed and denigrated. Environmental justice means recognizing the lives of animals as valuable in and of themselves, protecting those lives and livelihoods, and taking this to be a moral obligation to our fellow creatures. Why should conservation carry the ultimate burden for human injustice, corruption, and political ineptitude? What are the consequences when the environment is made to do so, and how should we go about addressing this injustice? The contested nature of wildlife conservation, land, community, and justice is at the heart of debates about the future of Ndumo Game Reserve and the communities it can and must continue to serve.

A QUESTION OF SURVIVAL

The community at ePhosheni have lived adjacent the game reserve for decades. Sula Ngwenya and his family know the area well because many of them are employed in the reserve as part of the Working for Water initiative. When I visited Sula in 2013, he had an Ezemvelo KZN Wildlife sign in his homestead to indicate that they are workers. Sula arranged for me to record the group of women whom the anthropologist Angela Impey had helped to form a group some years before.[58]

When I recorded the women from ePhosheni, I was struck by the lyrics of "Shaya mfana," one of their songs about wildlife. ◀))

EXAMPLE 7.1: "Shaya mfana" (Kill it, boy), Dledleni Gumede (2012)

Idla uthuli lwezinja.	Eat the dog's dust.
Idla uthuli lwenyamazane.	Eat the antelope's dust.
Ubothi ungayishaya mfana ungisikele iqatha.	If you get it, boy, cut a piece for me.
Idla uthuli lwezinja idla olwenyamazane.	Eat the dog's dust, eat the antelope.
Mayibabo,	My goodness,
Idla uthuli lwezinja idla uthuli lwenyamazane.	Eat the dog's dust, eat the antelope's dust.
Bothi ungayishaya mfana ungisikele iqatha.	If you get it, boy, cut a piece for me.
Idla uthuli lwezinja idla uthuli lwenyamazane.	Eat the dog's dust, eat the antelope's dust.
Khuluma naye woza wena ya.	I'm speaking to you, come here.

"Shaya mfana" reflects on hunting practices that were and remain common at Ndumo as well as in many other places like uMsinga. Gunshots and barking dogs shatter the illusion of an idyllic Ndumo wilderness. That dreamscape has always been more myth than reality, a de-historicized invention that bears no resemblance to the stories of those who live and work in the reserve. The land and environment at Ndumo have been contested by humans and animals for centuries, and the hunting, snaring, burning, and destruction that go on today are not new. When my father made *Sounds of Tongaland* in the early 1960s, he recorded sonic spaces that were contested in similar ways. People have long sounded its forests and grasslands, and will continue to do so. But that is not to deny the importance of it remaining a conservation area. In the context of global warming, mass extinctions, habitat loss, water insecurity, and the destruction of wildlife areas across the globe at an unprecedented rate, we need to think more urgently than ever before about what is meant by environmental justice. Communities need sustainable solutions to their immediate subsistence challenges. The ecosystems that support life on the Phongolo floodplain will be destroyed in the rush to exploit them. This destruction could well prove unsustainable for the communities responsible. Wildlife conservation cannot be managed independently of the land and communities surrounding these areas. The history of conservation in KwaZulu-Natal demonstrates that the protection of wildlife can be managed effectively, but only if systems of governance and the rule of law are upheld.

———

When I listen again to the sounds of wildlife and music, I realize that Tongaland, as it was known then, was inseparable in my father's mind from the sounds of people and wildlife, and of people *with* wildlife. The composition of *Sounds of Tongaland* was designed to imagine this powerful coexistence.[59] At the end of his book *Mashesha*, my father wrote: "for the future of the small wildlife oasis of Ndumu game reserve, and the entire floodplain, there are still many questions to be addressed and answered. For the future of the people and the unique fauna and flora, it is a question of survival."[60] And so it remains. The complexity of the challenges faced by the communities in and around the game reserve require long-term interventions to make a real difference. The state has a duty to protect the wildlife of Ndumo and to uphold the law while finding solutions for its distressed communities.[61] Resolutions of mutual benefit are needed in conflicts over land and conservation if we are to maintain the ecosystems upon which we depend for our well-being. Ndumo has never been a place without people, nor should it be. It is only through coexistence that we will secure a sound future for all.

EIGHT

Unsung Melodies
Reciprocity in Sound

FEBRUARY 2012

At the end of a long, sweltering day at Ndumo, Thulani and I venture into the bush to meet Mduduzi Mngomezulu. Mdu is a football friend of Thulani's and has been waiting for us on the dirt road near Makhane. Dressed in a waistcoat, smart trousers, and shoes, his guitar slung over one shoulder, Mdu is ready to sing. But we are late; it is almost quarter to five now. We were delayed in a meeting with the Isicathamiya Kings who sold us one of their cassettes. Time is short because I must get back to the game reserve before the gate closes at nightfall. Mdu takes us to a homestead on the opposite side of the road, a few hundred meters off a rough grassed track. His two friends and backing singers are Zakele and Bhekithemba. Sanele Ngomezulu is the last of the quartet but is missing for some reason. The afternoon is filled with the sound of bird chatter and chirp, chickens running about the yard, and children playing nearby. The trio set up on the grass and perform a set. I am astounded by Mdu's dexterous guitar playing. His izibongo are intricately crafted, fluently articulated, and lyrical. The harmonizing between the three singers—soprano, alto, tenor—is remarkably sweet and gentle. Mdu says that he has enough material to record three or four CDs right away. He has been working at eMpangeni on the sugarcane farms. Recently, he sustained an injury when he fell off the back of a truck, and now he can't continue working there as a laborer. But he will go back as soon as he's better. I must just phone him and he will come and record; he is very keen. This is an exciting prospect because he is unquestionably one of the most talented musicians I have met. Even so, there are clear challenges: Mdu needs new guitar strings, and where on earth will we record in this area? Makhane is a bustling place. The environment is flush with the sounds of people, birds, and livestock. Mdu says recording a demo CD would help him fulfill a dream. He has been saving to record a demo at a local studio but has not yet come up with the R400 needed to finance it.[1] My arrival is a stroke of good fortune, he says. Mdu and I reach an agreement. I will record him with his group when I return in April.

MAY 2017

I was to return four times to Ndumo in 2012, and many more times in the years thereafter. But each time I went back, Mdu was nowhere to be found. Having recovered from his injury, he returned to work as a laborer at the sugarcane plantations near eMpangeni (a city more than one hundred fifty miles from Ndumo). Or his number had changed, or he was looking for work, or Thulani just couldn't find him. I managed to get through to him once when he was at eMpangeni and offered to pay for his transport to eShowe to make a recording at the high school. But he could not convince his boss to allow him to take time off. Eventually, in May 2017, we made another appointment. I brought him new guitar strings from Pietermaritzburg, and we met at Makhane. We sat in my Ford and listened to a recording of the Bergville Blue Roses, an isicathamiya group I recorded and produced for Thukela Records. Mdu was excited at the prospect of making a "clean" record approaching studio quality. He told me about Jonathan Mathenjwa from Ndumo whom I had recorded with his group, Mqamuli Wezintambo (see chapter 5). Jonathan had now moved to Jozini, and his music was performed on Kosi FM, a local Zulu-language radio station. But for all Mdu's optimism, communication remained a problem. His cell phone was smashed in an argument, and he could not afford to replace it. I would have to communicate through Thulani again.

RECIPROCITY ON RECORD

The initial program of research that led to this book was not principally ethno-graphic in focus. My doctoral research was a study of Zulu tone systems and song focusing on the relationship of song to speech. The phonetic methods I used to analyze pitch patterning and melody relied on clean, high-definition recordings. But as soon as I began the fieldwork for that project, I realized that the contexts for the music were crucial to understanding its meanings. The social dimensions to fieldwork also impressed on me the need for an engaged approach to scholarship. Having studied ethnomusicology and the anthropology of music, I decided to combine ethnographic studies with research on the perception and cognition of music. (This interdisciplinary approach is advanced in chapter 5.) I was sensitive to the dynamics involved in making records, and so from the start I was careful to negotiate permissions and to find ways of establishing trusting working relationships built on reciprocity. Working with Gugu Mbatha and Rauri Alcock at the Mdukatshani Rural Development Project, and with a template developed by the Smithsonian Institution, I fashioned an informed consent form and protocol printed in English and isiZulu that set out the goals of the project and how the recordings would be used. This document was used for approaching and consulting with traditional leaders and performers in rural places. I wrote letters to the *amakhosi* (chiefs) and scheduled meetings at the tribal authority offices. Then I approached izinduna in the tribal wards, as well as the democratically elected ward councillors. Everyone whom I recorded met with me to talk about their expectations, and signed permissions that were read to them in English or isiZulu if they were unable to read them. Some decided not to record once they had heard my conditions, mostly because they expected substantial payment. I decided not to pay large sums to record professionals and semiprofessionals. My aim was principally to record performances in everyday life. Gradually, as word got around, I was invited to more and more events and rituals; and some musicians approached me directly. By the time I had completed my second year of research in 2013, I was taking a deeper interest in ethnography, and communities who knew me would send invitations to me or my contacts in their area.

At umemulo and other ceremonies, I became the ordained officer of record. This usually entailed directing photography and videography for the event. I was fitted to the lifeworlds of the community in ways they found natural and useful. In some places, I also recorded singers at community halls, in their homes, in communal dance areas, and at schools. The performances I recorded in these places were often composed for public display, or competition. Those considered sacred were reserved for spaces inside the homestead. These performances were less accessible but were ultimately crucial to understanding Zulu cultures (see chapters 3 and 4). And so I came to rely on field recordings for much of my work, and I participated in ways that I could scarcely have imagined at the outset. The reciprocal nature of my relationships with performers was negotiated. Tangible benefits were a priority for many, especially the audio and video recordings

FIGURE 8.1 uMemulo at the Mbhele umuzi in Dakeni, KwaZulu-Natal Province, South Africa, July 10, 2012.

that I agreed to make for them. But in some ways a more important factor was intangible. Relationships were measured on trust, a mutually reinforcing and relational understanding of our coexistence, and the commingling of our quite different worlds through this encounter in performance. Once I had proven my trustworthiness to the community, so relationships would strengthen, and it became much easier to talk about performance and its meanings. Both at Ndumo and uMsinga I was fortunate in that I already had long-standing connections to these communities and in some respects was a known quantity.

The relationships I forged were ultimately more important than any of the data collected. This chapter reflects on those unsung voices as well as on the ethics of reciprocity that guided my research and recording practices. The Zulu principle of ubuntu advances a way of being-in-the-world that is captured in the proverb "umuntu ngumuntu ngabantu" (a person is a person through others). The nature of our obligations to others is understood as mutually reinforcing. Recording was one component to the reciprocity upon which my presence was accepted and invited. My appreciation for performances as cultural artifacts in addition to my respect and commitment to the community were ultimately more important in establishing trusting relationships. The question of how reciprocity is maintained in ethnographic fieldwork is a priority for many ethnographers. Applied ethnomusicology advances scholarship that benefits communities as much as the research agendas and careers of its exponents.[2] This research was not initially conceived as applied ethnomusicology, but it very soon became a project designed to benefit all who participated in it. The negotiation of culture- and community-specific ways of contributing to outcomes was dialogic. It required a combination of careful planning and flexible engagement with community leaders and performers. I worked toward tangible benefits that were appropriate to the community concerned.

In the initial stages of the research, negotiations with communities were complicated by dealings with other field researchers, some of whom worked with musicians and dancers prior to my arrival. Most researchers worked in other disciplines, but their presence was keenly felt by the community. This led me to think carefully about my own shadows in the field. The cluttering of the field makes this complexity inevitable, but it raises important questions about research ethics and our responsibilities to others. The interests of the ethno-musicologist tend toward the longitudinal end of the research spectrum. Trust is earned over time, and knowledge is based on long periods of immersion. Researchers embarking on a one-off tour strike a different bargain altogether. When there exists a quid pro quo, immediate and transactional, the stakes are much higher. I offered modest remuneration and sustenance to all the perform-ers I recorded. This was to cover their travel costs and time, but no more than that. I offered each performer an edited audio or video recording on CD or DVD. The time it took to make and return these records was considerable and it stretched my budget. Interestingly, there were many other demands made of me as an ethnographer. Some musicians requested alcohol, such as 1818 (Smirnoff vodka) or beer. Others insisted that *umqombothi* (traditional beer) had to be brewed to invoke their amadlozi. I did not agree to such demands, refusing all requests for alcohol, and this cost me opportunities. Other researchers had paid in kind, and so I had to explain my position very carefully so as not to offend. With the ever-extending reach of the academy, it is becoming increasingly necessary to establish accepted standards for scholars who engage in this kind of research across disciplines.

The process of recording musicians raised a unique set of challenges. Two starkly contrastive positions emerged from these discussions: some performers feared that I would exploit them, run away with their music, and make millions on the world music market.[3] Others were hopeful that I would act as their agent, take their music to the world market, and establish their careers. Serious musicians considered music and dance to be ways out of their current jobs, or unemployment, and were desperate for promotion. All I could do was make CDs and DVDs for them to enjoy, and these could be used as demos for community radio stations and record labels. In some places, I found other ways to help. For instance, I hosted a music festival competition at Busingatha, not far from Mazizini, where I offered a cash prize and the opportunity of a paid performance in Pretoria. This was a way to encourage interest in performances in a community isolated from metropolitan opportunities. The practice of recording was thus an important component to my ethnographic research and to the reciprocity I aimed to establish. But the use of sound technology in any research domain has its own impact.

Recording technologies introduce a new dynamic in performance situations. Placing microphones and cameras in cultural spaces changes how people see and hear themselves. Expectations and focus shift when performers know that an objective record of the event will be preserved. Erika Brady observes how early recording devices like the phonograph "represented a means to mediate the differences of purpose that separated collector and informant."[4] The proliferation of digital recording technologies over the past two decades has altered this dynamic. The idea of "collector" and "informant," and the power dynamics between them, is anachronistic. The idea of reciprocity that grounds ethnographic research extends to recording practice. Field recording now takes place in a hypermediated world. Cell phone cameras and microphones are everywhere. In the past, the ethnographer's role was custodial in the sense that recordings were stored safely and independently for future generations to engage with. Today, the ethnographer is sharing one recording of the event among several, and sometimes receives recordings as a response to their own. Recordings enable a digital dialogue that can be used to generate feedback from participants. Recordings that circulate and are shared on social media proliferate, thereby establishing a virtual community. This can be helpful to the research process, but it also means that sensitive information needs to be carefully controlled in dialogue with interested parties. This balance of priorities is a dialogic process of consultation, adaptation, and collaboration. The making and sharing of recordings should thus give us pause in thinking through the impact and role of ethnographers.

It is a difficult day to record at Ndumo Hill. We are using a small school hall not far from Mafutha Enkukhu's homestead. There is a lot of noise and misunderstanding. The sense of anticipation created by this unusual event seems to have sown confusion among the community. Controlling for the elements has proven impossible. There are masses of spectators crowding around the building, and the dancing has excited them. Some have forced open the windows and are peeking through creaking doors. Whispering, coughing, laughing, and all manner of muttering punctuate a comical quietness. Crying children have been carried nearby, and their parents seem oblivious to our objectives. Some visitors use the opportunity to make their own recordings using handheld cameras and phones. It does not help that pigeon chicks nestled in the ceiling are screeching at irregular intervals.

The filming of ingoma takes place on a patch of grass adjacent the school entrance. Mafutha Enkhuku has plants a wooden sign in the ground with his name painted on it. When we record his group, I discover that half of them are young boys; few adults are present, he tells me. The dance troupe are wearing traditional outfits and have a battery of cowhide drums and an *ingulube* (friction drum). This resonates a powerful, deep rumbling sound that can be heard from afar. Mafutha Enkukhu dances izingilili, a style quite unlike that of the isishameni and umzansi styles I know from uMsinga and the Drakensberg further south. The dancers carry spears and shields and move as a tightly organized regiment, but capturing their singing and dancing across a broad dance circle is difficult. There is competitive gesturing between individuals, and finely wrought nuances that elicit laughter among the crowd of onlookers. Mafutha Enkukhu himself leads the way with somersaults and turns, dust billowing up around him. His circular movements are athletic and supple, completed with a freedom of movement quite unlike the martial dances of uMsinga. iZingilili is a stamping dance in which the dancers observe a crouching pose. It requires considerable flexibility and fitness with dancers standing on their heads, rolling and somersaulting, and using their sticks for carefully choreographed actions.[5]

The combination of young children and elderly men dancing with Mafutha Enkukhu signals a generational disconnect. The rhythms of the drums echo those my father recorded on *Sounds of Tongaland* fifty years before, but the sounds of this community cohere differently now. Many youngsters in the audience are watching through their devices, recording the event for themselves and a virtual community far away.

ON RECORDING

The conditions at Ndumo Hill were characteristic of the kinds of acoustic challenges I faced pretty much everywhere. Most venues were not well suited to recording. Classrooms, community halls, and rondavels seldom had electricity, lighting, or windows intact, and the corrugated iron roofing and concrete flooring created an echo. The "best" results came from recordings made in rondavels with polished dung floors and thatched roofs. At schools and community halls, my recording sessions were of great interest to the community and passersby. An audience would grow. Many, despite their best efforts, could not contain their excitement and curiosity. In retrospect, the results were sometimes comical: children climbing walls and hanging through open windows, babies crying on mothers' backs, excited ululations from elderly women, and a host of other complications. Initially, I was very concerned about the extraneous environmental sounds and worked hard to edit out the attendant noise. But as my work progressed, I came to understand these sounds as integral to the worlds I was recording, and as an extension of the acoustemology of the performances that marked each place.

I quickly had to establish a flexible field-recording technique using condenser microphones and a portable digital recorder. I recorded film and audio simultaneously on separate devices and synced these recordings later. Monitoring recording and noise levels, microphone placement, and the events unfolding in time and space was a constant juggling act. It was impossible to control environmental factors like rain, wind, livestock, and birds, of course, as well as the sheer excitement of the crowds in attendance. At ceremonies I would move around a lot during the proceedings, filming with a handheld high-definition video camera and using a tripod. For outdoor events, I relied on a shotgun microphone with a shock mount and wind shield. The challenge in recording a polyphonic event like an umsindo was to capture a range of performances taking places simultaneously while preserving their relationships in sonic space. There was no chance of rerecording these events later or of capturing individual voices, and so important decisions had to be made in real time.

Then there was the question of microphone technique and placement. It often required several takes before singers and instrumentalists were comfortable with the various microphones I used. At least one-third of all recordings were deleted. All of this led to a great deal of frustration on my part, and I had to rethink how the materials I collected would or could be used to address my initial research questions. Indeed, this became part of the process of rethinking those questions. Editing, rendering, and systematizing data proved enormously time consuming. Because most events take place over several days, I collected a substantial archive of video and audio data—most of which I did not intend to use for music or linguistic analysis, but which became important for my ethnography. In any case, the community enjoyed having access to these as a record of their own performances. Another complication was that many homes had only very basic DVD playback facilities. On follow-up trips, I made deliveries and checked that the DVDs and CDs I had made were playable on the available equipment. Sometimes I had to return two or even three times to try out different formats. In the end, I bought the Ndlovu family a new DVD player so that they could watch their wedding video! Such challenges were part of a research process established on trust, and on a reciprocal ethics to which I was bound.

Digital technologies have changed the nature of sociality. It is tempting to speak of a digital revolution, of a social media revolution, or even of a new virtual episteme. Digitization has changed how we make and consume information, as well as how we value it. Experiences are made accessible through digital recordings just as these technologies make possible new experiences. Recorded sound is rendered in images and representations that in turn are used as lenses to interpret the world. This marks a paradigm shift in the kind of ethnomusicology now possible. Conversely, it marks a shift in the worlds in which ethnomusicologists are themselves immersed. Fifty years ago, my father's microphone was a curiosity at Ndumo. Today, everyone has access to recording devices on their mobile phones. Most digital devices have built-in cameras and microphones for video and photography. Social media applications create hyperrealities of our everyday experiences. The saturation of devices has enabled the obsessive and sometimes voyeuristic consumption of everyday life experiences. Sharing is declaring. The immediacy of these technologies and the speed of digital information flows have changed how we communicate. The research for this book focused on communities transitioning to these new technologies; a decade on, that transition is now complete. What this will mean for the next generation of Zulu performances is anyone's guess, but the ubiquity of digital devices already appears to have changed how performers direct their attention and imagine their sound.

FIGURE 8.2 Drum shed at Mafutha Enkukhu's homestead
near the Phongolo River, July 29, 2012.

JULY 29, 2012

11:20 a.m. Thulani arrives at the T-junction at Shemula with his friend Bheki.
We are off to visit Mafutha Enkukhu. The umuzi really is *ehlathini* (in the deep
bush), as both Thulani and Bheki keep telling me. The road is red and very sandy.
The central mound is high, so I maneuver the car along the edges of the tracks
and onto the grass. The wheels are spinning with no traction. We could well get
stuck out here, and without Madolwane to guide us, I begin to wonder whether
we are lost. But just at that moment, we chance upon a young woman who directs
us, and sure enough, the familiar sight of the drum shed and plows comes into
view. There is no one to be seen among the outbuildings. Thulani wanders off
and hails a child in the nearby field. I try phoning Mafutha Enkukhu and his
brother, Jabulani, but there is no reception. They are plowing in the fields down at
the Phongolo River. The dry, winter foliage reveals to us their location below the
isibaya where Msani is irrigating and growing *amazambane* (potatoes) a stone's
throw from the game reserve. The cattle from these huge byres are being used to
plow his land. Mafutha Enkukhu returns up the hill, walking swiftly to greet us.

When I hand him the DVD recordings, he smiles. They'll watch the video later at his *indodana's* (son's) home, he says, with jubilant gesture. We part on good terms. The circle is complete.

———

I listen as the isizembe sounds a somber tone. This is the resonance of an internalized world of sound that Madolwane hums quietly to himself. The record spins to its needle emanating the warmly familiar sound of a time and a place that connect with me still. His enigmatic song has no words, but its unmeasured lines speak of a shared moment of consonance. Like the beating of wings and the thronging voices of birds on the Phongolo floodplain, this melody is unsung.

CONCLUSION

Land *is* belonging. Place matters as a locus for genealogy and spirituality in Zulu societies. A visceral and spiritual connection to place motivates the recognition of home. Being in place facilitates the web of social life. Performances of music, dance, and oratory are the vehicle through which the connections between land, genealogy, and identity are established. This book has argued that sound matters in the politics of place, and, more specifically, that sonic spaces are used to reinforce culture and custom in Zulu performances. Singing is a way of figuring land in memory, in imagination, and in consciousness. Dance extends the lifeworld in space and time, marking out a politics of proximity. Praise poetry is used to extol virtues and vices, to call upon ancestors, and to identify one's place of origin. I have argued that ways of being, knowing, and belonging are forged through all these modalities in Zulu performance; I have tied this to land as a symbol of indivisible association. In Zulu societies, land is not simply a physical entity that can be traded and developed. Land and being are inseparable. Psychological attachments to place are powerful. Because land is about relation, it can lead to alienation. Persons uprooted, displaced, and injured by their landlessness, as well as by the inaccessibility of their lands, suffer. If land is a way of thinking about and identifying oneself, of understanding the ways in which one moves and dreams, then land cannot be dissociated from soul and sensibility.

The diversity of Zulu performances documented in this book engage a series of debates on postapartheid culture, ethnicity, and politics. These explorations of performance speak to global challenges of land and landlessness, migrancy, displacement, and environmental degradation. I have adopted an ethnographic method rooted in the anthropology of the senses, sound studies, and ethnomusicology to engage these debates through a reflexive foregrounding of experience, and by employing a writing strategy that is dialogic and open-ended, sometimes resisting interpretation. While to some degree there is the inevitable need to draw conclusions, these summations need not preclude others. Enabling an open dialogue on land, culture, and performance is a primary aim of this book. Reaching across difference to understand one another in space and time is an ethical necessity.

This book is an ethnography of Zulu performances written in the post-Mandela phase of South Africa's democracy. But understanding the dynamics of post-apartheid governance and politics, and how these shape cultures of performance in rural KwaZulu-Natal, necessitates critical reflection on the traces of empire, colonialism, and apartheid on contemporary institutions. The Zulu and British Empires established administrative structures upon which twentieth-century Zulu societies were governed. Political elites continue to advance their interests through the construction and reinvention of traditional institutions in KwaZulu-Natal. For instance, the present system of communal land tenure under the governance of traditional authorities means that many Zulu communities continue to have access to land, but without title. What would full ownership of land mean for these communities? Would this empower a new generation of farmers and businesses to take advantage of their natural resources? Or would this result in further conflicts over boundaries and territorial limits, as well as more violence in an already turbulent region? The present land calculus means that although many Zulu families reside on tracts of land across the province, they are still only a tiny minority of landowners. Unfortunately, this perpetuates the racial inequalities that the Union and apartheid governments established by design.

The chapters on performances at Mdukatshani and Johannesburg show the tenacity of Zulu indigenous knowledge systems and the power of place in connecting migrant workers to their rural homes. Customs and rituals preserve bonds between and within communities. I have shown how the politics of sonic space in communal performances are used to articulate identity and status as well as to register difference. The resolution of land claims on the farms at Mdukatshani offer important case studies for how land can be returned and governed by and for communities in rural KwaZulu-Natal. The social dynamics of the tribal wards in the Inkosi Langalibalele and uMsinga Municipalities mean that many adults seek work elsewhere, returning only intermittently to their rural homes. This led me to a study of isishameni dance at Jeppe Hostel, where so many men spend their adult lives. This phenomenology of ingoma focused on the politics of proximity in Jeppestown, and on how migrants draw power from their rural networks to survive and compete in the inner city of South Africa's largest metropole.

The prosody and politics of popular praises are explored in chapter 5, which integrated new digital methods for linguistic and musical analysis to produce insights on melody and song prosody that are complementary to ethnographic and hermeneutic interpretation. The politics of place figure in performances of izibongo that invoke geographic and genealogical connections. Popular praises are used to inflict incisive social commentary directed at close friends, family, and leaders, in a space sanctioned for politics. iziBongo articulate the experiences, genealogy, and heritage of their orators, and are replete with idioms and lyrical encodings intelligible only to those familiar with the contexts, symbols, and sounds specific to umaskandi lifeworlds. A genealogy of izibongo linked umaskandi to other popular praises, to genres of dance and bow music, and to izibongo zamakhosi. This chapter shows the power of performance to assert identity and belonging in contested social contexts.

The second half of the book focuses on performances in the municipalities of Jozini and uMhlabuyalingana in northeast KwaZulu-Natal. Thulani Gumede and I spent much of our time visiting schools where we attended lessons, rehearsals, and competitions for choirs and dance troupes. The popular extracurricular activities in these schools are excluded from the formal curriculum, which recognizes only the literacies of Western staff and tonic solfa notations. This pattern is consistent with the music and dance activities at schools in the uMsinga and uThukela districts, and appears to contradict national imperatives to validate and promote indigenous knowledge systems. Finding ways to integrate these activities into the curriculum by rethinking literacies, and (re)training teachers, would be a major advance for synchronizing education and arts sectors in South Africa.

I returned to Ndumo with my father's album *Sounds of Tongaland* in mind. A powerful personal bond with this place shaped my experience of working there. I was welcomed by the community, and the relationships I established were important for the kind of work I completed. The umaskandi and ingoma I recorded at Ndumo and ePhosheni created a dialogue with my father's records. The performances of bow players, singers, and dancers included many songs in the same genres my father had recorded half a century earlier. The continuities and discontinuities in these records show that while the traces of some cultural practices have been retained, there is much that has been lost.

The politics of place at Ndumo Game Reserve is registered in a crisis that threatens the sanctity of the area. Unresolved land claims and aggressive occupation, hunting, and harvesting in large tracts of the reserve threaten sensitive ecosystems that harbor endangered wildlife. The invasion of Ndumo raises difficult questions about how subsistence in poverty-stricken regions can and should be supported, and how reserves can be used to provide resources to communities without compromising the project of conservation. These are critical issues in an age of climate change, mass extinction, and environmental degradation. How the case of Ndumo is settled will set an important precedent in law. How will government protect wildlife and the environment in accordance with the Constitution of the Republic? I approach the land issues at Ndumo, and the need for coexistence, through reflections on my own experiences in the reserve, and by using recorded wildlife sounds to give voice to our fellow creatures.

An ethics of reciprocity guided my fieldwork and recording practice, just as it has shaped the writing of this book. I have sought to work respectfully and dialogically with communities in a committed way to advance their interests. The use of recording technologies was a method for documenting the cultures I studied and for engaging dialogically in an increasingly digital world saturated with social media. I have argued that a pragmatic and engaged scholarship can be fashioned through recording practice when it is used as a flexible tool of dialogic engagement.

RITES OF RETURN

My return to South Africa from the United States precipitated the journey this book records. My experiences in researching and writing this ethnography compelled me to study and make sense of the everyday experiences expressed in Zulu performances. I was motivated not only by the richness and depth of cultural expression that I witnessed, but also by the plight of the rural poor and marginalized communities in South Africa. I have witnessed desperate conditions of poverty, violence, and decay. South Africa is a country struggling to emerge from decades of corruption and injustice, and still battling with the terrible legacies of segregation, racism, and apartheid. And yet, despite these seemingly intractable problems, I find myself drawn back again and again by those intangible powers of association and belonging that makes this land home, encouraged and reinvigorated by the beauty, wisdom, and generosity of so many who strive for a better life.

The nature of my relationship to the land of my birth, and to the many places

I have come to know over the past decade, has reshaped my sense of belonging. The memories, histories, and genealogies embodied in our relationships to land resonate to our inner songs. Singing is a vehicle for collective memory that connects us to our ancestors and to those from whom we depart. Performances of song and dance have the power to heal our sense of alienation and displacement. The renewal we experience in the sounds of place and in the songs of our forebears reveals to us our deep connections to land. The journey ahead will be challenging, but if we hold to the upward path, advancing justice in the pursuit of a better life, then perhaps we will find happiness and belonging in this land that is sung.

GLOSSARY

Where two terms appear, the first is singular and the second plural.

amasi—curdled milk

ibandla/amabandla—assembly of men or elders who inform the leadership

ibutho/amabutho—regiment/s, men of the same age grade

idlozi/amadlozi—ancestral spirit/s

igoso/amagoso—leader/s in dance or music

ihubo/amahubo—anthem/s

ikhetho—bridegroom's party at a wedding

ilobolo—bride wealth

indlamu—male dance style from central and northern KwaZulu-Natal

indlu enkhulu—principal dwelling in a homestead

induku/izinduku—fighting stick/s

induna—headman

ingoma—generic term for dance song; sometimes used for female dance styles only

inhlonipho—culturally sanctioned behavior that exhibits respect, reverence, and honor

inkosi/amakhosi—chief/s

intelezi—plants used for protection against witchcraft and misfortune

iphini/amaphini—second-in-command or lower-ranking officer/s

isibaya—cattle byre

isibongo/izibongo—praise/s, praise name/s; clan name/s

isicathamiya—an a cappella vocal genre with close-knit harmonies and call-and-response

isidwaba/izidwaba—leather skirt/s

isigodi/izigodi—tribal ward/s

isishameni—a style of ingoma dance characterized by its high kick and vertical movements

ubukhosi—kingship

umakho—gift

umakoti—bride/wife

umgonqo—place of seclusion

umhlwehlwe—caul, the white film that envelops a cow's gall bladder

umKhosi woMhlanga—ceremony of the first fruits performed by the king

umkhwenyana—bridegroom

umnumzane—homestead owner

umqombothi—traditional beer brewed for use at rituals involving ancestral spirits

umsamo—inner sanctum of the home

umsindo—sound, noise, uproar, quarrel; or wedding

umthetho/imithetho—law/s

umthimba—bridal party

umuthi—medicinal herbs for healing

umuzi/imizi—homestead/s

NOTES

Note on Language

Clement M. Doke, D. Mck. Malcolm, J. M. A. Sikakana, and Benedict W. Vilakazi. *English–isiZulu, isiZulu–English Dictionary*. 4th edition with revised orthography. Johannesburg: Wits University Press, 2014.

INTRODUCTION *Sounding a Way*

1. Tony Pooley, *Discoveries of a Crocodile Man* (London: Collins, 1982).

2. *umNyonyovu* is a species of wasp and is the name I was given at birth by the Zulu community at St. Lucia in northern KwaZulu-Natal (now part of the iSimangiliso Wetland Park). My mother was gardening at the St. Lucia Crocodile Education Centre my father had established for research and education. She was stung by umnyonyovu wasps beside a cycad and went into labor.

3. Mashesha means "he who hurries and takes" and is the isiZulu name given to my father.

4. *Hyphaene coriacea.*

5. Homes in the area do not have piped water or sewage. Women collect water daily from the Phongolo River. The municipality installed water tanks located at two-mile intervals along the main service roads. Each tank has a single tap from which to draw water for drinking, washing, and cleaning.

6. Working for Water is a government-funded poverty alleviation program in South Africa providing work to unemployed, unskilled workers who are trained to remove invasive non-native plants that suck up precious water reserves and negatively transform habitats threatening biodiversity. "Working for Water Programme," Department of Forestry, Fisheries & the Environment, Republic of South Africa, accessed September 24, 2022, https://www.dffe.gove.za/projectsprogrammes/wfw.

7. The Bill of Rights is enshrined in the Constitution of the Republic of South Africa (1996).

8. The notion of "being-in-the-world" used in this book draws on Martin Heidegger's notion of *Dasein*, which he developed in *Being and Time*. Heidegger, *Being and Time*, translated by John Macquarrie and Edward Robinson (New York: Harper Perennial, 1962).

9. Mahmood Mamdani, *Citizen and Subject: Contemporary Africa and the Legacy of Late Colonialism* (Braamfontein: Wits University Press, 2017); John L. Comaroff and Jean Comaroff, eds., *The Politics of Custom: Chiefship, Capital, and the State in Contemporary Africa* (Chicago: University of Chicago Press, 2018); Dineo Skosana, Mbongiseni Buthelezi, and Beth Vale, *Traditional Leaders in a Democracy: Resources, Respect and Resistance* (Woodmead: MISTRA, 2018).

10. Clifford Geertz, *The Interpretation of Cultures* (New York: Basic Books, 1973); James Clifford and George E. Marcus, eds., *Writing Culture: The Poetics and Politics of Ethnography* (Berkeley: University of California Press, [1986] 2010).

11. Geertz, *The Interpretation of Cultures*.

12. Maurice Merleau-Ponty, *Phenomenology of Perception*, translated by Colin Smith (New York: Routledge, 1962); Paul Stoller, *The Taste of Ethnographic Things: The Senses in Anthropology* (Philadelphia: University of Pennsylvania Press, 1989); Steven Feld and Donald Brenneis, "Doing Anthropology in Sound," *American Ethnologist* 31, no. 4 (2004): 461–474; David Samuels, Louise Meintjes, Ana Maria Ochoa, and Thomas Porcello, "Soundscapes: Toward a Sounded Anthropology," *Annual Review of Anthropology* 39 (2010): 329–345; Louise Meintjes, *Dust of the Zulu: Ngoma Aesthetics After Apartheid* (Durham, NC: Duke University Press, 2017).

13. Clifford and Marcus, *Writing Culture*.

14. James Clifford, "Introduction: Partial Truths," in James Clifford and George E. Marcus, eds., *Writing Culture: The Poetics and Politics of Ethnography* (Berkeley: University of California Press, [1986]2010), 5.

15. Clifford, "Introduction: Partial Truths," 5.

16. Clifford, "Introduction: Partial Truths," 5.

17. Ruth Hellier-Tinoco, "Experiencing People: Relationships, Responsibility and Reciprocity," *British Journal of Ethnomusicology* 12, no. 1 (2003): 19–34.

18. See Jeff Todd Titon, "Music, the Public Interest, and the Practice of Ethnomusicology," *Ethnomusicology* 63, no. 3 (1992): 315–322; and other essays in this volume.

19. Recent monographs that embrace the reflexive turn in southern African ethnography include Carol Muller, *Rituals of Fertility and the Sacrifice of Desire: Nazarite Women's Performance in South Africa* (Chicago: University of Chicago Press, 1999); Louise Meintjes, *Sound of Africa! Making Music Zulu in a South African Studio* (Durham, NC: Duke University Press, 2003); and Meintjes, *Dust of the Zulu*.

20. Michelle Kisliuk, *Seize the Dance! BaAka Musical Life and the Ethnography of Performance* (New York: Oxford University Press, 1998); Steven Friedson, *Dancing Prophets: Musical Experience in Tumbuka Healing* (Chicago: University of Chicago Press, 1996); Steven Friedson, *Remains of Ritual: Northern Gods in a Southern Land* (Chicago: University of Chicago Press, 2009).

21. Deborah Kapchan, "Body," in *Keywords in Sound*, edited by David Novak and Matt Sakakeeny (Durham, NC: Duke University Press, 2015), 33.

22. Steven Feld, *Sound and Sentiment: Birds, Weeping, Poetics, and Song in Kaluli Expression* (Philadelphia: University of Pennsylvania Press, 1982).

23. Jean Comaroff and John L. Comaroff, *Theory from the South: Or, How Euro-America Is Evolving Toward Africa* (New York: Routledge, 2010).

24. Gavin Steingo and Jim Sykes, eds., *Remapping Sound Studies* (Durham, NC: Duke University Press, 2019), 4.

25. R. Murray Schafer, *The Soundscape: Our Sonic Environment and the Tuning of the World* (Rochester, VT: Destiny Books, 1993), 15.

26. Schafer, *The Soundscape*, 17.

27. Veit Erlmann, "What of the Ethnographic Ear?" in *Hearing Cultures: Essays on Sound, Listening and Modernity*, edited by Veit Erlmann (New York: Routledge, [2004]2020), 3.

28. Erlmann, "What of the Ethnographic Ear?" 3.

29. Deborah Kapchan, "The Splash of Icarus: Theorizing Sound Writing/Writing Sound Theory," in *Theorizing Sound Writing*, edited by Deborah Kapchan (Middletown, CT: Wesleyan University Press, 2017), 12.

30. Steven Feld, "Acoustemology," in *Keywords in Sound*, edited by David Novak and Matt Sakakeeny (Durham, NC: Duke University Press, 2015), 12–21.

31. Feld, "Acoustemology."

32. Tim Ingold, "Against Soundscape," in *Autumn Leaves: Sound and the Environment in Artistic Practice*, edited by Angus Carlyle (Paris: Double Entendre, 2007), 10–13.

33. Naomi André, Yolanda Covington-Ward, and Jendele Hungbo, eds., *African Performance Arts and Political Action* (Ann Arbor: University of Michigan Press, 2021).

34. Gregory Barz and Timothy J. Cooley, "Casting Shadows," in *Shadows in the Field: New Perspectives for Fieldwork in Ethnomusicology*, 2nd ed., edited by Gregory Barz and Timothy J. Cooley (Chicago: University of Chicago Press, 2008), 4.

35. Barz and Cooley, "Casting Shadows," 19–20.

36. Peter J. Coertze, "Volkekunde," *South African Journal of Ethnology* 1, no. 1 (1978): 1–9; John S. Sharp, "The Roots and Development of Volkekunde in South Africa," *Journal of Southern African Studies* 8, no. 11 (1981): 16–36.

37. Being-in-the-world is very much a function of integrating mind, brain, and world in ways that philosopher Andy Clark writes about in *Being There: Putting Brain, Body, and World Together Again* (Cambridge, MA: MIT Press, 1997).

38. "On the one hand, the submerged, the unseen, the unrecognized may under certain conditions be called to awareness; on the other, things once perceived and explicitly marked may slip below the level of discourse into the unremarked recesses of the collective unconscious. The latter is emphatically *not* some form of group mind. It is the implicit structure of shared meaning that human beings absorb as they learn to be members of particular social worlds." Jean Comaroff and John Comaroff, *Of Revelation and Revolution, Volume 1: Christianity, Colonialism, and Consciousness in South Africa* (Chicago: University of Chicago Press, 1991), 29.

39. 22.7 percent of all South Africans recognize isiZulu as their first language. There are several mutually intelligible dialects of isiZulu. In 2018 the population of KwaZulu-Natal was estimated at 11,384,722 persons living in an area of 94,361 km^2 (roughly equivalent to the area of Portugal). "Mid-year Population Estimates, 2018. Statistical Release P0302" (Pretoria: *Statistics South Africa*, 2018), 17. The 2011 national census determined that 7,901,932 persons, or 78 percent, spoke isiZulu as their first language in this province. "Census 2011: Census in Brief," *Statistics South Africa* (Pretoria: Statistics South Africa, 2012).

40. The Nguni languages spoken in KwaZulu-Natal include isiZulu, isiXhosa, and siSwati. The focus of this research is principally on isiZulu-speaking cultures.

41. "The Swazi language, which is considered to be a distinct language from that of Zulu, is also said to be *ukuthekeza*." Clement Doke, "The Phonetics of the Zulu Language," *Bantu Studies*, Vol. 2., Reprint (Muenchen: Lincom Grammatica, [2012] 1926), 11.

42. Doke, "Phonetics," 12.

43. In a survey of Zulu dialects in Natal and Zululand conducted in 1979, Isaac Kubeka classified six main areas: Central Zululand, Zululand Coast, Natal Coast, Lower Natal Coast, Southwest Natal, and Northern Natal. Kubeka excludes dialects at the fringes of the province, including the Pondo area to the south, Tembe-Tongas to the north, and the influence of seSotho in the Nquthu District of central KwaZulu-Natal. Isaac Sibusiso Kubeka, "A Preliminary Survey of Zulu Dialects in Natal and Zululand" (master's thesis, University of Natal, Durban, 1979), 2–3.

44. For a detailed discussion of the politics of identity, see John Wright, "Reflections on the Politics of Being 'Zulu,'" in *Zulu Identities: Being Zulu, Past and Present*, edited by Benedict Carton, John Laband, and Jabulani Sithole (Pietermaritzburg: University of KwaZulu-Natal Press, 2008), 35–44. The invention of tradition in KwaZulu is the subject of Daphna Golan's book *Inventing Shaka: Using History in the Construction of Zulu Nationalism* (London: Lynne Rienner, 1994). The historical literature in this field is discussed in more detail in chapter 1.

45. The annual uMkhosi womHlanga (reed dance ceremony) held at the Enyokeni Royal Palace outside Nongoma is one instance of a bringing together of girls and young women from across the province to join in a community of singing and dancing (see chapter 3).

46. Carolyn Hamilton and Nessa Leibhammer, eds., *Tribing and Untribing the Archive:*

Identity and the Material Record in Southern KwaZulu-Natal in the Late Independent and Colonial Periods. 2 volumes (Scottsville: University of KwaZulu-Natal Press, 2016); John Guy, *Theophilus Shepstone and the Forging of Natal* (Scottsville: University of KwaZulu-Natal Press, 2013).

47. A note on race and terminology: I have used the terms "Black" and "White" throughout the book because this is the commonplace usage in South Africa today. Other racial terms, such as "Europeans" and "natives," are invoked only when discussing legislation or documentary sources specific to a period in South African history. Gavin Steingo's reflection on the language of race in South Africa explains the complexity of racial terminologies and their usage; see *Kwaito's Promise: Music and the Aesthetics of Freedom in South Africa* (Chicago: University of Chicago Press, 2016), xix–xx.

48. Mbongiseni Buthelezi, "The Empire Talks Back: Re-examining the Legacies of Shaka and Zulu Power in Post-apartheid South Africa," in *Zulu Identities: Being Zulu, Past and Present*, edited by Benedict Carton, John Laband, and Jabulani Sithole (Pietermaritzburg: University of KwaZulu-Natal Press, 2008), 23–34.

49. Golan, *Inventing Shaka.*

50. Meintjes, *Dust of the Zulu.*

51. "Yoked together in the service of colonial and later apartheid rule, the pernicious combination of tribe and tradition continues to tether modern South Africans to ideas about the region's remote past as primitive, timeless, and unchanging, despite substantial scholarly and public critical discussion of the fallacy of these notions. Any hunger for knowledge or understanding of the past before European imperialism thus remains to a significant degree unsated, even denied, in the face of a narrowly prescribed archive and repugnant, but insidiously resilient stereotypes." Hamilton and Leibhammer, *Tribing and Untribing the Archive*, vol. 1, 14.

52. Ibid.

53. "Despite the heterogeneity of groupings in this region [KwaZulu-Natal], a traditional and homogenous notion of Zulu identity has been promoted at various times throughout the twentieth century by Zulu royalists, white segregationists, the early twentieth-century black petite bourgeoisie, the apartheid government, KwaZulu Bantustan authorities and the Zulu nationalist organization, Inkatha, for political ends to unite and constrain a multitude of constituencies under the generic title 'Zulu.'" Grant McNulty, "(Re)discovering the Correct History: Tradition and Custom, the Archival Record and Identity in Contemporary KwaZulu-Natal," in *Tribing and Untribing the Archive: Identity and the Material Record in Southern KwaZulu-Natal in the Late Independent and Colonial Periods*, Volume 1, edited by Carolyn Hamilton and Nessa Leibhammer (Scottsville: University of KwaZulu-Natal Press, 2016), 115–145, 121.

54. Judith Temkin Irvine and Liz Gunner, "With Respect to Zulu: Revisiting ukuHlonipha," *Anthropological Quarterly* 91, no. 1 (2018): 173–207.

55. See Louise Meintjes, "Shoot the Sargeant, Shatter the Mountain: The Production of Masculinity in Zulu Ngoma Song and Dance in Post-Apartheid South Africa," *Ethnomusicology Forum* 13, no. 2 (2004): 173–201.

56. See Terence Ranger, *Dance and Society in Eastern Africa, 1890–1970: The Beni Ngoma* (Berkeley: University of California Press, 1975); Meintjes, *Dust of the Zulu.*

57. I recorded indlamu (central and northwest KwaZulu-Natal), isishameni (midlands), umzansi (south and Ukhahlamba-Drakensberg regions), and izingilili (northeast), among others.

58. David Rycroft and A. Bhekabantu Ngcobo, *Say It in Zulu* (London: School of Oriental and African Studies, 1979), D11.

59. Musa Xulu, "The Re-Emergence of Amahubo Song Styles and Ideas in Some Modern Zulu Musical Styles" (Unpublished PhD diss., University of Natal, 1992).

60. Rycroft and Ngcobo, *Say It in Zulu,* D15.

61. See Angela Impey, "Sound, Memory and Dis/placement: Exploring Sound, Song and Performance as Oral History in the Southern African Borderlands," *Oral History* 36, no. 1 (2008): 33–44.

62. isiCathamiya originated in the urban hostels of Johannesburg and Durban where groups of male migrant-workers would join in choral singing after hours and on weekends. These weekend competitions continue today at hostels like Jeppe and George Goch in Johannesburg. See Veit Erlmann, *Nightsong: Performance, Power, and Practice in South Africa* (Chicago: Chicago University Press, 1996).

63. Kwaito is a form of electronic house music. See Steingo, *Kwaito's Promise.*

64. Kofi Agawu, *The African Imagination in Music* (New York: Oxford University Press, 2016), 267.

ONE *The Politics of Belonging: Land, Culture, and Representation in KwaZulu-Natal*

1. The meaning of the word *iZulu* is "sky or heavens." Clement M. Doke et al., *English–isiZulu, isiZulu–English Dictionary*, 4th ed., with revised orthography (Johannesburg: Wits University Press, 2014), 1248.

2. *umZulu*, the condition of being Zulu, and isizwe, of nation and national identity are not coterminous.

3. Gavin Whitelaw, "A Brief Archaeology of Precolonial Farming in KwaZulu-Natal," in *Zulu Identities: Being Zulu, Past and Present*, edited by Benedict Carton, John Laband, and Jabulani Sithole (Pietermaritzburg: University of KwaZulu-Natal Press, 2008), 47–61.

4. isiZulu employs click consonants in its phonetic inventory, and these shape the patterning of melody and rhythm in singing. See David Rycroft, "The Relationships

between Speech-Tone and Melody in Southern African Music," in *South African Music Encyclopedia*, Vol. 2, edited by J. P. Malan (Pretoria: Human Sciences Research Council, 1982), 301–314; Thomas Pooley, "Depressing Melodies: Consonants and Tone in Zulu Song." *Journal of the Phonetic Society of Japan* 22, no. 3 (2018): 42–49; Thomas Pooley, "Linguistic Tone and Melody in the Singing of Sub-Saharan Africa," in F. Russo and A. Cohen, eds., *The Routledge Companion to Interdisciplinary Studies in Singing*, Volume 1: Development (New York: Routledge, 2020), 108–120.

5. Tim Huffman, "The Archaeology of the Nguni Past," *Southern African Humanities* 16, no. 1 (2004): 79–111; W. David Hammond-Tooke, "The Uniqueness of Nguni Mediumistic Divination in Southern Africa," *Africa* 72, no. 2 (2002): 277–292.

6. John Wright and Carolyn Hamilton, "Traditions and Transformations: The Phongolo-Mzimkhulu Region in the Late Eighteenth and Early Nineteenth Centuries," in *Natal and Zululand from Earliest Times to 1910: A New History*, edited by Andrew Duminy and Bill Guest (Pietermaritzburg: University of Natal Press, 2009), 56.

7. Tim Maggs, "The Iron Age Farming Communities," in *Natal and Zululand from Earliest Times to 1910: A New History*, edited by Andrew Duminy and Bill Guest (Pietermaritzburg: University of Natal Press, 1989), 37.

8. John Laband, *The Eight Zulu Kings: From Shaka to Goodwill Zwelithini* (Cape Town: Jonathan Ball, 2018).

9. Mbongiseni Buthelezi complicates the idea of a homogeneous Zulu culture in his doctoral dissertation, "Sifuna umlando wethu (We Are Searching for Our History): Oral Literature and the Meanings of the Past in Post-Apartheid South Africa" (PhD diss., Columbia University, 2012).

10. Roger Crowley, *Conquerors: How Portugal Seized the Indian Ocean and Forged the First Global Empire* (London: Faber, 2015).

11. David Smith, "Colonial Encounters through the Prism of Music: A Southern African Perspective," *International Review of the Aesthetics and Sociology of Music* 33, no. 1 (2002): 31–55.

12. T. V. Bulpin, *Natal and the Zulu Country* (Pretoria: Protea, 2013).

13. Charles Ballard, "Traders, Trekkers and Colonists," in *Natal and Zululand from Earliest Times to 1910*, edited by Andrew Duminy and Bill Guest (Pietermaritzburg: University of Natal Press, 1989), 116.

14. Pippa Skotnes, ed., *Miscast: Negotiating the Presence of the Bushmen* (Cape Town: University of Cape Town Press, 1996).

15. Edgar Brookes and Colin de Webb, *A History of Natal* (Scottsville: University of Natal Press, 1965), 154–155.

16. Jeff Guy, *The Maphumulo Uprising: War, Law, and Ritual in the Zulu Rebellion* (Pietermaritzburg: University of KwaZulu-Natal Press, 2005).

17. "The Commission, which began its investigations in 1902 and reported in 1904, demarcated Reserves totaling 3,887,000 acres. Thus 2,613,000 acres were excluded and much of this area [was subsequently] made up of privately owned European sugar and wattle plantations and vested European interests were thus created in the heart of Zululand." Brookes and de Webb, *A History of Natal*, 186.

18. Act No. 27 of 1913. The act states that "'native' shall mean any person, male or female, who is a member of an aboriginal race or tribe of Africa; and shall further include any company or other body of persons, corporate or unincorporate, if the persons who have a controlling interest therein are natives."

19. Louis Changuion and Bertus Steenkamp, *Disputed Land: The Historical Development of the South African Land Issue, 1652–2011* (Pretoria: Protea, 2012), 134.

20. Bill Freund, "South Africa: The Union Years, 1910–1948 – Political and Economic Foundations," in *The Cambridge History of South Africa, Volume 2, 1885–1994*, edited by Robert Ross, Anne Kelk Mager, and Bill Nasson (Cambridge: Cambridge University Press, 2016), 211–253.

21. Posel, "The Apartheid Project," 158.

22. Deborah Posel, "The Apartheid Project," in *The Cambridge History of South Africa, Volume 2, 1885–1994*, edited by Robert Ross, Anne Kelk Mager, and Bill Nasson (Cambridge: Cambridge University Press, 2016), 350.

23. Anne Kelk Mager and Maanda Mulaudzi, "Popular Responses to Apartheid: 1948—c. 1975," in *The Cambridge History of South Africa, Volume 2, 1885–1994*, edited by Robert Ross, Anne Kelk Mager, and Bill Nasson (Cambridge: Cambridge University Press, 2016), 393. Posel, "The Apartheid Project," 158.

24. Mager and Mulaudzi, "Popular Responses to Apartheid," 393–394.

25. Murders and assassinations are still commonplace, and events like umemulo ceremonies and weddings are sometimes zones of conflict at which skirmishes break out.

26. Zulu Chiefs and Headmen Act No. 8 of 1974 (revised 1980).

27. Jill Kelly, *To Swim with Crocodiles: Land, Violence, and Belonging in South Africa, 1800–1996* (Scottsville: University of KwaZulu-Natal Press, 2019).

28. "Media Release: Quarterly Labor Force Survey, Q4 2021" (Pretoria: Statistics South Africa, 2021).

29. Lawrence Hamilton, *Are South Africans Free?* (New York: Bloomsbury, 2014), chapter 2.

30. Laurence Piper argues that the Zulu ethnic group cannot be considered a nation owing to their disparate political factions. Laurence Piper, "Nationalism without a Nation: The Rise and Fall of Zulu Nationalism in South Africa's Transition to Democracy, 1975–99," *Nations and Nationalism* 8, no. 1 (2002).

31. Guy, *Theophilus Shepstone*, 532.

32. The word *igoso* also refers to the leader of a dance troupe. Doke et al., *Dictionary*, 655.

33. Rauri Alcock and Donna Hornby, *Traditional Land Matters—A Look into Land Administration in Tribal Areas in KwaZulu-Natal* (Mdukatshani: Legal Entity Assessment Project, 2004), 31. The term may also be spelled *iphini*, meaning "underling; inferior officer, personal representative." Doke et al., *Dictionary*, 1030.

34. "It is the *ibandla* that can initiate a process to have an *induna* or even *inkosi* removed from authority." Doke et al., *Dictionary*, 437.

35. A succession battle ensued that resulted in a schism within the royal house.

36. Mbongiseni Buthelezi and Dineo Skosana, "The Salience of Chiefs in Postapartheid South Africa: Reflections on the Nhlapo Commission," in *The Politics of Custom: Chiefship, Capital, and the State in Contemporary Africa*, edited by John L. Comaroff and Jean Comaroff (Chicago: University of Chicago Press, 2018), 111.

37. "Ingonyama Trust Home Page," Ingonyama Trust Board, last modified 2019, accessed June 15, 2019, http://www.ingonyamatrust.org.za.

38. "In 2017, former President Kgalema Motlanthe chaired a High-Level Panel (HLP) to review key legislation in South Africa. The panel met with individuals and communities across South Africa and reported to parliament on a range of issues, including land tenure and restitution. Their findings declare that the Ingonyama Trust legislation is unique to KwaZulu-Natal and has been used to exploit the land rights of rural communities to their detriment. The HLP recommended that the Ingonyama Trust Act be repealed or amended." Jabulani Sithole and Percy Ngonyama, "The Land Question – The Ingonyama Trust Controversy," *Polity* (website), published May 11, 2018, accessed June 15, 2019, https://www.polity.org.za/article/the-land-question-the-ingonyama-trust-controversy-2018-05-11.

39. Ibid.

40. "Report of the High Level Panel on the Assessment of Key Legislation and the Acceleration of Fundamental Change," November 2017, https://www.parliament.gov.za/storage/app/media/Pages/2017/october/High_Level_Panel_HLP_Report/HLP_report.pdf.

41. Ibid.

42. Lwandile Bhengu, "King Zwelithini Likens Land Question to Being 'Stripped of Our Blanket," *Timeslive*, September 8, 2019, accessed online: https://www.timeslive.co.za/politics/2019-09-08-king-zwelithini-likens-land-question-to-being-stripped-of-our-blanket/.

43. Mamdani, *Citizen and Subject*; Barbara Oomen, *Chiefs in South Africa: Law, Power & Culture in the Post-Apartheid Era* (New York: Palgrave MacMillan, 2006); Lungisile Ntsebeza, *Democracy Compromised: Chiefs and the Politics of the Land in South Africa* (Leiden: Brill, 2005); Comaroff and Comaroff, *Politics of Custom*.

44. Jo Beall, Sibongiseni Mkhize, and Shahid Vawda, "Emergent Democracy and 'Resurgent' Tradition: Institutions, Chieftaincy and Transition in KwaZulu-Natal," *Journal of Southern African Studies* 31, no. 4 (2005): 763.

45. Act No. 3 of 2019: Traditional and Khoi-San Leadership Act, 2019. November 28, 2019, Accessed online: https://www.gov.za/sites/default/files/gcis_document/201911/4286528 -11act3of2019tradkhoisanleadership.pdf.

46. Nhlapo Commission Report, "Determinations on the Position of the Paramount Chiefs," 2010, accessed October 2, 2022, https://www.gov.za/sites/default/files/gcis_document /201409/reports-paramountcieso.pdf.

47. Buthelezi and Skosana, "Salience of Chiefs."

48. When Zwelithini passed away in 2021, an acrimonious succession battle ensued. President Ramaphosa ultimately endorsed the new king in March 2022, a little over a year after Zwelithini's passing. Sizwe Sama Yende, "Ramaphosa Recognises Prince Misuzulu as AmaZulu King," *City Press*, March 17, 2022, https://www.news24.com/citypress/news /ramaphosa-recognises-prince-misuzulu-as-amazulu-king-20220317.

49. The system of traditional leadership was first established under Theophilus Shepstone in the mid-nineteenth century. Guy, *Theophilus Shepstone*.

50. Alfred T. Bryant, *Olden Times in Zululand and Natal: Containing Earlier Political History of the Eastern-Nguni Clans* (London: Longmans, 1929), chapters 30–32.

51. Guy, *Theophilus Shepstone*, 109. Note that variations in spelling are historical and so have been retained.

52. *Theophilus Shepstone*, 110.

53. Creina Alcock, "A Brief History of the Mchunu and Mthembu Tribes," in *Imithetho yomhlaba yaseMsinga: The Living Law of Land in Msinga, KwaZulu-Natal*, edited by Ben Cousins (Cape Town: University of the Western Cape, 2011), 23.

54. Alcock, "A Brief History," 24.

55. "Msinga had become the centre of the gun trade in South Africa, with the only fulltime Firearm Squad in the country. The Squad was moved into the area some time in 1957, and housed in tents on the riverbank at Tugela Ferry; they ran a token operation for the next 45 years." Alcock, "A Brief History," 27.

56. The relationship of White farmers and their Black tenants and workers was exploitative. It was continued because it enabled Black tenants to retain their livestock (and thus their wealth) while providing these farmers with cheap labor. But the hardships of this exploitation are not forgotten. On the farm Darkest Africa, I was told of a life of deprivation under apartheid. Ndididi Dladla recounted to me how those living at Nkaseni and in its surroundings struggled: "We could choose between buying one pair of shoes, or one pair of trousers each year. It was like working the dust for nothing."

57. Creina Alcock, "No Ordinary Farm," unpublished manuscript (1984), 5.

58. Sato, "Forced Removals, Land NGOs and Community Politics in KwaZulu-Natal, South Africa, 1953–2002" (PhD thesis: University of Oxford, 2006), 26.

59. Sato, "Forced Removals," 3.

60. "Forced Removals," 27.

61. "Forced Removals," 223.

62. Census data collected in the Weenen District between 1946 and 1980 show a 44 percent decrease in population; this in contrast to continuous population growth in neighboring districts like Estcourt. Sato, "Forced Removals," 219.

63. Jonathan Clegg, "An Examination of the Umzansi Dance Style," in *Papers Read at the 3rd Symposium on Ethnomusicology*, edited by Andrew Tracey (Rhodes University, Grahamstown, 1984), 1.

64. Creina explained the meaning of the name to me in a letter: "The farms were bare and eroded, and as rehabilitation had been an important part of our work at Maria Ratschitz, we imagined with care Mdukatshani would one day be covered with grasses too—and we wanted its history to be remembered."

65. "The Church Agricultural Project (CAP) was established in March 1965 at Maria Ratschitz Mission farm near Wasbank in northern Natal under the management of Neil Alcock. It was a joint venture by the Catholic, Anglican and Lutheran Churches in order to utilize the Mission farms more effectively and by so doing to provide its African residents with training and skills in agriculture. At first it was run on several mission-owned farms in Natal and Eastern Transvaal, but soon their center of operations was concentrated on Maria Ratschitz farm and Springvale near Ixopo." Chizuko Sato, "Forced Removals," 2.

66. Alcock, "No Ordinary Farm," 5.

67. Ibid.

68. Creina Alcock, "Koornspruit: The Story of an African Farm," in *Mdukatshani Rural Development Project Annual Report 2016* (2017), 4.

69. GG Alcock, *Third World Child: Born White, Zulu Bred* (Johannesburg: Tracey McDonald, 2014).

70. Presently, CAP is engaged with a number of projects focused on developing women and the youth through educational ventures, skills training for livestock, health initiatives, and a jewelry and art business. "Mdukatshani Rural Development Project Home Page," *Mdukatshani Rural Development Project*, accessed November 14, 2019, http://www.mdukatshani.com.

71. Brookes and de Webb, *A History of Natal*, 188.

72. David Leslie, *Among the Zulus and amaTongas*, 2nd ed. (Edinburgh: Edmonston & Douglas, 1875); Bryant, *Olden Times in Zululand and Natal*; Walter Felgate, *The Tembe Thonga of Natal and Mozambique: An Ecological Approach* (Durban: University of Natal, 1982); Angela Impey, *Song Walking: Environmental Justice in a Borderland* (Chicago: University of Chicago Press, 2018).

73. In a research survey completed in 1982, prior to its amalgamation with KwaZulu, Walter Felgate found that Zulu and Thonga were the two main languages. Men spoke mostly Zulu for reasons of "prestige," he wrote, while women spoke Thonga "almost exclusively." Most inhabitants of Tongaland did not practice Zulu customs even though

some would deny their Thonga ancestry. Felgate pointed to cultural dissimilarities between Zulu and Thonga: "The land tenure system, the arrangement of huts in the home, the laws that govern marriage, the way they bury their dead, their ritual life, their taboos, are all very much more closely related to Thonga customs, as Junod recorded them, than to Zulu customs. The women remain Thonga in activity and outlook and in Tongaland, where the women bear the burden of providing the food for the whole family, the Thonga way of life persists." Felgate, *The Tembe Thonga of Natal and Mozambique*, 27.

74. In 2017 I visited the traditional council of the Tembe at the KwaNgwanase Tribal Authority where I met with the induna mkhulu and the ibandla—mostly izinduna assembled from across the entire region from Lake Sibaya to Kosi Bay. The meeting took place exclusively in isiZulu but the ibandla insisted they wanted their Thonga heritage acknowledged, recorded, and respected on the national stage.

75. See Angela Impey, "Cartographic Encounters: Settling the Southeast African Border," in *Song Walking*, 94–115.

76. Eric Hobsbawm, "Introduction: Inventing Traditions," in *The Invention of Tradition*, edited by Eric Hobsbawm and Terence Ranger (Cambridge: Cambridge University Press, 1982), 9.

77. Terence Ranger, "The Invention of Tradition in Colonial Africa," in *The Invention of Tradition*, edited by Eric Hobsbawm and Terence Ranger (Cambridge: Cambridge University Press, 1982), 221.

78. Quoted in Ranger, "The Invention of Tradition," 252.

79. Ranger, "The Invention of Tradition," 212.

80. Ranger, "The Invention of Tradition," 212.

TWO *umSindo! The Politics of Sonic Space at a Zulu Wedding*

1. Doke et al., *Dictionary*, 1117.

2. Edward Evans-Pritchard, *The Nuer* (Oxford: Clarendon Press, [1940]1956); Alfred Radcliffe-Brown, *Structure and Function in Primitive Society* (London: Cohen &West, 1952); Hilda Kuper, "The Language of Sites in the Politics of Space," *American Anthropologist* 74, no. 3, 411–425.

3. Marie Jorritsma, *Sonic Spaces of the Karoo: The Sacred Music of a South African Colored Community* (Philadelphia: Temple University Press, 2011).

4. Kuper, "The Language of Sites," 413.

5. Maurice Merleau-Ponty, *The World of Perception*, translated by Oliver Davis (New York: Routledge, [1948]2004), 39.

6. Setha Low, "Claiming Space for an Engaged Anthropology: Spatial Inequality and Social Exclusion," *American Anthropologist* 113, no. 3 (2011): 392.

7. Setha Low, "Claiming Space for an Engaged Anthropology."

8. Doke et al., *Dictionary*, 858.

9. The term is relevant to dancing: "Horseshoe shape, circle (with only one opening or none at all). [cf *umkhumbi*.] *ukwakha isibaya sokugiya* (to make a horseshoe formation for dancing)." Doke et al., *Dictionary*, 441.

10. The significance of this sacrifice is detailed in chapter 3.

11. "The terms *idlozi* (plural: *amadlozi*) and *ithongo* (plural: *amathongo*) denote the dead who, according to Zulu thought patterns, maintain a close and intimate relationship and association with the living, especially their survivors, descendants or dependents." J. B. Ngubane, "The Role of Amadlozi/Amathongo as Seen in the Writings of B.W. Vilakazi," *Religion in Southern Africa* 5, no. 2 (1984): 57. Today the terms are used interchangeably, but there are still some who maintain the distinction recorded by Doke et al. in their *Dictionary* where *idlozi* refers to a departed spirit that has not "gained entrance into the body of the *amathongo*, ancestral spirits, by the *ukubuyisa* ceremony" (564).

12. "There is, in fact, a line of spiritual force linking the sacred locus of the *umsamo*, located in the world of men, with the byre, the home of the family herd, the place no woman who is not a daughter of the home may enter. . . . This symbolic link expresses a profound reality, for there is a fundamental identity between the members of the homestead and their cattle. In a very real sense household and herd are one; they constitute a single community." David Hammond-Tooke, "Cattle in Zulu Life," in *The Abundant Herds: A Celebration of the Cattle of the Zulu People*, edited by Marguerite Poland, David Hammond-Tooke, and Leigh Voight (Johannesburg: Fernwood Press, 2003), 22–23.

13. "The goat that 'opens' any sacrifice is taken to the umsamo, and introduced, and explained. Only after the speaking at the umsamo has been done, does the sacrifice take place in the isibaya. And all the sacrifice meat is then hung and stored at the umsamo. It's at the umsamo that the bride and groom get anointed with gall. It's an unseen ceremony." Creina Alcock, personal communication, May 2, 2022.

14. "If I am standing behind a wall and hear the ihubo, I will know these are my people." Fezela Zwane, personal communication, Beaulieu, Johannesburg, May 2019.

15. In the "KwaZulu Regulations for Chiefs and Headmen" of 1980, it states that "any chief or headman shall—(g) disperse or order the dispersal of any unauthorized assembly of armed persons or of any riotous or unlawful meeting or gathering; (h) if a state of lawlessness exists in his area or in his opinion cannot otherwise be prevented, order that all or any of the following shall be prohibited for any period in his discretion—(i) the gathering of men in groups; (ii) the brewing of beer or the holding of any feast within such area as he shall specify; (iii) the carrying by any person of a shield or more than one ordinary stick; (iv) the shouting of war cries or the blowing of bugles or whistles." Zulu Chiefs and Headmen Act No. 8 of 1974 (revised 1980), 230–231. War cries, bugles, and whistles are all understood to have the potential to incite violence and must thus be kept in check by the induna present.

16. "In her hand she carries a short assegai or knife which she points at her husband-to-be in dancing. It signifies that she is a virgin. The rest of the party is also beautifully dressed, the girls of the *intanga* of the bride also wearing an isidwaba like the bride, and carrying bunches of short sticks to make a rattling noise (*uluxhaba*), and small pouches of dry skins with stones inside fixed to a riem tied around the ankles (*isiWahla*) to make a noise in the dance." Eileen Krige, *The Social System of the Zulus*, 2nd ed. (Pietermaritzburg: Shuter & Shooter, 1950), 141.

17. Doke et al. provide this definition: "1. Rattling ornaments worn round the ankles when dancing (esp. by women). 2. Pupes of the Queen moth, used for making dancing rattles." Doke et al., *Dictionary*, 598.

18. The umbogisi can be bought at Tugela Ferry some thirty minutes' drive away, but in this isigodi, men often purchase the umbogisi at Mai Mai market in Johannesburg.

19. *Gongobala*: "contract, get stiff (from cold, death, etc.)." Doke et al., *Dictionary*, 653.

20. Louise Meintjes explains these gestures in dance as a "playful expressive resource. Military aesthetics incorporated into ngoma ambiguate ngoma's relationship to acts of violence, intensifying the performance." Meintjes, *Dust of the Zulu*, 18. I take this sense of *ulaka*, or "righteous anger," from Meintjes, who says that "when a man possesses *ulaka* his anger registers the potential to be violent. It is a deep emotive state, and a positive quality in men. In the context of men's singing and chanting (understood historically to precede fighting), *ulaka* is a spirit for the better, even in the context of fighting" (65).

21. Much is made of hidden gestures and meanings associated with the dancing of the umakoti. The subtle veiling and unveiling of the ummese is thought to be a provocation to her beloved. The umakoti may also have her own inkondlo song, although this is not so at the Ncunjane wedding where no special song was sung by the bride. Rosemary Joseph describes the *inkondlo kamakoti* as "the principal wedding dance" that women "treasure all their lives." Joseph, "Zulu Women's Music," *African Music* 6, no. 3 (1983): 70.

22. *Zamalek* refers to a favorite brand of beer in South Africa marketed as Carling Black Label.

23. Similar taunts accompany women's dances in which there is "lighthearted teasing of the bridegroom and his family by the bridal party" with some retaliation from his party. "Traditionally relations between the two families are difficult and restrained, and there are general forms of avoidance between them. These songs provide a vehicle whereby these traditional barriers are temporarily removed, in a ritualized expression of hostility. Much of the teasing centers around the payment of the lobola cattle by the bridegroom's family." Joseph, "Zulu Women's Music," 71.

24. *umKhongi*: "Bridegroom's man, entrusted with the business of arranging on his behalf with the girl's father concerning the marriage." Doke and Vilakazi, *Dictionary*, 787.

25. Phulula is the name of their ibutha, marked with an umqele leopard-skin headband to identify the group.

26. Joseph, "Zulu Women's Music," 62.

27. Ibid.

28. Eleanor Preston-Whyte, "Kinship and Marriage," in *The Bantu-Speaking Peoples of Southern Africa*, 2nd ed., edited by W. D. Hammond-Tooke (New York: Routledge, 1974), 179.

29. Krige, *The Social System of the Zulus*, 120.

30. *Social System of the Zulus*, 120.

THREE *Songs of Sacrifice: uMemulo and the Politics of Gender and Generation*

1. Doke et al., *Dictionary*, 731.

2. In cases where a father has passed on, or is no longer, a mother may arrange an umemulo for her daughter.

3. The Xhosa *iintonjane* ritual is similar. See Deirdre Hansen, "The Music of the Xhosa-Speaking People" (Unpublished PhD diss., University of the Witwatersrand, 1981); Dave Dargie, *The Music of the Xhosa* (Cape Town: David Phillip, 1988); and Luvuyo Dontsa, "*Intonjane* Music: A Forum of Identity Formation for Xhosa Women," in *Music and Identity: Transformation and Negotiation*, edited by E. Akrofi, M. Smit and S-M. Thorsén (Stellenbosch: African Sun Press, 2007), 383–407.

4. Alfred T. Bryant, *The Zulu People: As They Were Before the White Man Came* (Pietermaritzburg: Shuter and Shooter, 1949); Max Kohler, "Marriage Customs in Southern Natal," *Ethnological Publications Volume 4*, edited by N. J. V. Warmelo (Pretoria: Department of Native Affairs, 1931); Krige, *The Social System of the Zulus*; Joseph, "Zulu Women's Music"; Thenjiwe Magwaza, "'So That I Will Be a Marriageable Girl': *Umemulo* in Contemporary Zulu Society," in *Zulu Identities: Being Zulu, Past and Present*, edited by Benedict Carton (Scottsville: University of KwaZulu-Natal Press, 2009), 482–496; Nompumelelo Zondi, *Bahlabelelelani – Why Do They Sing? Gender and Power in Contemporary Women's Songs* (Scottsville: University of KwaZulu-Natal Press, 2020).

5. Ritual is defined here as "repeatable patterns of behavior that carry complex meanings." "Ritual," *Oxford Reference*, 2002, https://o-www-oxfordreference-com.oasis.unisa.ac.za/view/10.1093/acref/9780195123715.001.0001/acref-9780195123715-e-1455.

6. Richard Elphick, *The Equality of Believers: Protestant Missionaries and the Racial Politics of South Africa* (Scottsville: University of KwaZulu-Natal Press, 2012).

7. John Blacking, "Songs, Dances, Mimes, and Symbolism of Venda Girls' Initiation Schools, Parts 1–4." *African Studies* 28 (1969a): 1–4. Sindile Moitse made similar observations on the Basotho. See Moitse, *The Ethnomusicology of the Basotho* (Roma: National University of Lesotho, 1994).

8. Muller, *Rituals of Fertility and the Sacrifice of Desire*.

9. John W. Colenso, *The Colenso Zulu-English Dictionary*, 4th ed. (Pietermaritzburg: Shuter and Shooter, 1878), 445.

10. W. D. Hammond-Tooke, "Cattle Symbolism in Zulu Culture," in *Zulu Identities: Being Zulu, Past and Present*, edited by Benedict Carton, John Laband, and Jabulani Sithole (Scottsville: University of KwaZulu-Natal Press, 2009), 62–63.

11. Krige, *Social System of the Zulus*, 104.

12. Eileen Jensen Krige, "Girls' Puberty Songs and Their Relation to Fertility, Health, Morality and Religion Among the Zulu," *Africa: Journal of the International African Institute* 38, no. 2 (1968): 173–198; David K. Rycroft, "A Royal Account of Music in Zulu Life with Translation, Annotation, and Musical Transcription." *Bulletin of the School of Oriental and African Studies, University of London* 38, no. 2 (1975a): 351–402.

13. Kohler, "Marriage Customs," 15.

14. Bryant, *The Zulu People*, 648.

15. Bryant, 648.

16. Bryant, 649.

17. I obtained permission from Sthenjwa Dladla to attend and record this umemulo, and I did so through his sons, Phelelani and Ndididi.

18. Doke and Vilakazi, *Dictionary*, 529.

19. The word "homeboys" is a colloquialism used by men in the hostels to refer to their kith and kin.

20. Doke and Vilakazi, *Dictionary*, 491.

21. Virginity testing is practiced in many parts of KwaZulu-Natal today.

22. I witnessed this practice firsthand at Mazizini.

23. At the homestead of Siwakhe Wiseman Mabtha at Mazizini, I was told that no men are allowed into the girls' hut and that they may have no knowledge of what takes place in there. S. Mbatha, interview with the author, December 15, 2015.

24. "She is not allowed to leave the *umgonqo* except at night, when few people might see her. Social isolation ensures that she is not affected by sorcery, for her intention to go through *umemulo* means that she will be acquainted with the targets of sorcerers, and that the revered *amadlozi* will consecrate her." Magwaza, "A Marriageable Girl," 483.

25. Magwaza, "A Marriageable Girl," 485.

26. Ibid.

27. S. Khumalo, uMsinga, interview with the author, April 25, 2017.

28. C. Mbatha, uMsinga, interview with the author, April 27, 2017.

29. The color of the ocher varies by region. I have seen red and white ocher used at uMsinga, and white used exclusively at Mnweni.

30. Magwaza, "A Marriageable Girl," 486.

31. This I witnessed only at Dakeni on the lower Thukela, and not at uMsinga, Mazizini, or Shemula, but it is a practice recorded by Rosemary Joseph in her work in central Zululand.

32. The elder men will also have opportunity to sing and chant amahubo, and married women who are not permitted to sing publicly may retire to sing inside a dwelling, perhaps choosing to parade in their finery later on.

33. When I visited Wiseman to record his own songs and izibongo, he insisted on using this room for the recording because of its importance to the amadlozi. The residue of ashes resulted in a pungent odor that remained with us throughout the recording process. Wiseman's izibongo called his amadlozi into presence.

34. Clara Mbatha, interview with the author, as translated by Wiseman Mbatha, Mazizini, April 17, 2017.

35. The term may also refer to a cut, incised wound, or imitation. Doke et al., *Dictionary*, 755. Axel-Ivar Berglund explains the difference between ritual and ceremony in Zulu societies: "Ritual refers to celebrations which aim at a communion with the shades. The various rites of the complete ritual are religious in content and conservatively sanctioned by both age and the shades with whom communion is sought: while ceremony is a conventional and sometimes an elaborate form of voicing one's feelings, ritual aims at a communion with the shades which is efficacious." Berglund, *Zulu Thought-Patterns and Symbolism* (Bloomington: Indiana University Press, 1989), 27–28.

36. Monica Wilson, *Religion and the Transformation of Society: A Study in Social Change in Africa* (Cambridge: Cambridge University Press, 1971).

37. "The dead were repeatedly spoken of as being hungry (*bafuna ukudla ngaye*), and wanting attention, and sacrifice satisfied them." Wilson, *Religion*, 27.

38. Mazizini, interview with the author, April 27, 2017.

39. This is recorded in Benedict Vilakazi's novel *Noma Nini*. "She wore on her head an inflated gall-bladder of the beast slaughtered for her by her father on the day of *Ukwemulisa* ritual before leaving her home to start her own household. It was this bladder that symbolized that the girl was not rejected by her family, and that the *amathongo* of her 'fathers' were with her in the building up of her peaceful household. This bladder also symbolized good relationships between the families of the wedding couple. After the bride was given her hut, she hung this bladder at the rear of the hut or over the doorway." Ngubane, "The Role of Amadlozi," 67–68.

40. Nomusa Mbatha, Mazizini, interview with the author, April 17, 2017.

41. Krige, "Girls' Puberty Songs," 177.

42. Krige, 177.

43. Joseph, "Zulu Women's Music," 67.

44. Leigh Johnson et al., "The Effect of HIV Programs in South Africa on National HIV Incidence Trends, 2000-2019." *JAIDS: Journal of Acquired Immune Deficiency Syndrome* 90, no. 2 (2022): 115–123.

45. The practice of virginity testing is highly contested in postapartheid South Africa. The Commission for Gender Equality and the South African Human Rights Commis-

sion have objected to the practice, claiming that it violates the rights of individuals, but some Zulu women have protested in favor of the practice. See Fiona Scorgie, "Virginity Testing and the Politics of Sexual Responsibility: Implications for AIDS Intervention." *African Studies* 61, no. 1 (2002): 55–75.

46. Scorgie, "Virginity Testing."

47. Zazi (Know Your Strength) is a nongovernmental organization working to empower young women in South Africa. In 2013 Zazi was present at the umKhosi woMhlanga ceremony in KwaZulu-Natal. *U.S. Mission South Africa*, "Zazi Reaches Young Women at Zulu Reed Dance," https://za.usembassy.gov/zazi-reaches-young-women-at-zulu-reed-dance/.

48. I recorded three girls, Benzani Dladla, Kwenzekile Dladla, and Landiwe Dladla, singing these songs. Informed consent was obtained and permissions have been granted for reproducing the lyrics in this chapter. The singers reported that the songs are "traditional" and the composers unknown. Many of the songs sung at this particular umemulo were also sung at other umemulo events I attended in the district.

49. T. Mchunu, interview with the author, April 26, 2017.

50. Danced January 5–6, 2012.

51. N. Dladla, interview with the author, September 13, 2013.

52. L. Dladla, interview with the author, September 13, 2013.

53. Refer to the discussion on inhlonipho in chapter 2.

54. Sung by Landiwe Dladla.

FOUR *Phenomenology of iNgoma: isiShameni Dance and the Politics of Proximity*

1. Merleau-Ponty, *Phenomenology of Perception*, 284.

2. Stoller, *The Taste of Ethnographic Things*.

3. Stoller, 67.

4. This section is based on ethnographic research at Jeppe, and author's interviews with Ndididi Dladla and Sakhile Dladla conducted at Jeppe Hostel, Johannesburg, on December 1, 2013.

5. The ANC is the African National Congress, which has been the ruling party in South Africa since 1994.

6. Irvine and Gunner, "With Respect to Zulu," 173–207.

7. Dlamini, Penwell, July 31, 2017. Renovation of Johannesburg hostels to start soon. https://www.timeslive.co.za/news/south-africa/2017-07-31-renovation-of-johannesburg -hostels-to-start-soon/.

8. William Beinart, *Twentieth Century South Africa* (New York: Oxford, 2000).

9. Harold Wolpe, "Capitalism and Cheap Labor-Power in South Africa: From Segregation to Apartheid," *Economy and Society* 1, no. 43 (1972): 425–456; Cherryl Walker

and Ben Cousins, "Introduction," in *Land Divided, Land Restored: Land Reform in South Africa for the 21st Century*, edited by Cherryl Walker and Ben Cousins (Johannesburg: Jacana, 2015), 1–23.

10. Erlmann, *Nightsong*; Liz Gunner, "Zulu Choral Music—Performing Identities in a New State," *Research in African Literatures* 37, no. 2 (2006): 84–97.

11. Kathryn Olsen, *Music and Social Change in South Africa: Maskanda Past and Present* (Philadelphia: Temple University Press, 2014); Carol Muller, *Focus: Music of South Africa*, 2nd ed. (New York: Routledge, 2008).

12. Veit Erlmann, *African Stars: Studies in Black South African Performance* (Chicago: University of Chicago Press, 1991).

13. David Coplan, *In the Time of Cannibals: The Word Music of South Africa's Basotho Migrants* (Chicago: University of Chicago Press, 1994).

14. David Coplan, *In Township Tonight!: South Africa's Black City Music and Theatre*, 2nd ed. (Chicago: University of Chicago Press, 2007).

15. Todd Plummer, "Where to Go in Maboneng, the Coolest Neighborhood in Johannesburg," https://www.vogue.com/article/maboneng-guide-johannesburg-south-africa.

16. "Maboneng Precinct," https://www.gauteng.net/attractions/maboneng_precinct/.

17. "Maboneng Precinct."

18. Shannon Walsh, "We Won't Move," *City* 17, no. 3 (2013): 400–408.

19. Walsh, "We Won't Move."

20. Mikhaela Sack, "Innovation to Convention! An Exploratory Study on the Evolution of Urban Regeneration in Maboneng, Johannesburg" (Master of Science Research Report: University of the Witwatersrand, 2016).

21. Delia Ah Goo, "From Urban Decline to Gentrifying Spaces: The Case of the Maboneng Precinct in Johannesburg's Inner City," *South African Journal of Cultural History* 31, no. 1 (2015): 1–18.

22. Melissa T. Mnyambo, "Red Velvet Cheesecake in Maboneng, Pap and Steak in Jeppestown," in *Reversing Urban Inequality in Johannesburg*, edited by Melissa T. Mnyambo (New York: Routledge, 2015), 69–81.

23. Philip Bonner and Vusi Ndima, "The Roots of Violence on the East Rand, 1980–1990," Seminar Paper presented to the Wits Institute for Advanced Social Research, no. 450 (October 18, 1999).

24. GG Alcock, eHlathini, Johannesburg, interview with the author, June 2, 2017.

25. "South Africa's transition from apartheid to democracy is often heralded as a miracle, both bloodless and peaceful. But as Nelson Mandela walked proudly out of Victor Verster prison in 1990 after twenty-seven years in jail, civil war wracked the nation's townships and countryside. Over twenty thousand South Africans died in this conflict (1985–1996), more than in any other period of the struggle to overthrow apartheid. Conservative estimates suggest that the war displaced some two hundred thousand people.

The world watched with bewilderment as civil war-ravaged South Africa, particularly the Pretoria/Witwatersrand/Vaal (PWV) area that is now the Gauteng province and what became the province of KwaZulu-Natal." Kelly, *To Swim with Crocodiles*, xxviii.

26. Kelly, xxix.

27. Liz Gunner, "Jacob Zuma, the Social Body and the Unruly Power of Song," *African Affairs* 108, no. 430 (2009): 27–48.

28. "In May 2008 nearly 70 people were killed, many more were injured and over 100,000 were displaced in violent attacks on people perceived to be foreigners . . . This kind of outbreak was repeated in April 2015, and both events were spectacularly captured in media images." Danai Mupotswa and Dorothee Kreutzfeldt, "Xenophobia, Nationalism and Techniques of Difference," *Agenda: Empowering Women for Gender Equity* 30, no. 2 (2016): 13–20; Loren Landau, *Exorcizing the Demons Within: Xenophobia, Violence and Statecraft in Contemporary South Africa* (Johannesburg: Wits University Press, 2012); Michael Neocosmos, "From 'Foreign Natives' to 'Native Foreigners': Explaining Xenophobia in Post-Apartheid South Africa" (Dakar: Codesria, 2010); Danai Mupotswa and Dorothee Kreutzfeldt, "Xenophobia, Nationalism and Techniques of Difference," *Agenda: Empowering Women for Gender Equity* 30, no. 2 (2016): 13–20.

29. Shireen Hassim, Tawana Kupe, and Eric Worby, *Go Home or Die Here: Violence, Xenophobia and the Reinvention of Difference in South Africa* (Johannesburg: Wits University Press, 2008).

30. Mbali Phala, "Jeppe Hostel Residents Say Their Public Image Is Affecting Service Delivery to the Hostels," *Daily Vox*, June 9, 2016, https://www.thedailyvox.co.za/jeppe-hostel-residents-say-public-image-affecting-service-delivery-hostels/.

31. Nomsa Maseko, "Inside South Africa's 'Dangerous' Men's Hostels," *BBC*, 2015, http://www.bbc.com/news/world-africa-32692461.

32. Sakephi Mbatha, Mdukatshani, uMsinga, interview with the author, April 27, 2017.

33. Manyathela Mvelase, Jeppe Hostel, Johannesburg, interview with the author, June 4, 2017.

34. Maseko, "Inside South Africa's 'Dangerous' Men's Hostels."

35. Greg Nicolson, "Gauteng Xenophobia: Gigaba and Mashaba trade accusations," February 28, 2017, https://www.dailymaverick.co.za/article/2017-02-28-gauteng-xenophobia-gigaba-and-mashaba-trade-accusations/#.WTj_sSN97so.

36. Ibid.

37. Tankiso Makhetha, "Crime Surge in Eastern Suburbs," *The Star Late Edition*, May 2, 2017.

38. Ibid.

39. Fezela Zwane, Jeppe Hostel, Johannesburg, interview with the author, June 4, 2017.

40. Msukelwa Mvelase, Jeppe Hostel, Johannesburg, interview with the author, June 4, 2017.

41. Sizakele Zwane, Jeppestown, Johannesburg, interview with the author, June 4, 2017.

42. Afrikaans: "take and sit."

43. GG Alcock grew up at uMsinga speaking isiZulu with the same fluency he speaks English. Alcock, *Third World Child*. An imisebenzi is a return of the spirit ceremony that takes place one or more years after a person has died. The views in this paragraph were expressed in an interview with the author at eHlathini, Johannesburg, on June 2, 2017.

44. Sakephi Mbatha, Mdukatshani, uMsinga, interview with the author, April 27, 2017.

45. Erlmann, *Nightsong*.

46. Jonathan Clegg, "Dance and Society in Africa South of the Sahara" (BA Honors diss., University of the Witwatersrand, 1977), 74–75.

47. "In situations where there exists keen competition between groups or factions, the dance is an expression of group identity and membership." Jonathan Clegg, "Toward an Understanding of African Dance: The Zulu isiShameni Style," in *Papers Read at the 2nd Symposium on Ethnomusicology*, edited by Andrew Tracey (Grahamstown: International Library of African Music, Institute of Social and Economic Research, Rhodes University, 1982), 9.

48. Clegg, "African Dance," 9.

49. Clegg, "African Dance," 10.

50. Manyathela Mvelase, Jeppe Hostel, Johannesburg, interview with the author, June 4, 2017.

51. Sakephi Mbatha, Mdukatshani, uMsinga, interview with the author, April 27, 2017.

52. Mbatha, interview.

53. Meintjes, *Dust of the Zulu*.

54. Terence Ranger, *Dance and Society in Eastern Africa*.

55. Clegg, "African Dance."

56. The audience at umemulo events and weddings play a role in defining the limits of this space and in encouraging the dancers.

57. Kofi Agawu argues that a common, even essential, feature to African performances is shared and "based on an indispensable foundation: an inviolate periodicity or groove regulates musical utterance and provides the condition of possibility upon which basic articulation and necessary departure, play, or improvisation take place. Groove and associated repetition are the ultimate guarantors of meaningfulness in musical performance." Agawu, *The African Imagination in Music* (New York: Oxford University Press, 2016), 17.

58. Steingo, *Kwaito's Promise*, chapter 1.

59. Meintjes, *Dust of the Zulu*, 94–123.

60. Gary Tomlinson, *A Million Years of Music: The Emergence of Human Modernity* (New York: Zone Books, 2015), 77.

61. Martin Clayton, Rebecca Sager, and Udo Will, "In Time with the Music: The Concept of Entrainment and Its Significance for Ethnomusicology," *European Meetings in Ethnomusicology* (2005): 2.

62. Daniel Levitin, Jessica Grahn, and Justin London, "The Psychology of Music: Rhythm and Movement," *Annual Review of Psychology* 69 (2018): 56.

63. Clegg, "Dance and Society," 89. In his song "Heart of the Dancer," from the 1981 album *African Litany*, he sings: "The dance wants to dance the dancer, but the dancer wants to dance the dance. There's a war between the puppet and the master, between the master and the puppet-master's heart."

64. Ibid.

65. Clegg, "Dance and Society," 90.

66. Mihaly Csikszentmihalyi, *Flow and the Foundations of Positive Psychology* (Dordrecht: Springer, 2014).

67. "The African dance aesthetic is a transcended form of the real lived experience. It cannot be understood if it is seen as a magical world and reality apart from real life. It is an essential part of real lived experience and as I have tried to show, in many societies the dance aesthetic is a part and parcel of social reality, but because it is an art form, it is ideal and in it the society can enhance and unify the reality of the inter-subjective life-world." Clegg, "Dance and Society," 93–94.

68. Clegg, "Dance and Society," 115.

69. Penwell Dlamini and Alon Skuy, "Buthelezi begs angry crowd to calm down as he speaks against xenophobia," https://www.timeslive.co.za/news/south-africa/2019-09-08-hostel-residents-march-against-foreigners-as-buthelezi-tries-to-appeal-for-peace/.

FIVE *uMaskandi iziBongo: The Politics and Poetics of Popular Praises*

1. I use the isiZulu word *umaskandi* to refer to the genre of accompanied song often termed *maskanda* in the literature. Jonathan Clegg and Bongani Mthethwa use the term *umaskande*, while D. B. Z. Ntuli uses the orthographically correct *umaskandi* in his article on izibongo praise poetry rather than the Anglicized *maskanda*. All the musicians whom I interviewed during research describe themselves and the music they play as 'maskandi or *umaskandi*. CD compilations such as *Maskandi Hits* also reflect this usage. *Maskandi Hits: eyami lenduku*, Gallo. CDGSP3055, 2004. Jonathan Clegg, "The Music of Zulu Immigrant Workers in Johannesburg: A Focus on Concertina and Guitar," in *Papers Presented at the Symposium on Ethnomusicology*, edited by Andrew Tracey (Makhanda, Grahamstown, South Africa: International Library of African Music, 1981), 2–9; Deuteronomy Bhekinkosi Zeblon Ntuli, "Remarks on Maskandi Poetry," *South African Journal of African Languages* 10, no. 4 (1990): 302–306.

2. Popular praises are distinct from izibongo zamakhosi that are associated with the royal household and performed by imbongi for kings and patrons.

3. David Rycroft and A. Bhekabantu Ngcobo, eds., *The Praises of Dingana: Izibongo zikaDingana* (Pietermaritzburg, South Africa: University of Natal Press, 1988), 11.

4. Krige, *The Social System of the Zulus*, 340.

5. Leroy Vail and Landeg White, *Power and the Praise Poem: Southern African Voices in History* (Charlottesville: University of Virginia Press, 1991), 57.

6. The izibongo of the Thembu royal house that I recorded at the offices of the inkosi at Thukela Estates near Weenen, KwaZulu-Natal, in 2012, show how popular and royal praises differ. For instance, the demeanor of the imbongi is sincere and respectful, and his articulation of the praises lacks the melodic inflections characteristic of umaskandi. There are also stark differences in duration, meter, and tonality. iziBongo zamakhosi tend to be declaimed in a monotone, and at a steady almost metronomic pace. The emphasis is on the form and content of the praises. uMaskandi izibongo are performed with flare.

7. Anton Koopman, "The Praises of Young Zulu Men," *Theoria* 70 (1987): 52.

8. Liz Gunner and Mafika Gwala, trans. and eds., *Musho! Zulu Popular Praises* (East Lansing: Michigan State University Press, 1991), 1.

9. Ntuli, "Remarks on Maskandi Praise Poetry," 302.

10. Tom Collins, "Constructing Maskanda," *South African Music Studies* 26–27 (2006): 1–26; Coplan, *In Township Tonight!*; Nollene Davies, "A Study of the Guitar Styles in Zulu *Maskanda* Music" (MMus diss., University of Natal, Durban, 1992); Nollene Davies, "The Guitar in Zulu 'Maskanda' Tradition," *The World of Music* 36, no. 2 (1994): 118–137; Muller, *Focus*; Olsen, *Music and Social Change in South Africa*.

11. David Rycroft, "Evidence of Stylistic Continuity in Zulu 'Town' Music," in *Essays for a Humanist: An Offering to Klaus Wachsmann*, edited by Mantle Hood, 216–260 (New York: The Town House Press, 1977), 228–229.

12. Rycroft, "Evidence of Stylistic Continuity," 234.

13. Rosemary Joseph, "Zulu Women's Bow Songs: Ruminations on Love," *Bulletin of the School of Oriental and African Studies, University of London* 50, no. 1 (1987): 92.

14. Joseph, "Zulu Women's Bow Songs," 92.

15. Ibid.

16. Constance Magogo, *The Zulu Bow Songs of Princess Constance Magogo KaDinuzulu by Hugh Tracey*, Music of Africa Series 37 (Grahamstown: International Library of African Music, 2004). See also David Rycroft, "The Zulu Bow Songs of Princess Constance Magogo kaDinzulu." *African Music* 3, no. 2, (1975b): 351–402.

17. Ntuli, "Remarks on Maskandi Praise Poetry," 302.

18. Davies, "A Study of Guitar Styles," 44.

19. Meintjes, *Dust of the Zulu*, "The Crossing," 151–181.

20. Clegg, "The Music of Zulu Immigrant Workers in Johannesburg," 4.

21. Louise Meintjes, *Sound of Africa! Making Music Zulu in a South African Studio* (Durham, NC: Duke University Press, 2003).

22. Charles Hamm, "'The Constant Companion of Man': Separate Development, Radio Bantu and Music," *Popular Music* 10, no. 2 (1991): 147–173.

23. Saul Dubow, *Apartheid* (Oxford: Oxford University Press, 2012).

24. Phuzekhemisi noKhetani, *Imbizo* (Johannesburg: Gallo. CDGSP3105 (CD), 1992).

25. Olsen, *Music and Social Change in South Africa.*

26. Kathryn Olsen, "'Mina ngizokushaya ngengoma'/ 'I Will Challenge You With a Song': Constructions of Masculinity in *Maskanda*," *Agenda* 49 (2001): 51–60.

27. Davies, "A Study of the Guitar Styles," 31.

28. The song "Bafana Bafana" was written by Jonathan Mathenjwa and recorded here with the group Mqamuli Wezintambo. Field recording by Thomas Pooley. April 30, 2012, Ndumo.

29. Mfaz' Omnyama, from the album *Ngisebenzile Mama* (Johannesburg: Gallo, CDGMP40822, 2002).

30. Mfaz' Omnyama, *Khula Tshitshi Lami* (Johannesburg: Gallo. CDAFR172 (CD), 1997).

31. Kathryn Olsen, "Musical Characterizations of Transformation: An Exploration of Social and Political Trajectories in Contemporary Maskanda" (Unpublished PhD diss.: University of KwaZulu-Natal, 2009).

32. Olsen, "'Mina ngizokushaya ngengoma.'"

33. Barbara Titus, "'Global Maskanda, Global Historiography?' Some Preliminary Enquiries," *South African Music Studies* 28 (2008): 43–54; Barbara Titus, "'Walking Like a Crab': Analyzing Maskanda Music in Post-Apartheid South Africa." *Ethnomusicology* 57, no. 2 (2013): 286–310; Olsen, *Music and Social Change in South Africa.*

34. Titus, "'Walking Like a Crab,'" 287.

35. Rycroft, "A Royal Account."

36. Intonation refers to the tonal structure of linguistic utterances. Melody is the linear patterning of pitch in a phrase or group of related phrases.

37. Eric Clarke and Nicholas Cook, eds., *Empirical Musicology* (Oxford: Oxford University Press, 2004); David Cooper and Ian Sapiro, "Ethnomusicology in the Laboratory: From the Tonometer to the Digital Melograph," *Ethnomusicology Forum* 15, no. 2 (2006): 301–313.

38. Leonard Meyer, *Emotion and Meaning in Music* (Chicago: University of Chicago Press, 1956).

39. Peter Ladefoged, *A Course in Phonetics* (Boston: Thomson Wadsworth, 2006), 237.

40. J. H. Kwabena Nketia, "Musicology and Linguistics: Integrating the Phraseology of Text and Tune in the Creative Process," *Black Music Research Journal* 22, no. 2 (2002): 143–164, 145.

41. Arthur Morris Jones, *Studies in African Music* (Oxford: Oxford University Press, 1959); Kofi Agawu, *African Rhythm: A Northern Ewe Perspective* (Cambridge: Cambridge University Press, 1995c); Kofi Agawu, *Representing African Music: Postcolonial Thoughts, Queries, Positions* (New York: Routledge, 2003).

42. John Blacking, *Venda Children's Songs: A Study in Ethnomusicological Analysis* (Chicago: University of Chicago Press [1967]1995).

43. Thomas F. Johnston, "Speech-Tone and Other Forces in Tsonga Music," *Studies in African Linguistics* 4 (1973): 49–70; Hansen, "The Music of the Xhosa-Speaking People."

44. David Rycroft, "Melodic Features in Zulu Eulogistic Recitation," *African Language Studies* I (1960): 60–78; "Zulu and Xhosa Praise-Poetry and Song," *African Music* 3, no. 1 (1962): 79–85; "Tone in Zulu Nouns," *African Language Studies* IV (1963), 43–68.

45. David Rycroft, "Zulu Melodic and Non-Melodic Vocal Styles," in *Papers Presented at the Seventh Symposium on Ethnomusicology*, edited by Andrew Tracey (Grahamstown: South Africa: International Library of African Music, 1987), 23.

46. Rycroft, "Zulu Melodic," 24.

47. Rycroft, "Relationships," 306.

48. Ibid.

49. Depression refers to the lowering of pitch because of a conglomerate of tonal linguistic factors, including downdrift, downstep, declination, depressor consonants, and final lowering.

50. "For Zulu izibongo, four recurrent levels of pitch resembling Sol-fa notes *doh'*, *te*, *soh*, and *Doh* appear to predominate and serve as a basic tonality in the musical sense. But these are used mechanically, for essential tones, rather than melodically. The upper two notes take all non-final high and low syllables, respectively, except low tones when preceded by a 'lowering consonant' these take *soh*; and any low syllable in *final* position takes low *Doh* . . . Here it is to be noted that normal descending sentence intonation becomes replaced by sustained, equal levels of pitch for all high, low, and consonantally lowered syllables, respectively (until the final low tone)." Rycroft, "The Relationship between Speech-Tone and Melody," 308.

51. Rycroft and Ngcobo, *The Praises of Dingana*.

52. Rycroft, "Tone in Zulu Nouns."

53. Davies, "A Study of the Guitar Styles," 78.

54. This is perhaps unsurprising considering that the main imbongi in this case was James Stuart, who was not a native speaker, and who offered stylized representations of izibongo he had himself recorded and transcribed.

55. Olsen, *Music and Social Change in South Africa*.

56. Meter refers to the recurring pattern of strong and weak beats that underscore a melody.

57. Davies, "A Study of the Guitar Styles."

58. Declination refers to a gradual global descent over the course of a musical phrase.

59. Hey, I'm telling you!

1. According to the Office of the Treasury, "Consolidated Spending by Functional and Economic Classification, 2014/15" (National Treasury 2014, xi) will include 190.7 billion Rand on basic education, and 52.5 billion Rand on post-school education. This equates to 19.42 percent of total government expenditure of 1,252.3 billion Rand. "Budget Review: 2014," National Treasury, Republic of South Africa, February 26, 2014.

2. Rajendra Chetty, "Class Dismissed? Youth Resistance and the Politics of Race and Class in South African Education," *Critical Arts: South-North Cultural and Media Studies* 28, no. 1 (2014): 88–102.

3. Statistics South Africa reports that "the relationship between education and poverty appears strong—as the poverty measures reflect, the lower the level of education attained, the more likely adults were to be poor and experience more intense levels of poverty." "Poverty Trends in South Africa: An Examination of Absolute Poverty between 2006 and 2011," *Statistics South Africa* (Pretoria: Statistics South Africa, 2014). The poverty cycle is enabled by the low levels of education in so many parts of South Africa.

4. Etienne Nel and Tony Binns, "Changing the Geography of Apartheid Education in South Africa," *Geography* 84, no. 2 (1999): 119–128. Angie Motshekga, minister for education, attributed the drop in the national examination pass rate, and the prevalence of cheating in many schools across the country, to problems with the implementation of the new CAPS curriculum published in 2012.

5. "White Paper on Reconstruction and Development, Notice No. 1954 of 1994," Parliament of the Republic of South Africa. Cape Town, November 15, 1994.

6. Sibusiso Bengu, "White Paper on Education and Training. Notice 196 of 1995. Parliament of the Republic of South Africa" (Pretoria: Department of Education, 1995).

7. W. R. Johnson, "Education: Keystone of Apartheid," *Anthropology and Education Quarterly* 13, no. 3 (1982): 214–237.

8. Doreen Nteta, "Foreword." *White Paper on Arts Culture and Heritage* (Pretoria: Department of Arts, Culture and Heritage, 1996), 2.

9. Urvi Drummond, "Music Education in South African Schools after Apartheid: Teacher Perceptions of Western and African Music" (Ed.D diss., University of Glasgow, 2015), 14.

10. Drummond, "Music Education," 14.

11. Anri Herbst, Jacques de Wet, and Susan Rijsdijk. "A Survey of Music Education in the Primary Schools of South Africa's Cape Peninsula," *Journal of Research in Music Education* 53, no. 3 (2005): 261.

12. Herbst, de Wet, and Rijsdijk, "Survey," 273.

13. A brief history of the colonial impact on music education in South Africa is offered

by Herbst, de Wet, and Rijsdijk, "Survey." See also Christine Lucia, "How Critical Is Music Theory?" *Critical Arts: South-North Cultural and Media Studies* 21, no. 1 (2007): 166–189; and Drummond, "Music Education," chapter 3.

14. Herbst, de Wet, and Rijsdijk, "Survey," 274.

15. Meki Nzewi, "Strategies for Music Education in Africa," in *Musical Arts in Africa: Theory, Practice and Education*, edited by Anri Herbst, Meki Nzewi, and Kofi Agawu (Pretoria: University of South Africa, 2007), 13–37.

16. "National Curriculum and Assessment Policy Statement for Creative Arts," Department of Basic Education (Pretoria: Department of Basic Education, 2012), 4; emphasis added.

17. It is not useful to essentialize the features of indigenous practices to a set of ideal characteristics. Instead, I consider all musical genres that include features specific to the history and culture of local communities to be indigenous.

18. The Nguni dances practiced in KwaZulu-Natal are differentiated by region and include inter alia *umzansi*, isishameni, and many others, including the izingilili practiced at Jozini.

19. Since 2013 I have mentored hundreds of schoolteachers from across Gauteng as part of a community engagement project sponsored by the Department of Art History, Visual Arts and Musicology at the University of South Africa, and run in collaboration with the Gauteng Department of Education. On average, fifty teachers per year attend workshops where they are taught music and visual arts.

20. The performances that I recorded in schools were obtained with signed permission from education officials and legal guardians.

21. Phindile Mpetshwa, "The Adjudicating Rubric of Indigenous Folklore in South African Schools Choral Eisteddfodau: A Critical Analysis" (MTech diss., Tshwane University of Technology, 2016), 202.

22. Associated Board of the Royal Schools of Music, "Theory of Music," www.abrsm.org.

23. "Theory of Music." *Trinity College London*, October 21, 2014, http://www.trinitycollege .com/site/?id=1058.

24. Ibid.

25. Lucia, "How Critical Is Music Theory?" 177–178.

26. Ibid., 183.

27. Ibid., 183–184.

28. Enver Motala and Salim Vally, "Class, 'Race,' and State in Post-Apartheid Education," in *Class in Education: Knowledge, Pedagogy and Subjectivity*, edited by D. Kelsh, D. Hill, and S. Macrine (New York: Routledge, 2010), 88–89.

29. Pierre Bourdieu, *Distinction: A Social Critique of the Judgement of Taste*, translated by Richard Nice (New York: Routledge, 1984).

SEVEN *Sounds of Tongaland: Environmental Justice at Ndumo Game Reserve*

1. Philip P. De Moor, Elsa Pooley, G. Neville, and J. Barichievy. "The Vegetation of Ndumu Game Reserve, Natal: A Quantitative Physiognomic Survey," *Annals of the Natal Museum* 23, no. 1 (1997): 239–272, 259.

2. Nile crocodiles were hatched in captivity for the first time at this very spot, a story my father chronicled in his book *Discoveries of a Crocodile Man* (London: Collins, 1982). In 1973 my family departed for St. Lucia where my father established a much larger project for crocodile research and education, now called the St. Lucia Crocodile Education Centre.

3. In the preface to *Mashesha*, he writes: "It must be stressed that some of the opinions and philosophies expressed are purely personal. They are the thoughts of a young man seeking to understand the complex interactions and conflicts that existed, and some that still exist, between man and wildlife, over the utilization of land and natural resources." Tony Pooley, *Mashesha: The Making of a Game Ranger* (Cape Town: Southern, 1992), xiv.

4. Pooley, *Mashesha*, 172.

5. Tongaland was the name used to describe this remote region bordering Swaziland (eSwatini) and Mozambique, but it was changed to Maputaland when this region was placed under the jurisdiction of the KwaZulu government during apartheid. It is as the area stretching from Mkhuze in the south to Mozambique and Swaziland in the north, flanked by the Lebombo mountains and sea at its extremities.

6. Simon Emmerson and Denis Smalley, "Electro-acoustic Music," *Grove Music Online*, 2001.

7. "Today all sounds belong to a continuous field of possibilities lying within the comprehensive dominion of music. Behold the new orchestra: the sonic universe!" Schafer, *The Soundscape*, 12.

8. Steven Feld, "From Schizophonia to Schismogenesis: On the Discourses and Practices of World Music and World Beat," in *Music Grooves*, edited by Charles Keil and Steven Feld (Chicago: University of Chicago Press, 1994), 257–289; Steven Feld, "Pygmy POP: A Genealogy of Schizophonic Mimesis," *Yearbook for Traditional Music* 28 (1996): 1–35.

9. Colin Turnbull, *Music of the Ituri Forest*, LP, New York: Folkways, 1957, CD reissue, *Mbuti Pygmies of the Ituri Rainforest*, Washington, DC: Smithsonian Folkways, 1992; *The Pygmies of the Ituri Forest*, LP, New York: Folkways, 1958, CD reissue, *Mbuti Pygmies of the Ituri Rainforest*, Washington, DC: Smithsonian Folkways, 1992; *Music of the Rainforest Pygmies*, LP, New York: Lyrichord, CD reissue, 1992; Steven Feld and Donald Brenneis, "Doing Anthropology in Sound," *American Ethnologist* 31, no. 4 (2004): 461–474.

10. Greg Milner, *Perfecting Sound Forever: The Story of Recorded Music* (London: Granta, 2009).

11. Pooley, *Mashesha*, 170.

12. Cheryl Ogilvie, "Effectiveness of Environmental Education Programmes in Adverse Socio-economic Environments: A Case Study of the Ndumo Communities, KwaZulu-Natal, South Africa" (DTech diss., Tshwane University of Technology, 2019).

13. Pooley, *Mashesha*, 105. See also Henri-Alexandre Junod, *The Life of a South African Tribe, Volume II: Mental Life* (New York: University Books [1927] 1962).

14. A short history of Ndumo Game Reserve is included in Tony Pooley and Ian Player's book *KwaZulu/Natal Wildlife Destinations: A Guide to the Game Reserves, Resorts, Private Nature Reserves, Ranches and Wildlife Areas of KwaZulu/Natal* (Cape Town: Southern, 1995).

15. "That humans have occupied the Ndumu Game Reserve area for a considerable period of time is borne out by the finding of an iron smelting furnace, complete with fragments of slag, charcoal and broken funnels into which the bellows fitted, at a site below Ndumu hill on the Pongolo floodplain. Using the radiocarbon dating method, it was established that this furnace was used some 1,400 years ago." Pooley and Player, *KwaZulu/Natal Wildlife Destinations*, 228–229.

16. Pooley and Player, *KwaZulu/Natal Wildlife Destinations*, 229.

17. Ibid.

18. This makes it the oldest reserve in the province of KwaZulu-Natal.

19. "Capt. Harold Potter, Chief Conservator for Zululand game reserves, recorded that in 1951 there were 1159 adults residing in 631 huts and that they grazed 916 head of cattle." Pooley and Player, *KwaZulu/Natal Wildlife Destinations*, 229.

20. Pooley and Player, *KwaZulu/Natal Wildlife Destinations*, 230.

21. Impey, *Song Walking*.

22. Pooley, *Mashesha*, 82.

23. My mother surveyed the flora in the reserve between 1969 and 1974 and reported that poaching continued even after the reserve had been fenced and communities moved out. "Arson has always been a factor in the life of the game reserve," she wrote. "Fires are put in by poachers with regularity, particularly in the west but also on occasions, on Ndumu Hill." Elsa Pooley, "A Checklist of the Plants of Ndumu Game Reserve, North-Eastern Zululand," *Journal of South African Botany* 44, no. 1 (1978): 1–54.

24. Later it was renamed the KwaZulu Department of Nature Conservation.

25. Philip de Moor and collaborators mapped the reserve on foot using aerial photography to produce vegetation and soil maps. The findings of this survey indicate twenty-nine vegetations formations described according to physiognomic characteristics. The authors found that areas on the floodplain, including that near Madiphini, "was previously under cultivation." De Moor et al., "The Vegetation of Ndumu," 255.

26. "The floodplain before it was affected by Jozini dam was either inundated for several weeks each summer or sometimes not at all. However, once the dam started controlling

the flow of the river the floodplain was inundated to its highest levels at unseasonal times and for extended periods of time. This has had a great effect on the composition of grasses and sedges, which are changing steadily." Elsa Pooley, "Checklist," 5.

27. Ibid., 6.

28. "The Convention on Wetlands, called the Ramsar Convention, is the intergovernmental treaty that provides the framework for the conservation and wise use of wetlands and their resources. The Convention was adopted in the Iranian city of Ramsar in 1971 and came into force in 1975. Since then, almost 90 percent of UN member states, from all the world's geographic regions, have acceded to become 'Contracting Parties.'" "Ramsar Convention." *Ramsar*. https://www.ramsar.org/about-the-ramsar-convention.

29. Yolandi Groenewald, "Ndumo Reserve Hit by Invasion, Crime," *Mail and Guardian*, October 15, 2010, https://mg.co.za/article/2010-10-15-ndumo-reserve-hit-by-invasion -crime/.

30. Ibid.

31. Corrinne Louw, "Ndumo Land Wanted by Locals." *Sowetan Live*, October 7, 2010, https://www.sowetanlive.co.za/news/2010-10-07-ndumo-land-wanted-by-locals/.

32. Tamlyn Jolly, "The Killing of Ndumo Game Reserve," *The Zululand Observer*, November 4, 2014, https://zululandobserver.co.za/51169/the-killing-of-ndumo-game- reserve/.

33. Stephen Coan, "Land Invasions and Poaching Threaten Famed KZN Game Reserve," *The Witness*, November 13, 2014, https://www.news24.com/witness/archive/Land -invasions-and-poaching-threaten-famed-KZN-game-reserve-20150430.

34. Working for Water is a program hosted by the Department of Forestry, Fisheries, and the Environment in the South African government. "Working for Water Programme," Department of Forestry, Fisheries & the Environment, Republic of South Africa. https:// www.dffe.gov.za/projectsprogrammes/wfw.

35. Pooley, *Mashesha*, 207.

36. Anthony J. Conway and Peter S. Goodman, "Population Characteristics and Management of Black Rhinoceros *Diceros bicornis minor* and White Rhinoceros *Ceratotheirum simum simum* in Ndumu Game Reserve, South Africa." *Biological Conservation* 47, no. 2 (1989): 109–122.

37. Conway and Goodman, "Population Characteristics," 214.

38. Clive Walker and Anton Walker, *Rhino Revolution: Searching for New Solutions* (Auckland Park: Jacana, 2017), xxvii.

39. Walker, *Rhino Revolution*, 23.

40. Renamed the yellow-rumped tinkerbird.

41. Renamed the purple-crested turaco.

42. Ogilvie, "Effectiveness of Environmental Education."

43. Ogilvie, "Effectiveness of Environmental Education," 72.

44. Catherine Hanekom, regional ecologist, quoted in Ogilvie, "Effectiveness of Environmental Education."

45. Michelle Toxopeüs and Louis Kotzé, "Promoting Environmental Justice through Civil-Based Instruments in South Africa," *Law, Environment and Development Journal* 13, no. 1 (2017): 49.

46. Toxopeüs and Kotzé, "Promoting Environmental Justice," 49.

47. Tony Carnie, "Ndumo Game Reserve: The Complicated Balancing Act of Subsistence Farming and Nature Conservation in KwaZulu-Natal," *Daily Maverick*, December 6, 2021, https://www.dailymaverick.co.za/article/2021-12-06-ndumo-game-reserve-the-complicated-balancing-act-of-subsistence-farming-and-nature-conservation-in-kwa-zulu-natal/.

48. Simon Pooley quoted in Carnie, "Ndumo Game Reserve."

49. The literature on land and conservation at Ndumo includes, inter alia, Laurie Ashley, "Land Restitution and Protected Areas in KwaZulu-Natal South Africa: Challenges to Implementation," Graduate Student Theses, Dissertations, & Professional Papers, 4801 (2005), https://scholarworks.umt.edu/etd/4801; Andrew Blackmore, "Legal and Public Trust Considerations for the Ndumo Game Reserve and South Africa-Mozambique Border, Following the Migration of the Usuthu River," *South African Public Law* 30, no. 2 (2015): 347–378; Talia Meer and Matthew Schnurr, "The Community versus Community-Based Natural Resource Management: The Case of Ndumo Game Reserve, South Africa," *Canadian Journal of Development Studies* 34, no. 4 (2013): 482–497.

50. Anthony Barnosky et al., "Has the Earth's Sixth Mass Extinction Already Arrived?" *Nature* 471 (2011): 51–57.

51. Gerardo Ceballos et al., "Accelerated Modern Human-Induced Species Losses: Entering the Sixth Mass Extinction," *Science Advances* 1, no. 5 (2015): 1.

52. James Estes et al., "Trophic Downgrading of Planet Earth," *Science*, 333, no. 6040 (2011): 301–306.

53. Ibid.

54. Ceballos et al., "Accelerated Human-Induced Species Losses," 3.

55. Christine Korsgaard, *Fellow Creatures: Our Obligations to the Other Animals* (New York: Oxford University Press, 2018).

56. Korsgaard, *Fellow Creatures*, 21.

57. Korsgaard, *Fellow Creatures*, 33.

58. Angela Impey's work on environmental justice at Ndumo focuses on the experiences of two groups of women living at ePhosheni and in the uSuthu Gorge (to the southwest of the reserve) in the early 2000s, and on their claims to land in the reserve. Impey's project validates the voices of women who have for too long been ignored by anthropologists in this region. Some of these women were too young to remember the game reserve as home. Their parents and grandparents were forcibly removed from the reserve in the 1950s and

1960s. Impey relates these women's experiences and frustrations about access to land and resources. This chapter offers a counterpoint to her narratives and the discussion of game rangers' memoirs, including my father's.

59. Simon Pooley, Saloni Bhatia, and Anirudhkumar Vasava, "Rethinking the Study of Human-Wildlife Coexistence," *Conservation Biology* 35, no. 3 (2021): 784–793.

60. Pooley, *Mashesha*, 226.

61. I distinguish "wildlife"—animals, birds, insects, plants—from "conservation." The latter is an all too human practice fitted to its own ideals and ideologies that can and must adapt to the times. But conservation should not be conflated with wildlife. When this happens, conservation is constructed as the anthropomorphic ghost ship upon whose sails the futures of wildlife depend.

EIGHT *Unsung Melodies: Reciprocity in Sound*

1. R400 was roughly US$40 as of June 2013.

2. "Applied ethnomusicology is best regarded as a music-centered intervention in a particular community, whose purpose is to benefit that community—for example, a social movement, a musical benefit, a cultural good, an economic advantage, or a combination of these and other benefits. It is music-centered, but above all the intervention is people-centered, for the understanding that drives it toward reciprocity is based in the collaborative partnerships that arise from ethnomusicological fieldwork. Applied ethnomusicology is guided by ethical principles of social responsibility, human rights, and cultural and musical equity." Jeff Todd Titon, "Section 1. Applied Ethnomusicology: A Descriptive and Historical Account," in *The Oxford Handbook of Applied Ethnomusicology*, edited by Jeff Todd Titon and Svanibor Pettan (New York: Oxford, 2015), 4.

3. Many others would respond in the same way, often relating sad stories of exploitation by record producers and studios who made off with their money and music. My recording devices and basic expertise in editing and mixing would be their free entry into the music industry, or so they hoped.

4. Erika Brady, *A Spiral Way: How the Phonograph Changed Ethnography* (Jackson: University of Mississippi Press, 1999), 123.

5. There seems to be a link to the Zingili clan dances recorded by Hugh Tracey in the 1940s and 1950s at mines on the Witwatersrand. Tracey states that this clan is from the Ingwavuma District of Natal, suggesting a genealogy with these teams at Ndumo Hill. Hugh Tracey, *African Dances of the Witwatersrand Gold Mines*, Photographs by Merlyn Severn (Johannesburg: African Music Society, 1952).

BIBLIOGRAPHY

Act No. 3 of 2019: Traditional and Khoi-San Leadership Act, 2019. November 28, 2019. https://www.gov.za/sites/default/files/gcis_document/201911/4286528-11act3 of2019tradkhoisanleadership.pdf.

Agawu, Kofi. *African Rhythm: A Northern Ewe Perspective*. Cambridge: Cambridge University Press, 1995.

———. *The African Imagination in Music*. New York: Oxford University Press, 2016.

———. "How We Got Out of Analysis, and How to Get Back in Again." *Music Analysis* 23, no. ii–iii (2004): 267–286.

———. "The Invention of 'African Rhythm.'" *Journal of the American Musicological Society* 48, no. 3 (1995): 380–395.

———. "Representing African Music." *Critical Inquiry* 18, no. 2 (1992): 245–266.

———. *Representing African Music: Postcolonial Notes, Queries, Positions*. New York: Routledge, 2003.

"A Programme for Higher Education Transformation." *Government Gazette*, August 15, 1997. Pretoria, 1997.

Ah Goo, Delia. "From Urban Decline to Gentrifying Spaces: The Case of the Maboneng Precinct in Johannesburg's Inner City." *South African Journal of Cultural History* 31, no. 1 (2015): 1–18.

Alcock, Creina. "A Brief History of the Mchunu and Mthembu Tribes." In *Imithetho yomhlaba yaseMsinga: The Living Law of Land in Msinga, KwaZulu-Natal*, edited by Ben Cousins, 22–29. Cape Town: University of the Western Cape, 2011.

———. "Koornspruit: The Story of an African Farm." *Mdukatshani Rural Development Project Annual Report 2016*.

———. *Mdukatshani: Fifty Years of Beading, 1969–2019*. Hilton: Mdukatshani Craft and Welfare Trust, 2020.

———. "No Ordinary Farm." Unpublished manuscript, 1984.

Alcock, GG. *Third World Child: Born White, Zulu Bred*. Johannesburg: Tracey McDonald Publishers, 2014.

Alcock, Rauri, and Donna Hornby. "Traditional Land Matters—A Look into Land Administration in Tribal Areas in KwaZulu-Natal." *Legal Entity Assessment Project,* 2004.

André, Naomi, Yolanda Covington-Ward, and Jendele Hungbo, eds. *African Performance Arts and Political Action.* Ann Arbor: University of Michigan Press, 2021.

Ashley, Laurie. "Land Restitution and Protected Areas in KwaZulu-Natal South Africa: Challenges to Implementation." Graduate Student Theses, Dissertations, and Professional Papers. 4801 (2005). https://scholarworks.umt.edu/etd/4801.

Associated Board of the Royal Schools of Music. www.za.abrsm.org.

Ballard, Charles. "Traders, Trekkers and Colonists." In *Natal and Zululand from Earliest Times to 1910,* edited by Andrew Duminy and Bill Guest, 116–145. Pietermaritzburg: University of Natal Press, 1989.

Barnosky, Anthony, Nicholas Matzke, Susumu Tomiya, Guinevere Wogan, Brian Swartz, Tiago Quental, Charles Marshall, Jenny McGuire, Emily Lindsey, Kaitlin Maguire, Ben Mersey, and Elizabeth Ferrer. "Has the Earth's Sixth Mass Extinction Already Arrived?" *Nature* 471 (2011): 51–57.

Barz, Gregory, and Timothy J. Cooley, eds. *Shadows in the Field: New Perspectives for Fieldwork in Ethnomusicology.* 2nd ed. Oxford: Oxford University Press, 2008.

Beall, Jo, Sibongiseni Mkhize, and Shahid Vawda. "Emergent Democracy and 'Resurgent' Tradition: Institutions, Chieftaincy and Transition in KwaZulu-Natal." *Journal of Southern African Studies* 31, no. 4 (2005): 755–771.

Beinart, William. *Twentieth-Century South Africa.* Oxford: Oxford University Press, 2000.

Bengu, Sibusiso. "White Paper on Education and Training. Notice 196 of 1995. Parliament of the Republic of South Africa." Pretoria: Department of Education, 1995.

Berglund, Axel-Ivar. *Zulu Thought-Patterns and Symbolism.* Bloomington: Indiana University Press, 1989.

Bhengu, Lwandile. "King Zwelithini Likens Land Question to Being 'Stripped of Our Blanket.'" *Timeslive.* September 8, 2019. https://www.timeslive.co.za/politics/2019-09-08-king-zwelithini-likens-land-question-to-being-stripped-of-our-blanket/.

"Bill of Rights." *The Constitution of the Republic of South Africa.* South Africa, 1996.

Blacking, John. "Songs, Dances, Mimes and Symbolism of Venda Girls' Initiation Schools. Part 1: Vhusha." *African Studies* 28, no. 1 (1969a): 3–36.

———. "Songs, Dances, Mimes and Symbolism of Venda Girls' Initiation Schools. Part 2: Milayo." *African Studies* 28, no. 2 (1969b): 69–118.

———. "Songs, Dances, Mimes and Symbolism of Venda Girls' Initiation Schools. Part 3: Domba." *African Studies* 28, no. 3 (1969c): 149–199.

———. "Songs, Dances, Mimes and Symbolism of Venda Girls' Initiation Schools. Part 4: The Great *Domba* Song." *African* Studies 28, no. 4 (1969d): 215–266.

———. *Venda Children's Songs: A Study in Ethnomusicological Analysis.* Chicago: University of Chicago Press [1967] 1995.

Blackmore, Andrew. "Legal and Public Trust Considerations for the Ndumo Game Reserve and South Africa-Mozambique Border, Following the Migration of the Usuthu River." *South African Public Law* 30, no. 2 (2015): 347–378.

Bold, Edgar. *Ndumu*. South African Broadcasting Corporation, 1974.

Bonner, Philip, and Vusi Ndima. "The Roots of Violence on the East Rand, 1980–1990." Seminar Paper presented to the Wits Institute for Advanced Social Research, no. 450, October 18, 1999.

Bourdieu, Pierre. *Distinction: A Social Critique of the Judgment of Taste*, translated by Richard Nice. New York: Routledge, 1984.

Brady, Erika. *A Sprial Way: How the Phonograph Changed Ethnography*. Jackson: University of Mississippi Press, 1999.

Brookes, Edgar, and Colin de Webb. *A History of Natal*. Scottsville: University of Natal Press, 1965.

Bryant, Alfred T. *Olden Times in Zululand and Natal: Containing Earlier Political History of the Eastern-Nguni Clans*. Cape Town: C. Struik, 1965.

———. *The Zulu People: As They Were Before the White Man Came*. Pietermaritzburg: Shuter and Shooter, 1949.

"Budget Review: 2014." *National Treasury, Republic of South Africa*. Pretoria, 2014.

Bulpin, Thomas Victor. *Natal and the Zulu Country*. Pretoria: Protea, 2013.

Buthelezi, Mbongiseni. "The Empire Talks Back: Re-Examining the Legacies of Shaka and Zulu Power in Post-Apartheid South Africa." In *Zulu Identities: Being Zulu, Past and Present*, edited by Benedict Carton, John Laband, and Jabulani Sithole, 23–34. Pietermaritzburg: University of KwaZulu-Natal Press, 2008.

———. "Sifuna umlando wethu (We are Searching for Our History): Oral Literature and the Meanings of the Past in Post-Apartheid South Africa." PhD diss., Columbia University, 2012.

Buthelezi, Mbongiseni, and Dineo Skosana. "The Salience of Chiefs in Postapartheid South Africa: Reflections on the Nhlapo Commission." In *The Politics of Custom: Chiefship, Capital, and the State in Contemporary Africa*, edited by John L. Comaroff and Jean Comaroff, 110–133. Chicago: University of Chicago Press, 2018.

Carnie, Tony. "Ndumo Game Reserve: The Complicated Balancing Act of Subsistence Farming and Nature Conservation in KwaZulu-Natal." *Daily Maverick*. December 6, 2021. https://www.dailymaverick.co.za/article/2021-12-06-ndumo-game-reserve-the-complicated-balancing-act-of-subsistence-farming-and-nature-conservation-in-kwazulu-natal/.

"Census 2011: Census in Brief." *Statistics South Africa*. Pretoria: Statistics South Africa, 2012.

Ceballos, Gerardo, Paul Ehrlich, Anthony Barnosky, Andrés García, Robert Pringle, and Todd Palmer. "Accelerated Modern Human-Induced Species Losses: Entering the Sixth Mass Extinction." *Science Advances* 1, no. 5 (2015). https://doi.org/10.1126/sciadv.1400253

Changuion, Louis, and Bertus Steenkamp. *Disputed Land: The Historical Development of the South African Land Issue, 1652–2011*. Pretoria: Protea, 2012.

Chetty, Rajendra. "Class Dismissed? Youth Resistance and the Politics of Race and Class in South African Education." *Critical Arts: South-North Cultural and Media Studies* 28, no. 1 (2014): 88–102.

Clark, Andy. *Being There: Putting Brain, Body, and World Together Again*. Cambridge, MA: MIT Press, 1997.

Clarke, Eric, and Nicholas Cook, eds. *Empirical Musicology*. Oxford: Oxford University Press, 2004.

Clayton, Martin, Rebecca Sager, and Udo Will. "In Time with the Music: The Concept of Entrainment and Its Significance for Ethnomusicology." *European Meetings in Ethnomusicology* 11 (2005): 1–82.

Clegg, Jonathan. "An Examination of the Umzansi Dance Style." In *Papers Read at the 3rd Symposium on Ethnomusicology*, edited by Andrew Tracey, 64–70. Grahamstown: Rhodes University, 1984.

———. Dance and Society in Africa South of the Sahara. BA Honors dissertation: University of the Witwatersrand, 1977.

———. "The Music of Zulu Immigrant Workers in Johannesburg: A Focus on Concertina and Guitar." In *Papers Presented at the Symposium on Ethnomusicology*, edited by Andrew Tracey, 2–9. Grahamstown, South Africa: International Library of African Music, 1981.

———. "Toward an Understanding of African Dance: The Zulu isiShameni Style." In *Papers Read at the 2nd Symposium on Ethnomusicology*, edited by Andrew Tracey, 8–14. Grahamstown: International Library of African Music, Institute of Social and Economic Research, Rhodes University, 1982.

Clifford, James. "Introduction: Partial Truths." In James Clifford and George E. Marcus, eds., *Writing Culture: The Poetics and Politics of Ethnography*, 1-26. Berkeley: University of California Press, [1986]2010.

Clifford, James, and George E. Marcus, eds. *Writing Culture: The Poetics and Politics of Ethnography*. Berkeley: University of California Press [1986] 2010.

Coan, Stephen. "Land Invasions and Poaching Threaten Famed KZN Game Reserve. *The Witness*. November 13, 2014. https://www.news24.com/witness/archive/Land -invasions-and-poaching-threaten-famed-KZN-game-reserve-20150430.

Coertze, Pieter J. "Volkekunde." *South African Journal of Ethnology* 1, no. 1 (1978): 1–9.

Colenso, John W. *The Colenso Zulu-English Dictionary*. 4th ed. Pietermaritzburg: Shuter and Shooter, 1878.

Collins, Tom. "Constructing Maskanda." *South African Music Studies* 26–27, no. 1 (2006): 1–26.

Comaroff, Jean, and John Comaroff. *Of Revelation and Revolution, Volume 1: Christian-*

ity, Colonialism, and Consciousness in South Africa. Chicago: University of Chicago Press, 1991.

———. *Theory from the South: Or, How Euro-America Is Evolving Toward Africa*. New York: Routledge, 2010.

Comaroff, John L., and Jean Comaroff, eds. *The Politics of Custom: Chiefship, Capital, and the State in Contemporary Africa*. Chicago: University of Chicago Press, 2018.

Conway, Anthony J., and Peter S. Goodman. "Population Characteristics and Management of Black Rhinoceros *Diceros bicornis minor* and White Rhinoceros *Ceratotheirum simum simum* in Ndumu Game Reserve, South Africa." *Biological Conservation* 47, no. 2 (1989): 109–122.

Constitution of the Republic of South Africa. Act 108 of 1996.

Cooper, David, and Ian Sapiro. "Ethnomusicology in the Laboratory: From the Tonometer to the Digital Melograph." *Ethnomusicology Forum* 15, no. 2 (2006): 301–313.

Coplan, David. *In the Time of Cannibals: The Word Music of South Africa's Basotho Migrants*. Chicago, University of Chicago Press, 1994.

———. *In Township Tonight! South Africa's Black City Music and Theatre*. 2nd ed. Chicago: University of Chicago Press, 2007.

Crowley, Roger. *Conquerors: How Portugal Seized the Indian Ocean and Forged the First Global Empire*. London: Faber, 2015.

Csikszentmihalyi, Mihaly. *Flow and the Foundations of Positive Psychology*. Dordrecht: Springer, 2014.

Dargie, Dave. *The Music of the Xhosa*. Cape Town: David Phillip, 1988.

———. "Umakhweyane, A Musical Bow and its Contribution to Zulu Music." *African Music* 8, no. 1 (2007): 60–81.

Davies, Nollene. "A Study of the Guitar Styles in Zulu *Maskanda* Music." MMus diss., University of Natal, Durban, 1992.

———. "The Guitar in Zulu 'Maskanda' Tradition." *The World of Music* 36, no. 2 (1994): 118–137.

De Moor, Philip P., Elsa Pooley, Gill Neville, and Joey Barichievy. "The Vegetation of Ndumu Game Reserve, Natal: A Quantitative Physiognomic Survey." *Annals of the Natal Museum* 23, no. 1 (1977): 239–272.

Dlamini, Penwell. "Renovation of Johannesburg Hostels to Start Soon." *Timeslive*. July 31, 2017. https://www.timeslive.co.za/news/south-africa/2017-07-31-renovation-of-johannes burg-hostels-to-start-soon/.

Dlamini, Penwell, and Alon Skuy. "Buthelezi Begs Angry Crowd to Calm Down as He Speaks Against Xenophobia." *Timeslive*. https://www.timeslive.co.za/news/south africa/2019-09-08-hostel-residents-march-against-foreigners-as-buthelezi-tries-to -appeal-for-peace/.

Dlamini, Sazi. "Umakhweyana and Ugubhu Zulu Musical Bows as inKokha, imVingo, inKohlisa, uQwabe and isiQwemqwemana." In *Musical Bows of Southern Africa*, edited by Sazi Dlamini, 113–156. New York: Bloomsbury, 2021.

Doke, Clement. "The Phonetics of the Zulu Language." *Bantu Studies* 2 (1926). Reprint. Muenchen: Lincom Grammatica, 2012.

Doke, Clement M., D Mck. Malcolm, J.M.A. Sikakana, and Benedict W. Vilakazi. *English–isiZulu, isiZulu–English Dictionary*. 4th ed. with revised orthography. Johannesburg: Wits University Press, 2014.

Dontsa, Luvuyo. "*Intonjane* Music: A Forum of Identity Formation for Xhosa Women." In *Music and Identity: Transformation and Negotiation*, edited by E. Akrofi, M. Smit, and S-M. Thorsén, 383–407. Stellenbosch: African Sun Press, 2007.

Drummond, Urvi. "Music Education in South African Schools after Apartheid: Teacher Perceptions of Western and African Music." Ed.D diss., University of Glasgow, 2015.

Dubow, Saul. *Apartheid*. Oxford: Oxford University Press, 2012.

Elphick, Richard. *The Equality of Believers: Protestant Missionaries and the Racial Politics of South Africa*. Scottsville: University of KwaZulu-Natal Press, 2012.

Emmerson, Simon, and Denis Smalley. "Electro-Acoustic Music." *Grove Music Online*, 2001.

Erlmann, Veit. *African Stars: Studies in Black South African Performance*. Chicago: University of Chicago Press, 1991.

———. *Music, Modernity, and the Global Imagination*. New York: Oxford University Press, 1999.

———. *Nightsong: Performance, Power and Practice in South Africa*. Chicago: Chicago University Press, 1996.

———. "What of the Ethnographic Ear?" In *Hearing Cultures: Essays on Sound, Listening and Modernity*, edited by Veit Erlmann, 1–20. New York: Routledge [2004] 2020.

Estes, James A., John Terborgh, Justin S. Brashares, Mary E. Power, Joel Berger, William J. Bond, Stephen R. Carpenter, et al. "Trophic Downgrading of Planet Earth." *Science* 333, no. 6040 (2011): 301–306.

Evans-Pritchard, Edward. *The Nuer*. Oxford: Clarendon Press [1940] 1956.

Feld, Steven. "Acoustemology." In *Keywords in Sound*, edited by David Novak and Matt Sakakeeny, 12–21. Durham, NC: Duke University Press, 2015.

———. "From Schizophonia to Schismogenesis: On the Discourses and Practices of World Music and World Beat." In *Music Grooves*, edited by Charles Keil and Steven Feld, 257–289. Chicago: University of Chicago Press, 1994.

———. "Pygmy POP: A Genealogy of Schizophonic Mimesis." *Yearbook for Traditional Music* 28 (1996): 1–35.

———. *Sound and Sentiment: Birds, Weeping, Poetics, and Song in Kaluli Expression*. Philadelphia: University of Pennsylvania Press, 1982.

Feld, Steven, and Donald Brenneis. "Doing Anthropology in Sound." *American Ethnologist* 31, no. 4 (2004): 461–474.

Felgate, Walter. *The Tembe Thonga of Natal and Mozambique*. Durban: University of Natal, 1982.

Freund, Bill. "South Africa: The Union Years, 1910–1948; Political and Economic Foundations." In *The Cambridge History of South Africa, Volume 2, 1885–1994*, edited by Robert Ross, Anne Kelk Mager, and Bill Nasson, 211–253. Cambridge: Cambridge University Press, 2016.

Friedson, Steven. *Dancing Prophets: Musical Experience in Tumbuka Healing*. Chicago: University of Chicago Press, 1996.

———. *Remains of Ritual: Northern Gods in a Southern Land*. Chicago: University of Chicago Press, 2009.

Geertz, Clifford. *The Interpretation of Cultures*. New York: Basic Books, 1973.

"General Household Survey." *Statistics South Africa*. Pretoria: Statistics South Africa, 2018.

Golan, Daphna. *Inventing Shaka: Using History in the Construction of Zulu Nationalism*. London: Lynne Rienner, 1994.

Groenewald, Yolandi. "Ndumo Reserve Hit by Invasion, Crime." *Mail and Guardian*. October 15, 2010. https://mg.co.za/article/2010-10-15-ndumo-reserve-hit-by-invasion -crime/.

Gunner, Liz. "Jacob Zuma, the Social Body and the Unruly Power of Song." *African Affairs* 108, no. 430 (2009): 27–48.

———. "Zulu Choral Music—Performing Identities in a New State." *Research in African Literatures* 37, no. 2 (2006): 84–97.

Gunner, Liz, and Mafika Gwala, eds. *Musho! Zulu Popular Praises*, translated by Liz Gunner and Mafika Gwala. East Lansing: Michigan State University Press, 1991.

Guy, Jeff. *The Destruction of the Zulu Kingdom*. Pietermaritzburg: University of Natal Press, 1979.

———. *The Maphumulo Uprising: War, Law and Ritual in the Zulu Rebellion*. Pietermaritzburg: University of KwaZulu-Natal Press, 2005.

———. *Theophilus Shepstone and the Forging of Natal*. Scottsville: University of KwaZulu-Natal Press, 2013.

Hamilton, Carolyn, and Nessa Leibhammer, eds. *Tribing and Untribing the Archive: Identity and the Material Record in Southern KwaZulu-Natal in the Late Independent and Colonial Periods*. 2 Volumes. Scottsville: University of KwaZulu-Natal Press, 2016.

Hamilton, Lawrence. *Are South Africans Free?* New York: Bloomsbury, 2014.

———. *Freedom Is Power: Liberty through Political Representation*. Cambridge: Cambridge University Press, 2014.

Hamm, Charles. "'The Constant Companion of Man': Separate Development, Radio Bantu and Music." *Popular Music* 10, no. 2 (1991): 147–173.

Hammond-Tooke, W. David. "The Uniqueness of Nguni Mediumstic Divination in Southern Africa." *Africa* 72, no. 2 (2002): 277–292.

———. "Cattle in Zulu Life." In *The Abundant Herds: A Celebration of the Cattle of the Zulu People*, edited by Marguerite Poland, David Hammond-Tooke, and Leigh Voight, 14–33. Johannesburg: Fernwood Press, 2003.

———. "Cattle Symbolism in Zulu Culture." In *Zulu Identities: Being Zulu, Past and Present*, edited by Benedict Carton, John Laband, and Jabulani Sithole, 62–68. Scottsville: University of KwaZulu-Natal Press, 2009.

Hansen, Deirdre. "The Music of the Xhosa-Speaking People." Unpublished PhD diss., University of the Witwatersrand, 1981.

Hassim, Shireen, Tawana Kupe, and Eric Worby. *Go Home or Die Here: Violence, Xenophobia and the Reinvention of Difference in South Africa*. Johannesburg: Wits University Press, 2008.

Heidegger, Martin. *Being and Time*, translated by John Macquarrie and Edward Robinson. New York: Harper Perennial, 1962.

Hellier-Tinoco, Ruth. "Experiencing People: Relationships, Responsibility and Reciprocity." *British Journal of Ethnomusicology* 12, no. 1 (2003): 19–34.

Herbst, Anri, Jacques de Wet, and Susan Rijsdijk. "A Survey of Music Education in the Primary Schools of South Africa's Cape Peninsula." *Journal of Research in Music Education* 53, no. 3 (2005): 260–283.

Hobsbawm, Eric. "Introduction: Inventing Traditions." In *The Invention of Tradition*, edited by Eric Hobsbawm and Terence Ranger. Cambridge: Cambridge University Press, 1982.

Huffman, Tim. "The Achaeology of the Nguni Past." *Southern African Humanities* 16, no. 1 (2004): 79–111.

Impey, Angela. *Song Walking: Environmental Justice in a Borderland*. Chicago: University of Chicago Press, 2018.

———. "Sound, Memory and Dis/placement: Exploring Sound, Song and Performance as Oral History in the Southern African Borderlands." *Oral History* 36, no. 1 (2008): 33–44.

Ingold, Tim. "Against Soundscape." In *Autumn Leaves: Sound and the Environment in Artistic Practice*, edited by Angus Carlyle, 10–13. Paris: Double Entendre, 2007.

"Ingonyama Trust Home Page." Ingonyama Trust Board. Last modified 2019. http://www.ingonyamatrust.org.za.

Irvine, Judith Temkin, and Liz Gunner. "With Respect to Zulu: Revisiting ukuHlonipha." *Anthropological Quarterly* 91, no. 1 (2018): 173–207.

Johnson, Leigh, Gesine Meyer-Rath, Rob Dorrington, Adrian Puren, Thapelo Seathlodi, Khangelani Zuma, and Ali Feizzadeh. "The Effect of HIV Programs in South Africa on National HIV Incidence Trends, 2000-2019." *JAIDS: Journal of Acquired Immune Deficiency Syndrome* 90, no. 2 (2022): 115–123.

Johnson, W. R. "Education: Keystone of Apartheid." *Anthropology and Education Quarterly* 13, no. 3 (1982): 214–237.

Johnston, Thomas F. "Speech-Tone and Other Forces in Tsonga Music." *Studies in African Linguistics* 4 (1973): 49–70.

Jolly, Tamlyn. "The Killing of Ndumo Game Reserve." *The Zululand Observer*. November 4, 2014. https://zululandobserver.co.za/51169/the-killing-of-ndumo-game-reserve/.

Jones, Arthur Morris. *Studies in African Music*. Oxford: Oxford University Press, 1959.

Jorritsma, Marie. *Sonic Spaces of the Karoo: The Sacred Music of a South African Coloured Community*. Philadelphia: Temple University Press, 2011.

Joseph, Rosemary. "Zulu Women's Bow Songs: Ruminations on Love." *Bulletin of the School of Oriental and African Studies, University of London* 50, no. 1 (1987): 90–119.

———. "Zulu Women's Music." *African Music* 6, no. 3 (1983): 53–89.

Junod, Henri Alexandre. *The Life of a South African Tribe, Volume II: Mental Life*. New York: University Books [1927] 1962.

Kant, Immanuel. *Groundwork of the Metaphysics of Morals*, edited by Mary Gregor and Jens Timmermann. Cambridge: Cambridge University Press, 2012.

Kapchan, Deborah. "Body." In *Keywords in Sound*, edited by David Novak and Matt Sakakeeny, 33. Durham, NC: Duke University Press, 2015.

———. "The Splash of Icarus: Theorizing Sound Writing/Writing Sound Theory." In *Theorizing Sound Writing*, edited by Deborah Kapchan, 1–22. Middletown, CT: Wesleyan University Press, 2017.

Kelly, Jill. *To Swim with Crocodiles: Land, Violence, and Belonging in South Africa, 1800–1996*. Scottsville: University of KwaZulu-Natal Press, 2019.

Kirby, Percival. *The Musical Instruments of the Native Races of South Africa*. 2nd ed. Johannesburg: Wits University Press [1934] 1968.

———. *The Social System of the Zulus*. Pietermaritzburg: Shuter and Shooter, 1950.

Kisliuk, Michelle. *Seize the Dance! BaAka Musical Life and the Ethnography of Performance*. New York: Oxford University Press, 1998.

Kohler, Max. "Marriage Customs in Southern Natal." In *Ethnological Publications Vol. 4*, edited by N.J.V. Warmelo. Pretoria: Department of Native Affairs, 1931.

Koopman, Anton. "The Praises of Young Zulu Men." *Theoria* 70 (1987): 41–54.

Korsgaard, Christine. *Fellow Creatures: Our Obligations to the Other Animals*. New York: Oxford University Press, 2018.

Krige, Eileen Jensen. "Girls' Puberty Songs and Their Relation to Fertility, Health, Morality and Religion among the Zulu." *Africa: Journal of the International African Institute* 38, no. 2 (1968): 173–198.

———. *The Social System of the Zulus*. 2nd ed. Pietermaritzburg: Shuter & Shooter, 1950.

Kubeka, Isaac Sibusiso. "A Preliminary Survey of Zulu Dialects in Natal and Zululand." Master's thesis, University of Natal, Durban, 1979.

Kuper, Hilda. 'The Language of Sites in the Politics of Space,' *American Anthropologist*, Volume 74, no. 3: 411–425.

Laband, John. *The Eight Zulu Kings: From Shaka to Goodwill Zwelithini*. Cape Town: Jonathan Ball, 2018.

Ladefoged, Peter. *A Course in Phonetics*. Boston: Thomson Wadsworth, 2006.

Landau, Loren. *Exorcizing the Demons Within: Xenophobia, Violence and Statecraft in Contemporary South Africa*. Johannesburg: Wits University Press, 2012.

Lefebvre, Henri. *The Production of Space*, translated by Donald Nicholson-Smith. Oxford: Blackwell, 1984.

Leslie, David. *Among the Zulus and amaTongas*. 2nd ed. Edinburgh: Edmonston & Douglas, 1875.

Levitin, Daniel, J., Jessica A. Grahn, and Justin London. "The Psychology of Music: Rhythm and Movement." *Annual Review of Psychology* 69 (2018): 51–75.

Low, Setha. "Claiming Space for an Engaged Anthropology: Spatial Inequality and Social Exclusion," *American Anthropologist* 113, no. 3 (2011): 389–409.

Louw, Corrinne. "Ndumo Land Wanted by Locals." *Sowetan Live*. October 7, 2010. https://www.sowetanlive.co.za/news/2010-10-07-ndumo-land-wanted-by-locals/.

Lucia, Christine. "How Critical Is Music Theory?" *Critical Arts: South-North Cultural and Media Studies* 21, no. 1 (2007): 166–189.

———. *Music Notation: A South African Guide*. Pretoria: UNISA Press, 2011.

"Maboneng Precinct." *Gauteng.net*. https://www.gauteng.net/attractions/maboneng_precinct/.

Mager, Anne Kelk, and Maanda Mulaudzi, "Popular Responses to Apartheid: 1948—c. 1975." In *The Cambridge History of South Africa, Volume 2, 1885–1994*, ed. Robert Ross, Anne Kelk Mager, and Bill Nasson, 369–408. Cambridge: Cambridge University Press, 2016.

Maggs, Tim. "The Iron Age Farming Communities." In *Natal and Zululand from Earliest Times to 1910: A New History*, edited by Andrew Duminy and Bill Guest, 28–48. Pietermaritzburg: University of Natal Press, 1989.

Magwaza, Thenjiwe. "'So That I Will Be a Marriageable Girl': *Umemulo* in Contemporary Zulu Society." In *Zulu Identities: Being Zulu, Past and Present*, edited by Benedict Carton, 482–496. Scottsville: University of KwaZulu-Natal Press, 2009.

Mamdani, Mahmood. *Citizen and Subject: Contemporary Africa and the Legacy of Late Colonialism*. 2nd ed. Johannesburg: Wits University Press, 2017.

Maseko, Nomsa. "Inside South Africa's 'Dangerous' Men's Hostels." *BBC*. May 13, 2015. http://www.bbc.com/news/world-africa-32692461.

McNulty, Grant. "'(Re)discovering the Correct History': Tradition and Custom, the Archival Record and Identity in Contemporary KwaZulu-Natal." In *Tribing and Untribing the Archive: Identity and the Material Record in Southern KwaZulu-Natal in the Late Independent and Colonial Periods*. vol. 1, edited by Carolyn Hamilton and Nessa Leibhammer, 115–145. Scottsville: University of KwaZulu-Natal Press, 2016.

"Mdukatshani Rural Development Project Home Page." *Mdukatshani Rural Development Project*. http://www.mdukatshani.com.

"Media Release: Quarterly Labour Force Survey, Q4 2021." *Statistics South Africa*. Pretoria: Statistics South Africa, 2022. https://www.statssa.gov.za/publications/P0211/Media%20release%20QLFS%20Q4%202021.pdf

Meer, Talia, and Matthew Schnurr. "The Community versus Community-Based Natural Resource Management: The Case of Ndumo Game Reserve, South Africa." *Canadian Journal of Development Studies* 34, no. 4 (2013): 482–497.

Meintjes, Louise. *Dust of the Zulu: Ngoma Aesthetics after Apartheid*. Durham, NC: Duke University Press, 2017.

———. "Shoot the Sergeant, Shatter the Mountain: The Production of Masculinity in Zulu Ngoma Song and Dance in Post-Apartheid South Africa." *Ethnomusicology Forum* 13, no. 2 (2004): 173–201.

———. *Sound of Africa! Making Music Zulu in a South African Studio*. Durham, NC: Duke University Press, 2003.

Merleau-Ponty, Maurice. *The World of Perception*, translated by Oliver Davis. New York: Routledge, [1948]2004.

———. *Phenomenology of Perception*, translated by Colin Smith. New York: Routledge, [1945]1962.

Meyer, Leonard. *Emotion and Meaning in Music*. Chicago: University of Chicago Press, 1956.

"Mid-year Population Estimates, 2018. Statistical Release P0302." *Statistics South Africa*. Pretoria: Statistics South Africa, 2018.

Milner, Greg. *Perfecting Sound Forever: The Story of Recorded Music*. London: Granta, 2009.

Mnyambo, Melissa Tandiwe. "Red Velvet Cheesecake in Maboneng, Pap and Steak in Jeppestown." In *Reversing Urban Inequality in Johannesburg*, edited by Melissa Tandiwe Mnyambo, 69–81. New York: Routledge, 2015.

Moitse, Sindile A. "The Ethnomusicology of the Basotho." Master's thesis, National University of Lesotho, 1990.

———. *The Ethnomusicology of the Basotho*. Roma: National University of Lesotho, 1994.

Motala, Enver, and Salim Vally. "Class, 'Race,' and State in Post-Apartheid Education. In *Class in Education: Knowledge, Pedagogy and Subjectivity*, edited by D. Kelsh, D. Hill, and S. Macrine, 87–107. New York: Routledge, 2010.

Mpetshwa, Phindile. "The Adjudicating Rubric of Indigenous Folklore in South African Schools Choral Eisteddfodau: A Critical Analysis." Unpublished MTech diss., Tshwane University of Technology, 2016.

Muller, Carol. *Focus: Music of South Africa*. 2nd ed. New York: Routledge, 2004.

———. *Rituals of Fertility and the Sacrifice of Desire: Nazarite Women's Performance in South Africa*. Chicago: University of Chicago Press, 1999.

Mupotswa, Danai, and Dorothee Kreutzfeldt. "Xenophobia, Nationalism and Techniques of Difference." *Agenda: Empowering Women for Gender Equity* 30, no. 2 (2016): 13–20.

"National Curriculum and Assessment Policy Statement for Creative Arts. CAPS: Creative Arts." Pretoria: Department of Basic Education, 2012.

Nel, Etienne, and Tony Binns. "Changing the Geography of Apartheid Education in South Africa." *Geography* 84, no. 2 (1999): 119–128.

Neocosmos, Michael. "From 'Foreign Natives' to 'Native Foreigners': Explaining Xenophobia in Post-apartheid South Africa." Dakar: Codesria, 2010.

Nicolson, Greg. "Gauteng Xenophobia: Gigaba and Mashaba Trade Accusations." *Daily Maverick.* February 28, 2017. https://www.dailymaverick.co.za/article/2017-02-28-gauteng-xenophobia-gigaba-and-mashaba-trade-accusations/#.WTj_sSN97so.

Ngubane, J. B. "The Role of Amadlozi/Amathongo as Seen in the Writings of B.W. Vilakazi." *Religion in Southern Africa* 5, no. 2 (1984): 55–75.

Nhlapo Commission Report. "Determinations on the Position of the Paramount Chiefs," 2010. https://www.gov.za/sites/default/files/gcis_document/201409/reports-paramount cieso.pdf.

Nketia, J. H. Kwabena. "Musicology and Linguistics: Integrating the Phraseology of Text and Tune in the Creative Process." *Black Music Research Journal* 22, no. 2 (2002): 143–164.

Nteta, Doreen. "Foreword." *White Paper on Arts Culture and Heritage*. Pretoria: Department of Arts, Culture and Heritage, 1996.

Ntsebeza, Lungisile. *Democracy Compromised: Chiefs and the Politics of the Land in South Africa*. Leiden: Brill, 2005.

Ntuli, Deuteronomy Bhekinkosi Zeblon. "Remarks on Maskandi Poetry." *South African Journal of African Languages* 10, no. 4 (1990): 302–306.

Nzewi, Meki. "Strategies for Music Education in Africa." In *Musical Arts in Africa: Theory, Practice and Education*, edited by Anri Herbst, Meki Nzewi, and Kofi Agawu, 13–37. Pretoria: University of South Africa, 2007.

Ogilvie, Cheryl. "Effectiveness of Environmental Education Programmes in Adverse Socio-economic Environments: A Case Study of the Ndumo Communities, KwaZulu-Natal, South Africa." DTech diss., Tshwane University of Technology, 2019.

Olsen, Kathryn. "'Mina ngizokushaya ngengoma'/'I Will Challenge You with a Song': Constructions of Masculinity in *Maskanda*." *Agenda* 49 (2001): 51–60.

———. *Music and Social Change in South Africa: Maskanda Past and Present*. Philadelphia: Temple University Press, 2014.

———. "Musical Characterizations of Transformation: An Exploration of Social and Political Trajectories in Contemporary Maskanda." Unpublished PhD diss., University of KwaZulu-Natal, 2009.

Oomen, Barbara. *Chiefs in South Africa: Law, Power & Culture in the Post-Apartheid Era*. New York: Palgrave MacMillan, 2006.

Phala, Mbali. "Jeppe Hostel Residents Say Their Public Image Is Affecting Service Delivery to the Hostels." *Daily Vox.* June 9, 2016. https://www.thedailyvox.co.za/jeppe-hostel -residents-say-public-image-affecting-service-delivery-hostels/

Piper, Laurence. "Nationalism without a Nation: The Rise and Fall of Zulu Nationalism in South Africa's Transition to Democracy, 1975–99." *Nations and Nationalism* 8, no. 1 (2002): 73–94.

Plummer, Todd. "Where to Go in Maboneng, the Coolest Neighborhood in Johannesburg." *Vogue.* https://www.vogue.com/article/maboneng-guide-johannesburg-south-africa.

Pooley, Elsa. "A Checklist of the Plants of Ndumu Game Reserve, North-Eastern Zululand." *Journal of South African Botany* 44, no. 1 (1978): 1–54.

Pooley, Simon, Saloni Bhatia, and Anirudhkumar Vasava, "Rethinking the Study of Human-Wildlife Coexistence." *Conservation Biology* 35, no. 3 (2021): 784–793.

Pooley, Thomas. "Depressing Melodies: Consonants and Tone in Zulu Song." *Journal of the Phonetic Society of Japan* 22, no. 3 (2018): 42–49.

———. "Linguistic Tone and Melody in the Singing of Sub-Saharan Africa." In *The Routledge Companion to Interdisciplinary Studies in Singing, Volume 1: Development,* edited by F. Russo and A. Cohen, 108–120. New York: Routledge, 2020.

Pooley, Tony. *Discoveries of a Crocodile Man.* London: Collins, 1982.

———. *Mashesha: The Making of a Game Ranger.* Cape Town: Southern, 1992.

Pooley, Tony, and Ian Player. *KwaZulu/Natal Wildlife Destinations: A Guide to the Game Reserves, Resorts, Private Nature Reserves, Ranches and Wildlife Areas of KwaZulu/Natal.* Cape Town: Southern, 1995.

Posel, Deborah. "The Apartheid Project." In *The Cambridge History of South Africa, Volume 2, 1885–1994,* edited by Robert Ross, Anne Kelk Mager, and Bill Nasson, 319–368. Cambridge: Cambridge University Press, 2016.

"Poverty Trends in South Africa: An Examination of Absolute Poverty between 2006 and 2011." *Statistics South Africa.* Pretoria: Statistics South Africa, 2014.

Preston-Whyte, Eleanor. "Kinship and Marriage." In *The Bantu-Speaking Peoples of Southern Africa,* 2nd ed., edited by W. D. Hammond-Tooke. New York: Routledge, 1974.

"Quarterly Labour Force Survey, Q1 2021." *Statistics South Africa.* Pretoria: Statistics South Africa, 2021. http://www.statssa.gov.za/?page_id=1856&PPN=P0211&SCH=72943.

Radcliffe-Brown, Alfred. *Structure and Function in Primitive Society.* London: Cohen & West, 1952.

"Ramsar Convention." *Ramsar.* https://www.ramsar.org/about-the-ramsar-convention.

Ranger, Terence. *Dance and Society in Eastern Africa, 1890–1970: The Beni Ngoma.* Berkeley: University of California Press, 1975.

———. "The Invention of Tradition in Colonial Africa." In *The Invention of Tradition,* edited by Eric Hobsbawm and Terence Ranger. Cambridge: Cambridge University Press, 1982.

Reader, John. *Africa: A Biography of the Continent*. New York: Vintage, 1999.

"Report of the High Level Panel on the Assessment of Key Legislation and the Acceleration of Fundamental Change." November 2017. https://www.parliament.gov.za/storage/app/media/Pages/2017/october/High_Level_Panel_HLP_Report/HLP_report.pdf.

"Revised National Curriculum Statement (Schools). Introducing the Arts and Culture Learning Area." *National Department of Education*. Pretoria, South Africa, 2002. http://curriculum.wcape.school.za/ncs/index/lareas/view/6/#9.

"Ritual." *Oxford Reference*. 2002. https://o-www-oxfordreference-com.oasis.unisa.ac.za/view/10.1093/acref/9780195123715.001.0001/acref-9780195123715-e-1455.

Rycroft, David. "Zulu Melodic and Non-Melodic Vocal Styles." In *Papers Presented at the Seventh Symposium on Ethnomusicology*, edited by Andrew Tracey, 13–28. Grahamstown: International Library of African Music, 1987.

———. "The Relationships between Speech-Tone and Melody in Southern African Music." In *South African Music Encyclopedia*. vol. 2, edited by J. P. Malan. Pretoria: Human Sciences Research Council, 1982.

———. "Evidence of Stylistic Continuity in Zulu 'Town' Music." In *Essays for a Humanist: An Offering to Klaus Wachsmann*, edited by Mantle Hood, 216–260. New York: The Town House Press, 1977.

———. "A Royal Account of Music in Zulu Life with Translation, Annotation, and Musical Transcription." *Bulletin of the School of Oriental and African Studies, University of London* 38, no. 2 (1975a): 351–402.

———. "The Zulu Bow Songs of Princess Constance Magogo kaDinzulu." *African Music* 3, no. 2 (1975b): 351–402.

———. "Tone in Zulu Nouns." *African Language Studies* IV (1963): 43–68.

———. "Melodic Features in Zulu Eulogistic Recitation." *African Language Studies* I (1960): 60–78.

Rycroft, David, and A. Bhekabantu Ngcobo. *Say It in Zulu*. London: School of Oriental and African Studies, 1979.

Rycroft, David, and A. Bhekabantu Ngcobo, eds. *The Praises of Dingana: Izibongo zikaDingana*. Durban, South Africa: Killie Campbell Africana Library: Pietermaritzburg, South Africa: University of Natal Press, 1988.

Sack, Mikhaela. "Innovation to Convention! An Exploratory Study on the Evolution of Urban Regeneration in Maboneng, Johannesburg." Master of Science Research Report: University of the Witwatersrand, 2016.

Samuels, David, Louise Meintjes, Ana Maria Ochoa, and Thomas Porcello. "Soundscapes: Toward a Sounded Anthropology." *Annual Review of Anthropology* 39 (2010): 329–345.

Sato, Chizuko. "Forced Removals, Land NGOs and Community Politics in KwaZulu-Natal, South Africa, 1953–2002." PhD thesis, University of Oxford, 2006.

Schafer, R. Murray. *The Soundscape: Our Sonic Environment and the Tuning of the World.* Rochester, VT: Destiny Books, 1993.

Scorgie, Fiona. "Virginity Testing and the Politics of Sexual Responsibility: Implications for AIDS Intervention." *African Studies* 61, no. 1 (2002): 55–75.

Sharp, John S. "The Roots and Development of Volkekunde in South Africa." *Journal of Southern African Studies* 8, no. 11 (1981): 16–36.

Sithole, Jabulani, and Percy Ngonyama. "The Land Question – The Ingonyama Trust Controversy." *Polity.* May 11, 2018. https://www.polity.org.za/article/the-land-question -the-ingonyama-trust-controversy-2018-05-11.

Skosana, Dineo, Mbongiseni Buthelezi, and Beth Vale. *Traditional Leaders in a Democracy: Resources, Respect and Resistance.* Woodmead: MISTRA, 2018.

Skotnes, Pippa, ed. *Miscast: Negotiating the Presence of the Bushmen.* Cape Town: University of Cape Town Press, 1996.

Smith, David. "Colonial Encounters through the Prism of Music: A Southern African Perspective." *International Review of the Aesthetics and Sociology of Music* 33, no. 1 (2002): 31–55.

Steingo, Gavin. *Kwaito's Promise: Music and the Aesthetics of Freedom in South Africa.* Chicago: University of Chicago Press, 2016.

Steingo, Gavin, and Jim Sykes, eds. *Remapping Sound Studies.* Durham, NC: Duke University Press, 2019.

Stoller, Paul. *The Taste of Ethnographic Things: The Senses in Anthropology.* Philadelphia: University of Pennsylvania Press, 1989.

Tau, Poloko. "'Release King Dalindyebo from Prison' – Traditional Leaders to Ramaphosa." *News24.* April 7, 2019. https://www.news24.com/SouthAfrica/News/release -king-dalindyebo-from-prison-traditional-leaders-to-ramaphosa-20190407.

"Theory of Music." *Trinity College London.* October 21, 2014. http://www.trinitycollege .com/site/?id=1058.

———. *University of South Africa.* October 21, 2014. http://www.unisa.ac.za/default.asp ?Cmd=ViewContent&ContentID=95128.

Titon, Jeff Todd. "Music, the Public Interest, and the Practice of Ethnomusicology." *Ethnomusicology* 63, no. 3 (1992): 315–322.

———. "Section 1. Applied Ethnomusicology: A Descriptive and Historical Account." In *The Oxford Handbook of Applied Ethnomusicology*, edited by Jeff Todd Titon and Svanibor Pettan, 4–28. New York: Oxford, 2015.

Titus, Barbara. "'Global Maskanda, Global Historiography?' Some Preliminary Enquiries." *South African Music Studies* 28 (2008): 43–54.

———. "'Walking Like a Crab': Analyzing Maskanda Music in Post-Apartheid South Africa." *Ethnomusicology* 57, no. 2 (2013): 286–310.

Tomlinson, Gary. *A Million Years of Music: The Emergence of Human Modernity*. New York: Zone Books, 2015.

Toxopeüs, Michelle, and Louis Kotzé. "Promoting Environmental Justice through Civil-Based Instruments in South Africa." *Law, Environment and Development Journal* 13, no. 1 (2017): 49–72.

Tracey, Hugh. *African Dances of the Witwatersrand Gold Mines*. Photographs by Merlyn Severn. Johannesburg: African Music Society, 1952.

———. "New Catalogue: The 'Sound of Africa' Series." *African Music: Journal of the International Library of African Music* 5, no. 3 (1973): 108–109.

Treffry-Goatley, Astrid. *Brother Clement Sithole: A Musical Biography*. Outcomes Publishing, 2015.

Vail, Leroy, and Landeg White. *Power and the Praise Poem: Southern African Voices in History*. Charlottesville: University of Virginia Press, 1991.

Walker, Cherryl, and Ben Cousins. "Introduction." In *Land Divided, Land Restored: Land Reform in South Africa for the 21st Century*, edited by Cherryl Walker and Ben Cousins, 1–23. Johannesburg: Jacana, 2015.

Walker, Clive, and Anton Walker. *Rhino Revolution: Searching for New Solutions*. Auckland Park: Jacana, 2017.

Walsh, Shannon. "We Won't Move." *City* 17, no. 3 (2013): 400–408.

Whitelaw, Gavin. "A Brief Archaeology of Precolonial Farming in KwaZulu-Natal." In *Zulu Identities: Being Zulu, Past and Present*, edited by Benedict Carton, John Laband, and Jabulani Sithole, 47–61. Pietermaritzburg: University of KwaZulu-Natal Press, 2008.

"White Paper on Arts, Culture, and Heritage." *Department of Arts, Culture, Science and Technology*. Pretoria, 1996.

"White Paper on Reconstruction and Development, Notice No. 1954 of 1994." Parliament of the Republic of South Africa. Cape Town, November 15, 1994.

Wilson, Monica. *Reaction to Conquest*. 2nd ed. London: Oxford, 1964.

———. *Religion and the Transformation of Society: A Study in Social Change in Africa*. Cambridge: Cambridge University Press, 1971.

Wolpe, Harold. "Capitalism and Cheap Labor-Power in South Africa: From Segregation to Apartheid." *Economy and Society* 1, no. 43 (1972): 425–456.

"Working for Water Programme." Department of Forestry, Fisheries & the Environment, Republic of South Africa. Accessed September 24, 2022. https://www.dffe.gove.za/projectsprogrammes/wfw.

Wright, John. "Reflections on the Politics of Being 'Zulu.'" In *Zulu Identities: Being Zulu, Past and Present*, edited by Benedict Carton, John Laband, and Jabulani Sithole, 35–44. Pietermaritzburg: University of KwaZulu-Natal Press, 2008.

Wright, John, and Carolyn Hamilton. "Traditions and Transformations: The Phongolo-Mzimkhulu Region in the Late Eighteenth and Early Nineteenth Centuries." In *Natal and Zululand from Earliest Times to 1910: A New History*, edited by Andrew Duminy and Bill Guest, 49–82. Pietermaritzburg: University of Natal Press, 2009.

Wylie, Dan. *Savage Delight: White Myths of Shaka*. Pietermaritzburg: University of KwaZulu-Natal Press, 2000.

Xulu, Musa. "The Re-Emergence of Amahubo Song Styles and Ideas in Some Modern Zulu Musical Styles." PhD diss., University of Natal, 1992.

Yende, Sizwe Sama. "Ramaphosa Recognises Prince Misuzulu as AmaZulu King." *City Press*. March 17, 2022. https://www.news24.com/citypress/news/ramaphosa-recognises-prince-misuzulu-as-amazulu-king-20220317).

"Zazi Reaches Young Women at Zulu Reed Dance." *U.S. Mission South Africa*. November 30, 2017. https://za.usembassy.gov/zazi-reaches-young-women-at-zulu-reed-dance/.

Zondi, Nompumelelo. *Bahlabelelelani – Why Do They Sing? Gender and Power in Contemporary Women's Songs*. Scottsville: University of KwaZulu-Natal Press, 2020.

Zulu Chiefs and Headmen Act No. 8 of 1974 (revised 1980).

DISCOGRAPHY

Arom, Simha. *Centrafrique: Anthologie de la musique des Pygmées Aka.* 3 LPs. Paris: Ocora, 1978. CD reissue, 1993.

———. *Music of the Ba-Benzélé Pygmies.* LP. Kasel, Germany: Barenreiter UNESCO Collection of World Music, 1966. CD reissue, Rounder Records, Cambridge, MA, 1998.

Bergville Blue Roses. *UThembi.* Thukela Records. TR006 (CD), 2021.

Feld, Steven. *Bosavi: Rainforest Music from Papua New Guinea.* 3 CDs. Washington, DC: Smithsonian Folkways Recordings, 2001.

———. *Voices of the Rainforest: A Day in the Life of the Kaluli People.* CD. The Word series, edited by Mickey Hart. Boston: Rykodisc. 1991.

Juluka. *African Litany.* EMI/MINC, 1981.

Magogo, Constance. *The Zulu Songs of Princess Constance Magogo KaDinuzulu by Hugh Tracey.* Music of Africa Series 37. ILAM. CDMOA37 (CD), 2004. Originally released in 1972.

Mfaz' Omnyama. *Khula Tshitshi Lami.* Gallo. CDAFR172 (CD), 1997.

———. *Ngisebenzile Mama.* Gallo. CDGMP40822 (CD), 2000.

Mqamuli Wezintambo. "Bafana Bafana." Field recording by Thomas Pooley. Recorded April 30, 2012, at Ndumo.

Pooley, Tony. *Sounds of Tongaland.* LP. Durban: Olympia Studios, 1970.

———. *Wildlife Calls of Africa.* Script written by James Clarke. Narrator: Michael Mayer. Directed and produced by Dick Reucassel. LP. Johannesburg, 1966.

Pooley, Tony, and Tony Henley. *Birds of the Drakensberg.* LP. Durban: Olympia Studios, 1969.

Phuzekhemisi noKhetani. *Imbizo.* Gallo. CDGSP3105 (CD), 1992.

Reucassel, Dick, and Tony Pooley. *Calls of the Bushveld.* Commentary written and directed by Hugh Rouse. Narrator: Michael Mayer. LP. Johannesburg, 1968.

Turnbull, Colin. *Music of the Ituri Forest.* LP. New York: Folkways, 1958. CD reissue, *Mbuti Pygmies of the Ituri Rainforest.* Washington, DC: Smithsonian Folkways, 1992.

Various Artists. *Maskandi Hits: eyami lenduku.* Gallo. CDGSP3055 (CD), 1994.

Audio and Video Recordings
Available on the Companion Website

Look for the Reader's Companion here: https://www.weslpress.org/readers-companions/
The recordings included on the companion website were all made by the author and with
the informed consent of the performers. Access using the password: LIS00588

umSindo! The Politics of Sonic Space at a Zulu Wedding

"Ndlovu Wedding." Video showing events at Ncunjane on December 29, 2011 (p. 49).
"uMakoti." A wedding song performed by a group at Mashunka on September 2, 2013
   (p. 63).

Songs of Sacrifice: *uMemulo* and the Politics of Gender and Generation

"uMemulo." Video of umemulo ceremonies in KwaZulu-Natal, South Africa (p. 68).
   The following umemulo songs were performed by a group of girls and young women
   at Mashunka on February 7, 2012:
"Ngilinde" (p. 81)
"Webaba Omncane" (p. 82)
"Ngibongeleni Baba Wami" (p. 83)
"Abanoma" (p. 83)
"Ngisayozama" (pp. 83–84)
"Umthetho Walomuzi" (pp. 83–84)
"Mhlawumbe" (p. 84)

Phenomenology of iNgoma: *isiShameni* Dance and the Politics of Proximity

"iNgoma dance." Video showing Thembu dance troupes at Jeppe Park, Johannesburg, and Msinga, KwaZulu-Natal (p. 87).

uMaskandi iziBongo: The Politics and Poetics of Popular Praises

"Sondela." uMaskandi song performed by Khonazugcina Dladla on February 7, 2012 (p. 112).
"Bafana Bafana." uMaskandi song performed by Jonathan Mathenjwa and Mqamuli Wezintambo on April 30, 2012 (p. 124).

Inscribing Tradition: Poverty, Inequality, and the
Politics of Performance in Schools

"Music and Dance in KwaZulu-Natal Schools." Video based on recordings made between 2012 and 2017 (p. 145).
"Saze Sabulawa KwaZulu." iHubo (anthem) performed by the eShowe High School Choir on September 2, 2012 (p. 152).

Sounds of Tongaland: Environmental Justice at Ndumo Game Reserve

"Cicadas." Sound recording made at Ndumo Game Reserve on April 30, 2012 (p. 158).
"Shaya Mfana." Song performed on the umakhweyana musical bow by Dledleni Gumede on May 1, 2012 (p. 178).

INDEX

Page numbers in *italics* indicate illustrations.

race in South Africa: education and, 145–46; ideology of research and, 11–12; land tenure/governance and, 27–28, 34, 38–39, 164–65, 192, 208n56; "native," Act defining (1913), 206n18; racial terminology, 203n47; separate development doctrine, 11, 28–29; wildlife conservation and, 164–65, 172–73

Radio Bantu, 121

Ramaphosa, Cyril, 31, 35, 208n48

Ramsar Convention on Wetlands, 165, 228n28

Ranger, Terence, 45

RDP (Reconstruction and Development Plan), 145

reciprocity, 21, 180–90, 194; ethnographic ethics and, 11–12, 184, 185; exploitation concerns, 185, 230n3; *izingilili* dance recorded at Ndumo, 186–87; justice for the environment and, 175–76; Mduduzi Mngomezulu, efforts to locate and record, 180–81; performance as, 79; sonic spaces constructed on basis of, 20; trust and fairness in making recordings, 181–85

Reconstruction and Development Plan (RDP), 145

recordings: challenges of making, 186, 187–88; on companion website, 6, 251–52; digital technology, effects of, 185, 186–88; trust, fairness, and reciprocity in making, 181–85

Red Cliffs, Ndumo Game Reserve, 168, 169, 170

red duiker, 164, 171

reflexive ethnography, 8, 11, 19

Reitz, Deneys, 163

Remapping Sound Studies (Steingo and Sykes), 8–9

Reucassel, Dick, 159

Revised National Curriculum Statement (2002), 147

rhinoceros, 162, 165, 167–68, 170, 171, 177

Richards Bay, 149

Rijsdijk, Susan, 148

rinderpest, 162

ritual: ceremony versus, 215n35; colonialism, Christianity, and outlawing of, 68; defined, 213n5; *isibaya* (cattle byre), ritual significance of, 50, 111; land, conflicts over, 39; syncretism and fluidity of, 46, 68; traditional leaders and, 33. *See also specific rituals*

Rycroft, David, 114, 118, 130–33, 135

sacrifices: for *umemulo* events, 66, 69–70, 71, 73, 74–79, *77*; *umhlwehlwe* (gall bladder and entrail fat), 66, 71, 74, 76, *77*, 79, 85; wedding ceremonies, sacrifice, food preparation, and food at, 49–50, 51, 55, 62, 64, 211n13

Sahlumbe, 39

San language, culture, and people, 24, 26

Sato, Chizuko, 39

Sawers, Richard Penn, 166

Schaefer, Pierre, 160

Schafer, R. Murray, 9, 160, 226n7

schizophonia, 160

schools and education, 21, 142–57, 193; challenges to transforming musical arts curriculum, 153–54, 156; competitions in dance and music, 142–43, *143*, 150–53; government spending on, 224n1; inequality of educational opportunity, 143–45, 156–57, 224n3; in Jozini Local Municipality, 145, 148–51, 155, 156–57, 193; migrancy, generational disconnect, and rising importance of, 21, 103–4, 148–49, 153; music education, 144, 145, 146–50, 152–54, 156–57; music examinations, 154–56; postapartheid education policy and practice, 145–48; poverty and education, relationship between, 224n3; prescribed texts for, 152; private versus public schools, 144, 145, 154–57; survey of music education and, 148–53; Unisa Department of Art History, Visual Arts and Musicology, teacher mentoring program, 225n19; Western norms/values, imposition of, 145–46, 148, 151, 154–56, 193; Zulu identity and, 14

war cries. See *izaga*

website, 6, 251–52

wedding ceremonies, 19–20, 47–65; *amahubo* at, *51*, 51–56, 59–61, 62, 63, 211n14; arrival and assembly of attendees, 50–52, *51*; audience, role of, 219n56; competitive singing/dancing between *ikhetho* and *umthimbo*, 55–57, 63, 64, 212n20, 212n23; dedicated spaces, use of, 62; dress and accoutrements at, 52–53, 57–59, 61, 212n16; as genre of Zulu performance, 17; *ikhetho* (bridegroom's party), *51*, 54–61, 62, 63, 65; *ilobolo* (bride wealth), 50, 63–64, 67, 73; *ingoma* dance at migrant hostels as preparation for, 105; invitation of author to, 49; marriage rite, 57–59, *58*; Ncunjane, thick description of wedding at, 20, 47, 49–62, *51*, *53*, *58*, *62*; post-marital-rite singing/dancing, 59–62, *62*; sacrifices, food preparation, and food, 49–50, 51, 55, 62, 64, 211n13; sonic space, concept of, 20, 47–48, 64–65; transition of bride from one lifeworld to another through, 62–64; *umakoti* (bride/married woman), 49, 52, 53, 55, 57–61, 62, 63, 212n21; *umemulo* and, 17–18, 63, 64; *umkhwenyana* (bridegroom), 49, 52, 57, 59, 60, 62; *umsindo* as colloquial term for, 19–20, 47, 50; *umthimba* (bridal party), 49, 52, *53*, 53–58, 60–61, 63, 65

Weenen, 36–40, 48–49, 120–21, 209n62, 221n6

whistles, 52, 61, 211n15

White, Landeg, 116

white-faced duck, 171

White Paper on Arts, Culture and Heritage (1996), 146

White Paper on Education and Training (1995), 145

white rhino, 162, 165, 167, 168, 170

Whites and Blacks. *See* race in South Africa

Wildlife Calls of Africa (Tony Pooley recording, 1966), 159, 160

Wilson, Monica, 78, 215n37

Wiseman Mbatha, Siwakhe, 75–79, *77*, 214n23, 215n33

Wolhuter men's hostel, Jeppestown, Johannesburg. See *ingoma* dance and migrant hostel life

Working for Water Initiative, 5, 167, 199n7, 228n34

writing culture, in ethnography, 7–8, 19

xenophobia, 31, 87, 98, 99, 105, 154, 218n28

Xhosa: *iintonjane* ritual, 213n3; music, pitch analysis of, 132

Xulu, Musa, 18

young men. See *ibutho/amabutho*; *izinsizwa*

Zakele (backing singer), 180

Zazi (nongovernmental organization), 216n47

Zingili clan dances, 230n5

"Zulu," as term, xvi

Zulu Chiefs and Headmen Act No. 8 (1974), 211n15

Zulu cosmologies, 7, 16–17, 64, 114

Zulu identity, 12–17, 31, 121, 123, 203n53

Zululand District Municipality, 36

Zululand Wildlife forum, 166

Zululand/Zulu kingdom (nineteenth century), 25–27, 47

Zulu monarchy: nineteenth century, 25–27; twentieth to twenty-first century, 28–29, 33–36. *See also specific kings*

Zulu nationalism, 31, 202n44, 206n30

Zulu performances and politics of place, 1–22, 191–95; ethnography and ethnographic ethics, 7–8, 10–12, 19, 184, 185, 230n3; genres of, 17–19; geographic region of study, 6, 13; methodological approach, 7–9; performance[s], concept of, 6, 12; postapartheid state and, 5–7, 12, 15, 22; research practices, 1–5; singing the land, 23; sound studies and sound writing, 7–10, 19; Zulu identity and, 12–17. See also *ingoma* dance and migrant hostel life; land tenure, governance, and representation; Ndumo Game Reserve and its sonic

Harris M. Berger
*Stance: Ideas about Emotion, Style,
and Meaning for the Study
of Expressive Culture*

Harris M. Berger and
Giovanna P. Del Negro
*Identity and Everyday Life: Essays
in the Study of Folklore, Music,
and Popular Culture*

Franya J. Berkman
*Monument Eternal: The Music
of Alice Coltrane*

Dick Blau, Angeliki Vellou Keil,
and Charles Keil
*Bright Balkan Morning:
Romani Lives and the Power
of Music in Greek Macedonia*

Susan Boynton and
Roe-Min Kok, editors
*Musical Childhoods and the
Cultures of Youth*

James Buhler, Caryl Flinn,
and David Neumeyer, editors
Music and Cinema

Thomas Burkhalter, Kay Dickinson,
and Benjamin J. Harbert, editors
*The Arab Avant-Garde: Music,
Politics, Modernity*

Patrick Burkart
Music and Cyberliberties

Julia Byl
*Antiphonal Histories: Resonant Pasts
in the Toba Batak Musical Present*

Corinna Campbell
*Parameters and Peripheries of Culture:
Interpreting Maroon Music and Dance
in Paramaribo, Suriname*

Alexander M. Cannon
*Seeding the Tradition: Musical Creativity
in Southern Vietnam*

Daniel Cavicchi
*Listening and Longing: Music Lovers
in the Age of Barnum*

Susan D. Crafts, Daniel Cavicchi,
Charles Keil, and the
Music in Daily Life Project
*My Music: Explorations
of Music in Daily Life*

Jim Cullen
*Born in the USA: Bruce Springsteen
and the American Tradition*

Anne Danielsen
*Presence and Pleasure: The Funk Grooves
of James Brown and Parliament*

Peter Doyle
*Echo and Reverb: Fabricating
Space in Popular Music Recording,
1900–1960*

Ron Emoff
*Recollecting from the Past: Musical
Practice and Spirit Possession on the East
Coast of Madagascar*

Yayoi Uno Everett and
Frederick Lau, editors
Locating East Asia in Western Art Music

Susan Fast and Kip Pegley, editors
Music, Politics, and Violence

Heidi Feldman
*Black Rhythms of Peru: Reviving African
Musical Heritage in the Black Pacific*

Kai Fikentscher
*"You Better Work!" Underground
Dance Music in New York City*

Helena Simonett
*Banda: Mexican Musical Life
across Borders*

Mark Slobin
*Subcultural Sounds: Micromusics
of the West*

Mark Slobin, editor
Global Soundtracks: Worlds of Film Music

Tes Slominski
*Trad Nation: Gender, Sexuality, and Race
in Irish Traditional Music*

Christopher Small
The Christopher Small Reader

Christopher Small
*Music of the Common Tongue:
Survival and Celebration
in African American Music*

Christopher Small
Music, Society, Education

Christopher Small
*Musicking: The Meanings
of Performing and Listening*

Andrew Snyder
*Critical Brass: Street Carnival and Musical
Activism in Rio de Janeiro*

Maria Sonevytsky
*Wild Music: Sound and Sovereignty
in Ukraine*

Tore Størvold
*Dissonant Landscapes: Music, Nature,
and the Performance of Iceland*

Regina M. Sweeney
*Singing Our Way to Victory:
French Cultural Politics and Music
during the Great War*

Colin Symes
*Setting the Record Straight: A Material
History of Classical Recording*

Kelley Tatro
*Love and Rage: Autonomy in
Mexico City's Punk Scene*

Steven Taylor
*False Prophet: Field Notes
from the Punk Underground*

Paul Théberge
*Any Sound You Can Imagine: Making
Music/Consuming Technology*

Sarah Thornton
*Club Cultures: Music, Media,
and Subcultural Capital*

Michael E. Veal
*Dub: Songscape and Shattered Songs
in Jamaican Reggae*

Michael E. Veal and
E. Tammy Kim, editors
*Punk Ethnography: Artists and Scholars
Listen to Sublime Frequencies*

Robert Walser
*Running with the Devil: Power, Gender,
and Madness in Heavy Metal Music*

Dennis Waring
*Manufacturing the Muse:
Estey Organs and Consumer Culture
in Victorian America*

Lise A. Waxer
*The City of Musical Memory:
Salsa, Record Grooves, and Popular
Culture in Cali, Colombia*

Mina Yang
*Planet Beethoven: Classical Music
at the Turn of the Millennium*

Acknowledgments for previously published material used with permission:

"Singing in South African Schools." In *The Routledge Companion to Interdisciplinary Studies in Singing, Volume 2: Education*, edited by Helga R. Gudmundsdottir, Carol Beynon, Karen M. Ludke, and Annabel J. Cohen, 123–133. New York: Routledge, 2020.

"Songs of Gender and Generation: Ethnographic Perspectives on Initiation Songs and Wellbeing in Southern Africa." In *The Routledge Companion to Interdisciplinary Studies in Singing, Volume 3: Wellbeing*, edited by Rachel Heydon, Daisy Fancourt, and Annabel J. Cohen, 357–367. New York: Routledge, 2020.

"The Phenomenology of Collapsing Worlds: isiShameni Dance and the Politics of Proximity in Jeppestown, Johannesburg." In *African Performance Arts and Political Acts*, edited by Naomi André, Yolanda Covington-Ward, and Jendele Hungbo, 85–105. Ann Arbor: University of Michigan Press, 2021.

"*Umaskandi Izibongo*': Semantic, Prosodic, and Musical Dimensions of Voice in Zulu Popular Praises." *African Music: Journal of the International Library of African Music* 10, no. 2 (2016): 7–34.

"'Extracurricular Arts': Poverty, Inequality, and Indigenous Musical Arts Education in Post-Apartheid South Africa." *Critical Arts: South-North Cultural and Media Studies* 30, no. 5 (2016): 639–654.

ABOUT THE AUTHOR

Thomas M. Pooley is an associate professor of musicology and chair of the Department of Art and Music at the University of South Africa. He holds a PhD in musicology from the University of Pennsylvania and is editor in chief of *Muziki: Journal of Music Research in Africa*. He has published widely on music, language, and dance in Africa, and is the founding director of the independent label Thukela Records.